Social need

Library of social work

General Editor:
Noel Timms
Professor of Social Work Studies
University of Newcastle upon Tyne

Social need
Policy, practice and
research

Gilbert Smith

Department of Social Administration and Social Work
University of Glasgow

Routledge & Kegan Paul
London, Boston and Henley

First published in 1980
by Routledge & Kegan Paul Ltd
39 Store Street, London WC1E 7DD,
Broadway House, Newtown Road,
Henley-on-Thames, Oxon RG9 1EN and
9 Park Street, Boston, Mass. 02108, USA
Set in Times
and printed in Great Britain by
The Lavenham Press Ltd, Lavenham, Suffolk
© Gilbert Smith 1980

British Library Cataloguing in Publication Data

Smith, Gilbert

Social need, policy, practice and research. —
(Library of social work).
1. Social service
I. Title II. Series
361   HV40   79-41430

ISBN 0 7100 0484 2

Contents

'Of course it is not really so cut-and-dried as all this; but often the only way of attempting to express the truth is to build it up, like a card-house, of a pack of lies.'

(Richard Hughes, *A High Wind in Jamaica*)

Acknowledgments

I did the research on which this book is based while I was a Research Fellow in Sociology and was attached to the Medical Research Council Medical Sociology Unit at the University of Aberdeen. Professor Raymond Illsley established and supervised the project and I am extremely grateful to him. Mr Gordon Horobin made detailed comments on the complete report in its various earlier drafts. For part of the period of the research Mr Robert Harris worked on a related project and I am grateful for his assistance in collecting some of the data used in Chapter 5. Financial support for the original research was provided by grants from the Nuffield Provincial Hospitals Trust and the Social Work Services Group, Edinburgh.

I also wish to thank those many members of staff in Social Work Departments who discussed their ideas with me and allowed me to observe them at work. In particular I want to acknowledge help from the senior staff who negotiated research access and the clerical staff in reception offices who bore the brunt of many of my most detailed enquiries.

Seldom do the results of an empirical research project fit neatly between the covers of a single book and this study is no exception. Some points have been made in preliminary form elsewhere and others have been developed more fully subsequently. The discussion of the Seebohm Report in Chapter 2 draws upon Smith (1971) in *The British Journal of Sociology*. The discussion of the Kilbrandon Report in the same chapter is presented at greater length in Smith (1978) in *Public Administration*. A short section of Chapter 2 is a summarised and slightly altered version of an argument developed more fully in Smith and Stockman (1972) in *The Sociological Review*. Data in Chapter 5 were first described in Smith and Harris (1972) in *The British Journal of Social Work* and are reproduced by permission of the Editor. An example of how material from

Acknowledgments

Chapter 6 may be used for teaching purposes can be found in Unit 5 of the Open University Course DE206 *Social Work, Community Work and Society* (pp. 44-7), and is reproduced by permission of the Open University.

The final version of this book was prepared while I was a member of the Department of Social Administration and Social Work at Glasgow University. I am grateful to Professor F. M. Martin for his general encouragement and to Mrs Kathleen Davidson who handled my secretarial work with considerable efficiency.

Prelude

Chapter one

Introduction

The idea of social need is used in very different ways by different groups, at different times, in different contexts, for different purposes and with different effects. This book is about some of these differences. The idea of need pervades social work practice and it pervades also the social policies that shape the institutions within which that practice takes place. As a result it plays an important part too in the social research which examines these policies, institutions and practices. Yet for all its importance it remains a confused and sometimes confusing concept, all the more so because the confusions frequently pass unacknowledged. This book is also about some of those confusions.

I think that the concept of social need has been made to work too hard in policy, practice and research. I shall argue that some groups who now use it—particularly social researchers—may be well advised to look elsewhere for this tool of their trade. There are points in the book therefore when I shall say how I think the idea of social need *should* be used, for selected purposes. For much of the book, however, I shall simply describe how the concept 'social need' *is* managed differently and, more ambitiously, I shall try to suggest why it is managed in some of the ways that it is. I am not offering a philosophical or linguistic analysis. The book reports an exercise in empirical sociology which I hope may contribute to debate about, research on, and treatment of, the needs of clients and potential clients of the welfare services. These needs have been widely debated, studied and treated but the idea of need itself, used in all these tasks, remains surprisingly crude.

Plan of the book

The book is divided into three parts, each of which looks at the concept of social need in a different context: in social policy, in

1

social research and in one area of professional practice, social work. Initially the focus is on social policy. And here I have selected one area of social policy for particular attention: the proposals for the reorganisation of British social work in the late 1960s and early 1970s. These proposals are particularly relevant to a study of social need for they were deliberately designed to structure the institutions of the personal social services more efficiently to meet social need. The concept of social need is central to the reorganisation process. I shall look in some detail at the important government reports and proposals that preceded that reorganisation. There are empirical assertions within these proposals that are capable of research investigation. Causal models about the functioning of welfare organisations at the local authority level were implicitly adopted by those supporting the creation of Social Work and Social Services Departments and one assumption in particular was especially significant. It was an assumption about the relationship between notions of need and forms of organisation. It was not a well-formulated assumption, it is possibly false and it is certainly worthy of further research study.

The second part of the book describes a search for a viable notion of need that might adequately serve such research purposes. I shall review several major studies of the provision of welfare services in Britain to see how different notions of need have actually been worked out in the practice of different strategies of research. I shall argue that a quite radical reformulation of traditional concepts of need is required if a number of serious theoretical and methodological pitfalls are to be avoided.

In the third part of the book I shall turn to the study of social work practice, again selectively, focusing on the intake and allocation of cases in local authority social work agencies. By studying the way in which people with problems become 'clients' in 'need' we can examine empirically the relationship between notions of need and forms of organisation and thus explore that policy assumption so crucial to the whole reorganisation process. On the basis of some original data I shall argue that need in social work practice must be understood not merely as the measurable property of individual clients but also as the outcome of administrative procedures which function to cope with the routine management of clients of the agency. For the practitioner, the problem of managing clients becomes the problem of successfully managing the concept of social need. For the social scientist, the problem of understanding social need becomes, in part, the problem of understanding the management techniques that the practitioner employs.

In a brief conclusion I shall return to the original policy debate. The empirical materials seem relevant not only to theoretical and methodological issues in research on social work but they cast some doubt also on the validity of an assumption basic to the reorganisation of British social work.

Starting point

When the Secretary of State for Scotland appointed a committee, in May 1961, to consider the provisions of Scottish law for the treatment of juvenile delinquents and juveniles in need of care and protection, there began a process that, over the next ten years or so, was to lead to a major reorganisation of the personal social services in Britain. These changes involved, in England and Wales, the creation of Social Services Departments to replace the existing Children's and Welfare Departments and, in Scotland, the creation of Social Work Departments formed from a merger of the Children's, Welfare and Probation services.

With hindsight it is possible to trace, as some writers have done (Rowntree, 1969; Seed, 1973; Thomas, 1973) the historical origins of the recent expansion and reorganisation of social work in Britain back at least as far as the immediate post-war developments of the National Health Act of 1946 and the National Assistance and particularly the Children's Acts of 1948. Alternatively the appointment of the Ingleby Committee in 1956 might be seen as a crucial milestone. Certainly no systematic historical record of recent administrative changes in social work can neglect the importance of the Ingleby Committee report, the Children and Young Persons Act 1963, the related developments of the two white papers, *The Child, The Family and the Young Offender* and *Children in Trouble*, and the subsequent Children and Young Persons Act, 1969. In Scotland a record of recent changes might well begin with the report of the McBoyle Committee in 1963 on the *Prevention of Neglect of Children*.

All these and other developments have been very fully described and their interrelationships explored elsewhere (see especially Rowntree, 1969; Hall, 1976; and Murray, 1976). It is unnecessary to elaborate here. In order to make a start to this book I want only to set down one or two general points about these developments.

The first point to note is that although a number of government reports (of various kinds) played a part in the social work reorganisation process, a limited number of documents are by far and away the most important for a study of the idea of social need. The Social Work Departments, established in Scotland in the autumn of 1969, resulted from the Social Work (Scotland) Act 1968. This legislation broadly implemented the proposals of the Kilbrandon Report, *Children and Young Persons, Scotland* and the 1966 White Paper

Social Work and the Community. These documents are important but *the* most prominent influence was the Seebohm Report, the *Report of the Committee on Local Authority and Allied Personal Social Services.* It led to the Local Authority Social Services Act 1970 and to the formation of Social Services Departments in England and Wales in April 1971. Although not the earliest, the Seebohm Report was certainly the fullest discussion of the proposals for organisational change in social work and it embodied the major ideas, including that of social need, upon which the reorganisation of social work throughout Britain was based.

There are differences as between England and Wales on the one hand and Scotland on the other, but in general terms the reorganisation of social work took the same form throughout Britain. There was created both north and south of the border a unified social work service in the form of a single agency charged with providing the majority of personal social services at the local authority level. So far as the broad strategy for meeting social need is concerned, differences in timing in creating the agencies and other variations are not significant. Even the differential impact of excluding probation from this agency in England and Wales should not be overestimated given that the working of the Children and Young Persons Act increasingly concentrates work with juvenile delinquents in the hands of professionals in Social Services Departments and confines probation to prison welfare and work with adult offenders and accused. The main difference remains the working of the Children's Panel System in Scotland.

A second general point that I want to make by way of an introduction to the discussion of social need in this book, is that the reorganisation of social work in Britain took place within the historical context of an expanding notion of what domains of social life were appropriately the concern of the professional social worker. Social work ceased to be viewed as a set of specific remedies to precisely defined conditions. Rather it was viewed as an umbrella service designed to meet social need in a much broader way.

This process entailed, particularly, the incursion of the world of social work upon areas that were previously the province of the judicial and penal systems. Social work made especially noticeable in-roads on the organisation of juvenile justice. But this was not the only example. Social work expanded too at its interface with health care systems. Patients' medical problems were seen to be accompanied by social needs which were soon to become, along with much else, the responsibility of local authority social work organisations. In short a revised notion of social work, promoted by Kilbrandon and Seebohm, put the idea of social need also, up for renegotiation.

This then is the starting point for this book, albeit stated in a rather general way at this stage. The reorganisation of British social work was based on a number of important assumptions about the fundamental nature of social need and the way in which the social services function to meet these needs. I am going to start by discussing these assumptions. I shall then set this review of important policy documents against some research data collected in social work agencies, and question a notion of need that has gained wide credence amongst policy makers, administrators, social workers and some researchers in the social services field. I shall explore, too, the truth of a number of empirical propositions that lie at the heart of the reorganisation of British social work, focusing, in particular, upon beliefs about the relationship between social need and the organisational and administrative structure of the services.

Some objectives

In concluding this introductory chapter I want to explain why an investigation of the topic of social need within the context of the reorganisation of British social work is potentially fruitful.

First, it seems useful as an exercise in research in social policy and social work practice. In a recent general discussion of knowledge and beliefs, Armstrong (1973) noted:

> Many of the beliefs which guide our actions never enter consciousness while the action is being performed, yet the belief must be causally active at that time. Sometimes a confidently held belief turns out to be false and as a result the action based on it is unsuccessful yet only with failure do we become conscious that we had been all along assuming the truth of that belief (p. 21).

Social policy proposals and the practice of social work similarly rest upon sets of 'causally active' beliefs. Yet the beliefs, as is the case in other spheres of social activity too, frequently remain unexplicated. Implicitly they are adopted and assumed to be true although in fact that may not be the case. It is only with the occurrence of failure, or sets of unanticipated consequences, as action based upon a particular body of policy begins to take effect, that doubt is cast on the validity of the assumption in which the policy was rooted initially. And even then the impact of basic premises may pass unacknowledged, explanation for the failure being sought in some other, often relatively trivial factor. Many of the supposed defects of social work reorganisation, for example, tend to be blamed upon 'staff shortage'. True, that may not be a trivial factor but then it may not be the correct explanation either.

Thus one task that the social scientist can usefully perform in relation to social policy and practice is that of teasing out basic assumptions and subjecting them to research investigation with a view to suggesting in what ways they are well founded and in what ways they seem to be mistaken.

But in spite of the fact that research of this kind has high policy relevance critics and commentators on the reorganisation of British social work have been slow to adopt such an empirical approach. With a few exceptions (Hall, 1976) discussion has focused largely either upon the value components of the debate or has been rooted in the sectional interests of the professional groups most affected by the reorganisation process. The arguments and assumptions on which the reorganisation proposals are founded have not been studied as closely as they might have been. In particular we lack explicit statement of those models of the internal social stucture of welfare agencies which underpin the arguments throughout. Still less has there been any extended attempt to *test*, in any sense, these models.

Now the research reported in this book is in no way a full-scale evaluation of the organisational changes that led to Social Work and Social Services Departments. What I shall try to do is to bring at least some data to bear upon questions that have all too often been debated in the absence of empirical evidence.

However, I am not only concerned with questions of social policy. Any study, however clearly it is primarily focused on questions of policy or on practical matters, necessarily touches upon theoretical issues pertinent to the research design and methods adopted. In this book therefore I shall also be concerned with some issues of theory, relevant to the research study of welfare organisations.

The central topic of the book, and the research it reports, is the concept of 'social need' and the way welfare agencies function to 'meet need'. This is not very novel. Put in this general way, it is a question that lies at the heart of the vast majority of the research in the field of social work. But traditionally there has been a tendency, again for the vast majority of this research, to analyse such problems by adopting, implicitly if not explicitly, a theoretical stance rooted in two premises.

First, 'need' tends to have been viewed as an objective and measurable property of that group of individuals who either were or should have been clients of welfare organisations. A 'medical model' of need has prevailed—or at least a model of need has prevailed closely akin to that which was thought to be the medical model of disease. Researchers thus spent their time in pursuing the accurate and independent diagnosis and measurement of social need (measurement was considered particularly difficult) and in locating its major causes with a view to its more effective treatment. As more recent studies have shown, this medical model was itself largely an illusion. Professional medicine in practice bears only partial resemblance to the way in which it has sometimes been characterised by other professional groups. As Freidson (1970) notes in discussing disease as an ideology, 'In practice the notion of disease is at once an objective *and an evaluative or moral concept*' (my italics). Nevertheless, medicine persists, for many, as an example of 'scientific' method and practice and much 'needs research' has been conducted in pursuit of this ideal.

The second premise concerns the nature of welfare organisations. Their central function has been assumed to be the more effective treatment of social need. Welfare agencies have been studied as if they were social structures in rational and co-ordinated pursuit of a set of objectively defined corporate goals. Research became the explication of these goals and the study of the effectiveness with which they were pursued under various conditions. Study after study has concluded that the goals are unclear and the agencies ineffective.

Recently however, this approach to the study of organisations, sometimes referred to as the 'orthodox' stance, has been criticised on a number of counts. Sociologists studying phenomena closely related to social need, such as delinquency (Cicourel, 1968), death (Sudnow, 1967), blindness (Scott, 1969) or mental illness (Scheff, 1966) have suggested that it is most helpful to view such phenomena not simply as properties of the individual client but as the outcome of a rather complex interaction pattern between clients on the one hand and professionals on the other. To complicate matters even further the interaction usually takes place within a set of organisational constraints in which the notions and activities of the professional workers are quite as significant as the properties of their clientele.

This kind of departure from the 'orthodox' stance in the study of professional practice in organisations is especially apparent in research which explores the use of particular concepts as actually sited within the social milieu in which they are employed from day to day. There is a very marked difference in approach in studies which are mainly concerned with *rates* of crime, or of the incidence of mental illness, for example, as compared with studies based on the participant observation of the way the police or judiciary handle criminals, or psychiatrists treat their patients. One very good example of the debate that has taken place between different approaches to the study of such phenomena can be found in the sociological study of suicide (Douglas, 1967). As far as the study of social need is concerned, this debate directs our attention to the

7

professional and to the contextual aspects of social need which considerations of the concept hitherto have largely ignored.

There is also a good deal of doubt about the value of an 'orthodox' approach to the study of welfare organisations as contexts for the interaction between professionals and their clients. Etzioni (1960), Perrow (1961), Bittner (1965) and Albrow (1968) amongst others have all undermined the central and established position occupied by the notion of organisational goal in this field of research. The central point is that the orthodox model of organisational functioning fails to assign a significant role to the organisational members' own subjective ideas about the phenomena in question. So far as the study of social need is concerned, the implication of this point is that we cannot expect successfully to study either the needs of clients or the administrative procedures of agencies for managing these needs, without also studying the concepts and ideologies of social workers about these needs.

These comments ride roughshod over many important points of detail that I shall come back to later in this book. At this stage I want only to indicate the general theoretical debates to which some discussion of the concept of social need may contribute.

Finally, apart from social policy and theoretical objectives, it seems that a research approach to the idea of social need is potentially useful methodologically. Most studies of the way welfare agencies meet social need in Britain have relied on limited sources of data; the research interview (sometimes only with senior staff in the organisation) and the records and statistics generated routinely by the agency. Although a second method may be used in providing an introductory background, it is most usual to rely heavily upon one type of data. Observational data are hardly ever used. There exists very little work on the functioning of British welfare agencies which is based on direct observational research methods.

These tendencies—the reliance upon a single data source and the sparse use of observational materials—are partly the result of practical difficulties. It is simply much easier to rely on one method of data collection. Many students feel (I think mistakenly) that if they are going to make a contribution to policy debate then they must base their work on large samples, which makes collecting a variety of data types even more difficult. It has also been suggested that observational techniques pose insurmountable problems of research access (raising severe problems of confidentiality) and that the impact of observer effect is difficult to control. I suspect that these difficulties have been overestimated and sometimes, almost certainly, the privacy of the client has been used as a screen to shield the professional from investigation. But most significantly the methods used have reflected the predominant 'objectivist' theoretical approach to 'need' that I have already mentioned. The general suggestion that reality, including 'need', is socially and in important ways subjectively constructed (Berger and Luckmann, 1967) has not been taken very seriously in this field of research. Certainly it has had little impact on the methods of data collection used in studies of welfare services.

If we do take this suggestion seriously we encounter several rather interesting methodological problems. Quickly it becomes apparent that official records and statistics, interview material and observational field notes, generate quite different types of description of what is going on in an agency. The meaning of official statistics has recently received especially close scrutiny (Kitsuse and Cicourel, 1963; Sudnow, 1965; Wheeler, 1967, 1969). This kind of data must be viewed as a highly specialised type of 'account'. The data are the outcome of specific rate-producing processes. That is not to say that such data are useless. Far from it. But if we are going to know how to use them we must comprehend the rate-producing processes and that means we must use other kinds of research techniques as well. Interview data similarly generate only particular forms of description (Cicourel, 1964) to be interpreted in the context of professional ideologies that generate such accounts.

The problem being referred to here is the central problem of establishing the validity of instruments of research. This problem refers to the extent to which the events being measured correspond to what it is that they are assumed to be measuring (Denzin, 1970). It is a very important question and insufficient attention has been paid to it within social work research. We require to know far more than we do about the major sources of data typically employed in research on welfare agencies. For example, we should know more about how closely professional behaviour with clients corresponds to reported behaviour in interviews. We should know more about the actions of social workers, secretaries, administrators, civil servants, statisticians and politicians as they assemble official statistics. We should know more about how files and records are produced if we are to interpret them correctly. But knowledge of this kind must await further research. Meanwhile there are precautions which research designs should embody.

First, as Denzin explains, 'One technique for establishing validity is to link the empirical measurement of a concept directly with its theoretical definition. This method asks to what extent the measurement process complements and draws upon the theoretical perspective under analysis' (1970, p. 104). In this report I shall seek to place a description of the research techniques employed in the context of a discussion of important conceptual problems associated with the idea of social need.

Second, the weakness of being bound to a single-method source of data may be avoided by approaching problems from different angles in the use of multiple methods. We can tap both behavioural and attitudinal dimensions. If we observe an event, examine the records which others have made on the basis of that event and talk to participants in that event about it, we have at least some protection against the distortions that might arise if we did only one of those things. This approach Denzin refers to as 'methodological triangulation'. Data of different kinds are brought to bear upon the same question. Events are studied through a combination, for example, of interviewing, participant observation and the analysis of files and records. In that way we have more chance of eliminating the distortions that may be inherent in any one type of data and which may be particularly misleading because they are not fully understood.

These are some of the methodological issues that I shall discuss at various points in this book. I shall take up Denzin's suggestions. I shall present some interview data and some observational material on social workers' interactions with clients and I shall describe how these data were collected. I shall also be paying particular attention to the ways in which documents and statistics are generated in social work and the implications of these processes for researchers, administrators and professional practitioners who seek to use them as objective indices of social need.

Part One

'Need' in policy

Chapter two

Reorganising social work

Although there have been some differences between recent developments in the reorganisation of social work in Scotland, and in England and Wales, the changes throughout Britain have had one central feature in common: the creation of 'unified departments' at the local authority level charged with administering the great majority of the personal social services. The proposal for these changes was the outcome of a policy debate in which three reports— Seebohm, Kilbrandon and the White Paper *Social Work and the Community*—featured prominently, providing the basis for later legislation and organisational change.

In this chapter I am going to look quite closely at these reports since their arguments and proposals are rooted in a number of important assumptions about the nature of social need. I shall try to systematise the arguments on which they depend in the form of causal models about the functioning of social service provision, paying particularly close attention to the way in which the idea of social need is managed in this policy debate. In Part three I shall present some research material which puts to the test one central assumption about the reorganisation of British social work, which will be highlighted during the discussion in this chapter.

The case for change in Seebohm

Originally appointed in December 1965, the Seebohm Committee received the commission: 'to review the organisation and responsibilities of the Local Authority Personal Social Services in England and Wales and to consider what changes are desirable to secure an effective family service' (para. 1). The Committee's central recommendation that the numerous existing social work and social welfare services then provided by a range of local authority agencies should in future be provided by a single Social Services Department, is now well known and has been much discussed. So too have Seebohm's more specific suggestions about the qualification of directors, the size of area teams, the role of research, the provision of services to the courts for children under seventeen and much else besides. They were linked by a common theme. As a package, it was argued, they would allow for the more 'effective' provision of personal social services in terms of meeting the 'consumers' need'. And it is this theme—the relationship between the effective meeting of social need and particular forms of administrative structure—that recurred throughout the Report.

Now in setting out these recommendations the Committee presented its reasoning in stages. First it established the grounds for some kind of organisational change. It described deficiencies in the existing personal social services and accounted for them, ultimately, in terms of the existing organisational structure. Several possible forms of reorganisation were then considered, but each was rejected in turn until, finally, the reorganisation of the personal social services as a single Social Services Department was proposed.

Let us take the general case first, and consider the large number of assumptions about the relation between organisational structures and social service efficiency in meeting clients' needs, on which the argument for organisational change in general was based. Initially the Committee detected shortcomings in the existing services. These it described as (1) inadequacies in the amount, range and quality of provision, which bore no systematic relation to differences in the levels of relevant social needs, (2) poor co-ordination of services to meet related needs, (3) problems of client access to services, and (4) low levels of adaptability of services to meet changing social needs. Together these deficiencies reflected what Seebohm viewed as the rigid and artificial notions of social need endemic to the prevailing structure of service provision. It was argued that these notions did not reflect the true nature of social need, were not amenable to change within the existing administrative framework, and could be viewed as little more than merely arbitrary.

Collectively the shortcomings Seebohm detailed were then accounted for in terms of three factors, lack of resources, inadequate knowledge and divided responsibility and these in turn, it was claimed, were rooted in the existing organisational structure. Inadequate knowledge and divided responsibility were seen as directly dependent, in substantial part, on the way the services were organised. The social services' lack of resources, on the other hand, was explained as a function of the services' organisational structure only via three further intervening variables: (1) the career prospects, salaries and conditions of staff, (2) local influence on central government and (3) efficiency in the use of resources.

The assumed links between all these factors are spelled out in considerable detail in the Seebohm Report (especially in paragraphs 86-100). It would be tedious to rehearse them all here. (See Smith, 1971 for a fuller discussion.) What I have done is to summarise the argument in diagrammatic form in Figure 1. It consists in essence of a series of empirical assumptions, a model of the social services which was implicit in this stage of the Seebohm Report. In this model the organisational structure of the social services at the local government level was posited as the major independent variable to account, via intervening variables, for the failure of the social services to meet clients' needs.

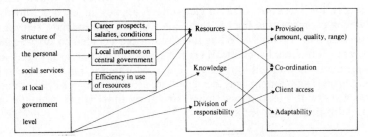

Figure 1 A model of service provision underlying the Seebohm report

Having established the general desirability of change, the Committee then considered in more detail some alternative proposals. It did this by applying the causal model it had implicitly developed (Figure 1) to those defects of the situation which it had diagnosed. The Seebohm Report therefore continued to focus upon organisational factors in its pursuit of a new service structure that would efficiently meet real social need.

Throughout the process of collecting evidence the Committee had, of course, been presented with various proposals for change. But it rejected most of them for the following reason. At the heart of Seebohm's arguments lay the idea of social need and its dissatisfaction with the way in which current notions of need were being operationally employed within the then prevailing structure of service provision. It felt that supposed needs were merely reflections of administrative categories and not accounts of 'true need'. It felt that most of the alternative proposals similarly reflected artificial, rigid or administrative notions which did not tally with what is viewed as the genuine underlying nature of the social needs and problems of the services' clientele. Only the creation of a much broader unitary welfare agency, it was suggested, would not be subject to this defect and it was on this basis that a single Social Services Department in each local authority was suggested.

So what was Seebohm proposing? The Report did not simply recommend administrative change. The point is that it was proposing administrative change in pursuit of the operational employment of revised notions of social need. The Committee opted for a complete reconceptualisation of social need on the part of professionals operating the services. It argued that neither the clients' presenting problems nor the legal or administrative categories of the services were indicative of the fundamental problems with which the services should be concerned. Rather these problems should be located within the family and community contexts in which they arose; the structure of a single welfare agency in each authority would promote this line of thinking and the appropriate relevant professional practices. What the Committee decided to do was to press professional social workers for a redefinition of social need in terms of 'the unified approach'. The recommendation for a Social Services Department was designed to provide the personal social services with an organisational structure that would promote a redefinition of this kind.

'Social need' in Seebohm

Summarised in this way, the Seebohm Report soon poses an important question in the mind of anyone interested in the evaluation of social policy. If pre-Seebohm notions of need were invalid, how can we tell whether the new ones are any better? That is, how did the Seebohm Report define 'social need'? In short, it did not—at least not clearly. Although the criticism of existing social service provision is based upon its failure to meet social needs, the concept of need itself remains ambiguous and ill-defined throughout the Committee Report. And this is something which we will encounter repeatedly in studying the idea of need in policy, practice and research. It is used without being explicitly defined. We can infer a definition only by observing the practices of its management which is why the empirical study of the management of the concept is so interesting. We must explore Seebohm's use of the idea a little further.

The problem is that although initial analysis was based upon assessment of social need in terms of the existing administrative categories, it was a basic recommendation of the Report that these categories should be abandoned because they were rigid and artificial. Needs should be reconceptualised but the reconceptualisation was again only spelled out in terms of an alternative administrative structure. The Report suggested that the proposed service should remain sensitive to new and emergent needs, but it remained unclear as to how these might be measured and detected in the absence of criteria independent of the organisational categories of the social services.

Townsend (1968) criticised the Committee for its imprecision in assessing social need. He called for three types of information: estimates of the number who are in general conditions of need, estimates of current need by service, and estimates of current need by local authority. But since the Seebohm proposals for administrative change were designed not only to increase levels of provision for need but also to bring the administrative categories for provision into line with some more realistic notions, there is a problem prior to the calculation of estimates of this sort. The criteria for measuring need must first be established, for the categories in terms of which needs should be estimated or measured are by no means self-evident. The differences, for example, between what have been termed normative need (measured by expert assessment), felt need (measured as want), expressed need (measured as demand) and comparative need (measured by comparing service receivers and non-receivers) may be considerable (Bradshaw, 1972). A careful reading of the text of the Report shows that in fact the Committee moved between several meanings of the term. Sometimes by 'social need' the Committee meant administrative categories (either existing or proposed), sometimes it meant conceptions of need implicit in current social work thinking, sometimes it meant the clients' perceptions of their own needs, sometimes it referred to an assumed consensus within the 'community' as to what counted as social need and on one occasion it referred to 'true need (sometimes a matter for expert diagnosis)'. Occasionally, too, 'social need' and 'social problems' were equated.

Nevertheless, it would be wrong to imply that the idea of social need was so confused as to be entirely devoid of meaning in the Seebohm Report. For although it lacked precise definition the Committee gave some indication as to what would count as appropriate notions of need by referring quite frequently to two other concepts. We are told that a service would be viewed as effectively meeting need only if it were 'family-oriented' and 'community based'. Thus, whatever else was meant by social need in Seebohm, it did have something to do with family and community structures.

To take the idea of a family-oriented service first, we should remember that it was built into the very terms of reference of the Committee. The enquiry arose in the first place from the government's detection of growing public concern at the increase in officially recorded juvenile deliquency rates in recent years. It was in the White Paper *The Child, the Family and the Young Offender,* which stressed the importance of preventing 'family breakdown' in reducing the level of delinquent behaviour, that the government announced its intention of setting up a committee to make recommendations about the personal social services with this end, the prevention of family breakdown, in view. So Seebohm was bound to take 'the family' as a basic unit of social structure in the design of any new form of social service which it might propose, the focus upon the family deriving at least in part from a belief which was widespread in social work thought (although more recently it has been challenged) that family breakdown was a major factor in explaining social need in general and the increase in officially recorded delinquency in particular. This was the conclusion of the preceding White Paper also. Its acceptance as a premise in Seebohm was reflected in the overall recommendation for a department providing a family-oriented service.

Yet in spite of its widespread use in conjunction with the notion of need the Committee was far from happy with the term 'family'. For in defining it such a broad answer to the question 'What is a family?' was offered that the term seemed to retain little meaning at all. The answer is given: 'In other words, everybody' (para. 32). Frequently thereafter the term 'family' appears between quotation marks as if it were being employed in some highly distinctive ways.

This uncertainty reflected a tension in the Report. On the one hand it did seek to escape from the rigid classification of need implied by the 'symptom-centred approach' and one way of doing this was to look beyond the presenting symptoms of distress to the structure of the family as the basic underlying problem. On the other hand there are some categories of need, by almost any definition, that are manifestly not well met by a family-oriented service as it is generally understood. It is well known that many individuals are clients of the social services precisely because they do not have any close relatives. The tension was also apparent in the Report's discussion on social worker specialisation. The Committee expected the 'symptom-centred approach' to be replaced by specialised skills newly emergent in the unified departments, but it failed to specify what the criteria for these new specialisations would or should be.

Thus in its attempt to spell out the idea of need in terms of the family unit the Seebohm Committee equivocated between proposing a fundamental rethinking of the client's problems (all manifest problems should be seen as functions of family need), and proposing merely administrative simplification (there should be just one social worker to deal with what would still be regarded as the many separate needs of each of the family members). The important point for studying the management of the idea of social need is that in the absence of a more rigorous statement of the concept of a family-oriented service, 'need' still remained an ill-defined and ambiguous notion.

The Seebohm Report recommended, too, that if the services of the new department were to meet need effectively they would have to be 'community based'. Thus the notions of 'need' and 'community' were also closely linked, the concept of community being taken to imply: 'the existence of a network of reciprocal social relationships, which among other things, ensure mutual aid and give those who experience it a sense of well-being' (para. 476). Social disintegration and loose-knit social networks were seen to play an important part in promoting 'social pathology' and hindering 'healthy individual development'. A lack of 'community identity' and 'mutual aid' were seen as major factors in the incidence of areas of social need. The Committee's picture of a healthy community was based upon the view that social needs were directly related to people's awareness of their community identity and to close-knit patterns of social relations.

This all remains quite general. As with the concept of a family-based service, it is difficult to tell what Seebohm meant by 'need' without a more rigorous specification of the concept of a community-based service. At times indeed the Report seemed fully aware of its lack of specificity but argued that the spelling out of its intentions should be left to local and central government and the heads of the new departments. (In the event what happened was that at least some aspects of Seebohm's policies were spelled out at levels considerably below that of Chief Officer; by secretaries, receptionists and fieldworkers in area teams. I shall describe some of these practices in Chapter 6.) The point I want to make here is simply that since the Committee's policy was not spelled out in more detail it is difficult to tell what its intentions were.

Indeed there are times when apparently quite contradictory proposals were advanced. It was suggested, for instance, that the Social Services Department should adopt a general orientation to community needs and should foster conditions that were favourable to a sense of community identity. But in view of the Report's comments that 'different members of a family may belong to different communities of interest', this suggestion appeared to be in conflict with the earlier stress upon a family-based service. The Committee also recommended that clients should be encouraged to provide each other with service, but the implication that a good deal of social work could as well be provided by a competent good neighbour contrasted with the Committee's views elsewhere that social work was a matter for skilled professionals who required both pre- and in-service training. As a final example of an apparent contradiction, the Committee recommended that clients should be encouraged to exercise control over professional and bureaucratic power. On occasions it was recognised that this might mean direct community protest against professional decisions although the principle of 'professional autonomy' is also a principle which the Committee appeared to defend.

Thus although at first sight the notion of a community-based service appeared to offer some guidelines as to what Seebohm meant by a service aimed at 'need', it is apparent on close inspection that the idea of community, like the concepts of 'the family' and 'need' itself, is characterised by a rather high degree of ambiguity. The point is that, at least so far as the Seebohm Report is concerned, the idea of the Social Services Department offering a community-based and family-oriented service does not move us far forward in search of any operational definition of social need. Social workers in the new unified departments would have to manage without precise policy guidance in seeking any new notions of social need to replace those previously dependent upon legal and administrative categories.

Before coming to any conclusions, however, we must also have a look at how the idea of social need was managed in the policy debate that preceded the reorganisation of social work in Scotland: in the Kilbrandon Report and in the Government White Paper, *Social Work and the Community*. But before proceeding to do that I want to consider an important possible objection to the way in which I have approached the study of how 'need' is managed in the context of social policy.

An objection overruled

In discussing the Seebohm Report and in reviewing White Papers and the reports of other government commissions or committees of enquiry that together go to make up the 'policy debate' that is the subject of this chapter, I am making two important assumptions. I presume first that we are justified in expecting such reports to be unambiguous in their recommendations and to define as clearly as possible the basic ideas and concepts which they employ. Second, I take it that the basic assumptions upon which a report's recommendations rest can reasonably be expected to be true. Thus in reviewing the part played by the concept of social need in policy debate about the reorganisation of social work I have used for guidance the general standards of clarity and validity that would be held appropriate to any discussions within social science.

However, it is important to establish that these criteria are, in fact, appropriate. For it might well be argued that since government reports are really a part of the political arena, then factors such as political ideology, pressure-group activity, the availability of resources, or the dynamics of large committees, for instance, are far more likely to be significant and relevant than any standards derived from some kind of scientific rationality. P. Hall (1976) has studied some of the politicking that surrounded the production of the Seebohm Report. It might well be objected that, although rational critical standards may well be appropriate to a social scientific report, it is simply naive even to expect them to be sustained by government reports or other policy documents. It could be argued that a policy proposal should really be judged by, for example, the success with which it reconciles opposing views, brings about change without increased cost or encourages reforms in advance of public opinion without prompting undue opposition. That may be so, but my argument is that political and other factors may be used to explain confusions or inaccuracies in social policy *once* these have been detected. That is the first thing to do. I want therefore to take a little space at this point to establish: (1) that the reports of government committees of enquiry and similar bodies *do* consist, in large part, of sets of factual assertions and (2) that the task of producing such a report is, at least in major part, a scientific enterprise in the sense that it takes place in what has been described as a 'context of assertion'. These points have been argued at length in Smith and Stockman (1972). But I want to recall the significant points of the argument here since it is important, as the basis for much that follows in this book, to confirm the relevance of assessment criteria drawn from social scientific method to social policy debate.

I said in the introduction to this book that it reported an empirical study in sociology. More precisely it reports an empirical study in the sociology of knowledge since it is with the *idea* of social need that I am primarily concerned. So, without our delving too deeply into the philosophy of social science, there are one or two issues involved in studying 'knowledge' that we cannot avoid. In particular, in formulating an approach to the study of the policy basis of social work reorganisation, I want to take issue with a tendency in the sociology of knowledge to study the causes and consequences of beliefs separate from questions about their validity.

Certainly, it seems clear that we *can* distinguish valid from invalid assumptions or beliefs in the sense that it is quite *possible* for us to do so. (At any particular point in time, of course, social scientists may disagree about standards of acceptability and these may change over time but that does not affect the essential point of the argument.) The more significant question, however, is whether or not it is *appropriate* to examine the truth of an assumption or belief if we are to understand how it is being used. I think it is and to support the point it is helpful to refer to a couple of fairly basic distinctions.

First, we may be concerned not only with the causes of a particular belief or assumption but also with its consequences. In discussing 'knowledge' in general and the assumptions of social policy in particular, it is important to be clear whether the causes or effects are the main point of interest, for the considerations which are relevant do differ. I shall return to this point later. Second, it is important to draw the distinction between the criteria of rationality and those of truth (or validity), for they are not the same. It is not irrational to believe something or to make an assumption that only later or elsewhere is discovered to be false, so long as at that particular time and in that particular place the view was a reasonable one. Thus we can define a rational belief as one which is held by an individual or group of people while consistently pursuing the activities normally considered appropriate to arriving at that particular type of belief. But of course a rational belief is not necessarily true.

On the other hand a true belief is not necessarily a rational one. An assumption might be made quite irrationally but nevertheless turn out by chance to be true. Presumably that does not happen very often. Most frequently people arrive at the truth by trying to do so, claiming to do so, and doing so in a way that is generally reckoned to be fruitful in this respect (for example by collecting evidence or seeking the views of informed people rather than by spinning roulette wheels). That is, people who are in the business of making statements that they intend to be true operate in what we may term a 'context of assertion'. Philosophers and philosophers of science have, of course, given a good deal of attention both to the problems of truth and rationality (e.g. MacIntyre, 1964; Wilson, 1970). Our problem here is to decide when each type of criteria is relevant. The point I am making is that although criteria of rationality may be applicable to all kinds of beliefs and assumptions (because the explanation of rational and irrational beliefs must follow different courses) criteria of truth (whether or not there be universal truth criteria) are applicable to 'contexts of assertion'. So, in order to make use of criteria of truth or validity drawn from social science, we must be able to identify the social context as one of assertion and we do this by noting the activities people engage in while advancing a belief or adopting an assumption.

We can now return to the point about whether our main interest is in causes or effects. If attention is exclusively on the *causes* of a particular belief, then truth criteria are not really relevant. Here it is the criteria of rationality, rather than the truth or not of beliefs which is appropriate, for whether an assumption is true or false does not tell us very much about why it should have been adopted. But if we are concerned with the consequences of an assumption, the question of truth is much more relevant. If a group making some assumptions gives every appearance of seeking to sustain empirically verifiable statements about the world then the clarity and scientific validity of these beliefs are highly relevant criteria both in the critical examination of the internal structure of those beliefs and in researching the consequences of their adoption.

The relevance of this whole discussion to the study of government committee reports and other sources of policy debate lies in considering whether it is really naive to expect the assumptions and arguments of a report to be clear and true. It seems that we can dismiss the objection that we should be using political or some other criteria, but certainly not the criteria of social science, on two grounds. (I am not, of course, wanting to argue that political and other factors have *no* part to play in policy analysis and research. But I do want to counteract the argument that the criteria of scientific rationality have no part to play.) First, whatever factors may have influenced the production of a report, if, as we most often are in the field of social policy, we are concerned with the likely results of implementing its proposals, then the validity of its basic assumptions are most relevant. Second, if we can establish that reports are produced within a context of assertion, then again it is clear that questions of truth and clarity are relevant.

With this discussion in mind I can now explain why I am treating the policy debate on which the reorganisation of social work was based as having taken place within a context of assertion. In discussing the Seebohm Report in the first part of this chapter I referred to the defects in service provision which the committee diagnosed, to the policy objectives which it spelled out and to the recommendations that it made in suggesting how to make improvements in the services. The important point to note is that each of these sets of statements consisted of, or presupposed, factual statements about the social world or assumed causal relationships between variables. Figure 1 set out many of these relationships as a causal model. It is, perhaps, not entirely clear that policy objectives are exclusively statements of fact, since it is often thought that the formation of policy objectives is a purely evaluative task. But even here matters of fact are highly relevant since what distinguishes a specifically *policy* objective is that it is intended to be (and is seen to be) potentially realisable. When Seebohm talks about improving the amount, quality and range of provision, and improving service co-ordination, client access and the adaptability of the services, I take it that the Committee is not simply in the business of playing with Utopias.

This prima facie case for suggesting that in social policy discussion we are operating in contexts of assertion is supported by the fact that a commission or committee also generally reports that it did engage in a series of activities which are normally pursued only by people who are trying to make true statements about the real world. Committees, for example, invariably claim to have collected material which they refer to as 'evidence'. Seebohm and Kilbrandon certainly did. Sometimes they call upon the views of independent consultants who are asked to offer advice on the basis of their acknowledged scientific expertise. In appointing a 'working group'to draw up the reorganisation proposals that appeared in *Social Work and the Community* (1966), the Secretary of State for Scotland had 'the benefit of the advice of Professor R. M. Titmuss, Professor of Social Administration, London School of Economics; Miss M. Browne, Department of Social Study, University of Edinburgh and Mrs C. M. Carmichael, School of Social Study, University of Glasgow.' Spencer (1973) reports that this group of 'independent advisers' actually drafted this particular paper. Committees also often conduct 'research' which may either be done by outside academic teams or by the Government Social Survey. Certainly the Seebohm Committee commissioned some pieces of research and it also reported that it would like to have done very much more research than it did had time constraints allowed. In the field of education there have been some particularly notable examples, in the reports of the Robbins Committee on higher education and the Plowden Committee on primary schools, of the role of research in policy debate.

The case for the relevance of scientific criteria in reviewing policy discussions is, finally, supported by some historical evidence about the way in which government enquiries have developed. Since the early nineteenth century the Registrar General's Office and the Statistical Office have developed in parallel with the statistical section of the British Association and the founding of statistical societies in major British cities (Perkin, 1969). The process of Benthamite 'factual enlightenment' in the process of administration was clearly exhibited in the Reports of the Poor Law Commissioners and subsequently in later Royal Commissions. Currently the reports of the Supplementary Benefits Commission are relatively sophisticated social scientific documents. Government committees have made increasing use of official statistics. The Government Social Survey set up in 1941 has come to be an important link between departmental committee enquiries and academic social science (Moser, 1958). Not only do committees commission research but it tends to be of an increasingly academic nature. All this lends support to the appropriateness of applying the criteria of social science to the arguments and assumptions contained in those policy documents which formed the basis for the reorganisation of social work throughout Britain.

In Scotland the most important of the ideas on which reorganisation was based are found in the Kilbrandon Report and in a subsequent government White Paper, *Social Work and the Community*. In parallel with the comments on the Seebohm Report in the first part of this chapter I shall now turn to the debate which began a little earlier, in 1964, north of the border. Again, the purpose of this review is to see how the idea of social need was managed within an area of social policy.

Kilbrandon

The Kilbrandon Committee began with a familiar problem: a supposed increase in the level of juvenile delinquency as indicated by rates calculated on the basis of officially recorded statistics. Early in its report the Committee stressed the importance of caution in drawing conclusions from official criminal statistics but nevertheless concluded that rises in the level of juvenile delinquency were outstepping rises in the juvenile population. Kilbrandon's solution to this problem was to propose (1) a system of Children's Panels and (2) a social education department to provide welfare services in support. This solution rested upon a model of the influence of control agencies which asserted both the organisational structure of juvenile justice and the organisational structure of associated welfare services as the major independent variables to account, at least substantially and via intervening variables, for the prevailing level of juvenile delinquency rates.

The arguments in the report were based upon this model. To begin with, the Committee argued that a disturbingly high level of delinquency arose from the inefficient nature of the then existing treatment measures and the inefficiency of these measures could in turn be accounted for in terms of four factors. First the Committee observed a widespread failure to involve the parents of a delinquent child in the treatment and felt that this process of excluding the parents began with the child's appearance in court. It was not that the parents were not physically at the court sitting. Section 42 of the 1937 Children and Young Persons (Scotland) Act required at least one parent to be there. (Although the Committee noted that the power to compel the presence of the second parent was rarely used.) It was simply that the 'nature of proceedings in the juvenile court' did not encourage parent participation. The procedures for ensuring adequate parental co-operation were far from ideal. The pressure of work upon each court also, it was thought, prevented it from spending sufficient time on each case.

A second reason given for inefficiency in the treatment process of juvenile delinquents was the failure of the existing court system to draw a clear distinction between its two quite separate functions; namely the task of determining guilt or innocence on the one hand and the question of sentencing, if guilty, on the other. Kilbrandon argued that these two functions should be dealt with apart from each other. The report indicated the very practical point that in 95 per cent of the cases in juvenile courts the facts alleged were not disputed anyway. Those concerned pleaded guilty. A rational system should be designed with this majority in mind. The Committee sought to establish an agency whose sole concern would be in deciding upon treatment measures for cases that would in effect amount to an agreed referral. A separate trial would be arranged only in the minority of cases where the guilt of the child was in dispute.

But the Report also indicated a more fundamental reason for proposing a separation of the court's two functions. The Committee concluded that in fact a court of law was not very effective as a treatment agency. Kilbrandon argued that the skills involved in performing the two quite separate functions were really of very different kinds. The question of guilt or innocence was a legal matter which rested on questions of fact about a particular instance of behaviour, the 'act'. The sentencing question, however, was an entirely separate one and called for quite different skills. Here the particular piece of behaviour was, in itself, relatively unimportant. As the Report explained: 'The offence, while the essential basis for judicial action, has significance only as a pointer to the need for intervention.' Legal classifications and standards, it was implied, might well be quite inappropriate to what should be the central concern of any body dealing with sentencing. Here it was the child's underlying needs which should be the central concern and any new agency designed exclusively with sentencing in mind should be structured to focus primarily upon these needs:

> [The Agency] would have no concern whatsoever with the determination of legal issues, its sole function being the consideration and application of training measures *appropriate to the child's needs.* Such an agency would clearly not be a criminal court of law, or indeed a court in any accepted sense. It would be the duly constituted public agency authorised to deal with juvenile offenders, where necessary by the application of compulsory measures. Within the range of measures

authorised by law, it would have the widest discretion in their application *appropriate to the needs of the individual child* (para. 73; italics mine).

Thus, like Seebohm, Kilbrandon was not merely concerned with administrative changes of a procedural kind. The Report was also concerned with the fundamental nature of juvenile delinquency. I mentioned in the introduction that the reorganisation of social work took place within the context of an expanding notion of what phenomena properly fell within the domain of social welfare. In important sections of its Report the Kilbrandon Committee was arguing that the nature of delinquency was such that the treatment process would be inefficient if questions of guilt and innocence and the nature of the offence were uppermost. It would be preferable, it was argued, to remove delinquency completely from the legal framework and assign it to a new type of agency which would be an aspect of welfare provision rather than of the framework of the law. And here the issue of social need should be uppermost.

Now, given that the question of social need was to figure prominently in dealings with juvenile delinquents, what was then clearly required was some appropriate framework for coding different types of need. The third reason which Kilbrandon gave for the inefficiency of existing treatment measures was that the categories of classification which did then exist were quite unrealistic. The Committee explained: 'we have had to consider how far the present treatment measures, as available and as applied, can be said to fulfil the criterion of actual need' (para. 15). They found the measures wanting in this respect and offered an explanation in close parallel to that of the Seebohm Committee which argued that many categories of social service provision were rigid and artificial and did not reflect 'true need'.

When the Kilbrandon Committee reported, children appearing before a juvenile court were divided by the law into four groups— those accused of having committed a crime, those in need of care and protection, those beyond parental control, and persistent truants. Kilbrandon insisted that these were completely fictitious groupings as far as the reality of the underlying problems was concerned.

> The great majority of the witnesses with whom we discussed this matter agreed . . . that in terms of the child's actual needs, the legal distinction between juvenile offenders and children in need of care or protection was—looking to the underlying realities—very often of little practical significance . . . these various classifications can not in practice be usefully considered as presenting a series of distinct and separately defineable

problems, calling in turn for distinct and separate principles
of treatment. The basic similarity of underlying situation far
outweighs the differences (paras. 13 and 15).

I have again quoted at some length from the Report here because in
this section of its argument the Committee was making an extremely
important point. Kilbrandon was not only attempting to demolish
the distinction between four types of legally defined delinquency but
also the distinction between the underlying 'needs' or 'problems' of
children and 'delinquency' *per se*. The suggestion that the treatment
process was inefficient because the parents were not fully involved
might be interpreted as merely a procedural suggestion about the
time that a court should devote to each case and the manner in
which the hearing should occur. The idea that a new framework for
coding social need was required, was rather more fundamental than
this. The Seebohm Report proposed not only administrative simplification but also a complete rethinking of the nature of social need.
Likewise Kilbrandon was recommending, not only a limited set of
modifications to the juvenile courts but also that 'delinquency' was
not a matter for the courts at all but rather fell within the domain of
some kind of welfare institution whose primary objective would be
that of meeting social need.

So far, I have referred to three factors which Kilbrandon suggested accounted for inefficient treatment of delinquents: a low level of
parental involvement, the confusion of questions of fact and welfare
and unrealistic categories of classification of need. The Committee
suggested that these deficiencies could be corrected by the creation
of Children's Panels in each local authority area. The most important
features of a Panel, the Committee explained, would be (1) that it
would be neither a court of law nor a local authority committee, (2)
that it would be peopled by those who were especially skilled at
assessing children's needs, (3) that the children would clearly remain
within the existing ambit of the law and (4) that in some areas the
Panel would have powers of intervention between parent and child
greater than those of the juvenile courts of the time. These were the
Panel's 'salient features'. (For a fuller and later discussion of various
aspects of the Children's Panel system, together with a bibliography,
see Martin and Murray (eds), 1976.)

But Kilbrandon did not see the Panels alone as a solution to the
deficiencies that the Committee had diagnosed. In conjunction with
this recommendation, it proposed too a reorganisation of local
government services. I said that Kilbrandon believed four factors to
be causing inefficiency in the treatment process. The fourth was the
existence of a multiplicity of agencies charged with the delinquent's
training needs. Kilbrandon was critical of the 'process of shuffling

from one agency to another' and felt that there should be one single agency with a remit more comprehensive in relation to the needs of children than that of any of the existing authorities. This was the origin of those organisations which now exist as Social Work Departments in Scotland and which closely resemble the Social Services Department in England and Wales. They began life, in the Kilbrandon Report, as 'social education departments', and were proposed as (relatively) minor adjuncts to the Children's Panels in a chapter headed 'The Matching Field Organisation' (ch. XII). Under these proposals it was the primary function of the social education departments to provide a service to the Panels, thus contributing to the greater efficiency of the treatment process and the reduction of juvenile crime. Under these proposals, too, the Committee hoped that a single organisation would be recognised as the point for co-ordinating information about all cases of children in need.

` Specifically, Kilbrandon made various suggestions about the powers and internal structure of the new agency. The members of the Committee were clear in saying that 'we do not think the importance of organisational matters should be under-emphasised'. The new organisation should assume the most important powers and duties of the existing Children's Departments and with the child care service would be merged 'a substantial number of those at present serving in the probation service'. Kilbrandon saw what it felt to be arbitrary distinctions between the child care and probation services, at least as far as the needs of children were concerned, as having 'no basis in reality'. (Since Kilbrandon's terms of reference confined discussion to children and young persons the Committee could say little about the adult probation service. This was included within the new organisation in the later White Paper.) The new agency would also take charge of the child guidance service, school welfare service and, in Kilbrandon, the school medical service. It would, too, be responsible for operating assessment centres and the approved school aftercare service. Overall the agency represented 'A merging and reorganisation of those existing services whose primary concern is with the problems of the children in special need' (para. 233).

This, then, is the line of reasoning in the Kilbrandon Report that led the Committee to recommend the creation of a system of Children's Panels and the reorganisation of major sections of Scotland's social work services. This argument consists in major part of a set of empirical assumptions. These I have tried to highlight and they are set out in diagrammatic form in Figure 2. As in the Seebohm Report, they constitute, in essence, a causal model which accounts for the level of delinquency rates and efficiency of welfare service provision to children and young persons in terms (via intervening variables) of the organisation of juvenile justice and the organisation of associated social work services aimed at meeting the juvenile's needs. As in Seebohm, one central assumption was that the ineffectiveness of existing welfare services reflected the 'unrealistic' or 'artificial' notions of need which were embodied within the prevailing service structure. The promotion of a reorganised structure, it was assumed, would promote the operational use of new categories closer to the realities of social need.

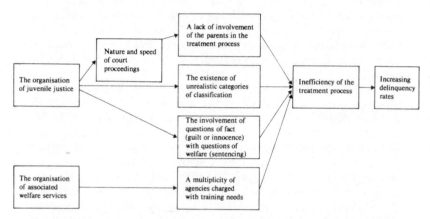

Figure 2   A model of service provision underlying the Kilbrandon Report

So although the aim of the proposed new social work agencies was initially rather limited in scope, being confined to reducing delinquency and being advanced primarily as a more efficient mechanism for collating information towards this end, Kilbrandon's proposals also contained the basis for a more far-reaching reorganisation of the personal social services in Scotland than was actually spelled out in detail at that stage. And even what Kilbrandon called the 'social education department', would, he envisaged, operate in practice as a fairly wide ranging social work agency. Supervision would take place 'within the community' and would 'involve the application of family case work' practised most often by qualified social workers. Kilbrandon saw fit, too, to mention that in the evidence collected by the Committee the proposal to extend a reorganised service to adults as well as children had received strong support.

In discussions before us, reference was made by some of the witnesses to the possibility in the long term of an even wider measure of reorganisation of services so as to provide a comprehensive 'family service' catering for the needs of adults of all ages, as well as those of children in the family (para. 246).

It was a view of which the Committee approved. Although its own proposals were, given the terms of reference, limited to children it noted;

we would expect that our own proposals, if adopted, would go a considerable way to improve the channels of communication necessary for concerted action relating to those, *young or old*, within a particular family unit, and irrespective of the initial source of referral (para. 246) (italics mine).

and added

Such an approach [that of family service] is, we believe, a proper and appropriate one as catering for the needs of children, and insofar as the idea of a 'family service' is a practical and achievable aim we consider that its centre and core will continue to be found in a service of the kind which we have recommended (para. 246).

It is important to quote directly from the Report here. The point we are making is that once the problem of delinquency has been redefined from terms of crime and guilt to terms of social need, and reorganisation proposed to give effect to this view, then there is no obvious reason, apart from Kilbrandon's initial terms of reference, why those proposals should be limited to children and young persons. Indeed, if social need has something to do with the local community and the family unit there is every reason to propose a comprehensive service on a much wider scale. Kilbrandon was aware of this view and was at pains to express it, by implication with approval, in the concluding paragraphs of the Report. The logic of the position was to be taken up and developed more fully, in the subsequent White Paper, *Social Work and the Community*.

But before I conclude discussion of the Kilbrandon Report and turn to the White Paper there is one further point that I want to make. And it is a point very closely related indeed to one I made about the Seebohm Report. I noted that, although Seebohm's criticism of existing services was based upon their embodiment of artificial notions of need, what would count as a more appropriate set of categories was not clearly indicated. The same is true of Kilbrandon. The Committee argued as I have explained, that the legal and administrative ideas of need were unreal. It did not, however, spell out what it did mean by real need nor how such needs might be identified or assessed. Like Seebohm, Kilbrandon indicated that the idea of need bore some relation to the community within which the need occurred and should also be met within the context of a comprehensive family service. But in Kilbrandon both notions received even slighter elaboration than in Seebohm and do little to clarify the idea of need. In short, while both Kilbrandon and Seebohm assumed that the reorganisation and integration of welfare services which they both proposed would promote operational notions of need closer to reality, neither specified the criteria for determining what that reality might be.

Social work and the Community

The Government White Paper *Social Work and the Community* published in October 1966 was the third of the most important official policy documents on which the reorganisation of British social work was based. The White Paper was at pains to stress its continuity with the proposals of the Kilbrandon Report, and the proposals of the White Paper have subsequently been widely referred to as being consistent with those of Kilbrandon. Although there were some differences, so far as our interests here are concerned it is true that in broad outline the dual recommendation for a system of Panels of lay members on the one hand, and a social work organisation unifying the previously disparate social services, on the other, was the same. In summarising the framework of argument in *Social Work and the Community* we can see too that, as in the Seebohm and Kilbrandon Reports, it consisted in essence, of a model of social service provision which posited the organisational structure of welfare services (together with the associated organisation of juvenile justice) as a major independent variable to account, via a set of intervening variables, for the effectiveness of service provision in coping with the problem of social need.

The question with which the White Paper began was not actually the specific problem of increasing delinquency rates, as was the case with Kilbrandon, but the more diffuse one of the failures of individuals and communities to solve social problems. The White Paper did not believe that social problems could be entirely annihilated but it did believe that under ideal conditions these problems could be solved by the individuals, who were involved, themselves. Although, it was argued, some kind of community development programmes which had been lacking in the past might help to avoid the creation of some difficulties, in the long run, difficulties would continue to occur.

Now normally, the White Paper suggested, the individual should be able to cope, of his own accord. If he is unable to it could be as a result of one of two factors. First it might be a matter of individual personal development related to child-rearing, upbringing and education. On the other hand it might be that the individual is unable to call upon the support of those family or community relations which are usually available when individuals encounter problems from time to time which they are unable to solve by their personal efforts alone.

Thus in setting down policy objectives for social work in Scotland the White Paper argued that a wider approach to community development could prevent the occurrence of some social problems but that, once they have occurred, social problems are rightly solved in the first instance by the individual himself and if this is not possible through the support of community and family relations. It should therefore be the central objective of service provision aimed at solving problems (1) to promote the individual's full personal development and (2) to strengthen family and community ties. The White Paper diagnosed that this had, in fact, not been satisfactorily achieved. This was because of defects in the quality and economy of the social work services which could in turn be accounted for in terms of five deficiencies of a more specific kind.

First, a serious overlap in service provision was thought to have occurred. Different service agencies had previously provided different kinds of service but since different types of social need were now thought to derive from the same root causes this specialisation by agency was seen as spurious and wasteful. The multiple visitation of a family by several social workers, who were now seen to be dealing not with separate problems but with separate facets of the underlying need, was regarded as an unnecessary overlap.

Second, it was argued, as Seebohm also argued, that insufficient numbers of trained staff were available to provide a social service of high quality. Additional staff were required. But, third, even those staff which had been available were inefficiently and uneconomically deployed. In particular, since they were all exercising the same basic skills, it was argued that the specialisation of social workers at an early stage in their careers was premature and inefficient. The resultant competition between agencies for trained staff was seen as inefficient too.

Fourth, the White Paper suggested, again as Seebohm suggested, that there were problems of client access to those services which did exist since families seeking help were often referred from one service to another and did not know which one really should be meeting their need.

The fifth reason offered for the poor quality of service was the inadequacy of the powers for insisting on compulsory measures for children in need of protection or care. The White Paper did not present any detailed comments on the juvenile courts but argued, with Kilbrandon, that some changes were required. It was thought that a new set of procedures for endowing welfare agencies with those compulsory powers would improve the quality of service. These were the arguments upon which the White Paper based its case.

Recommendations were thus made for major organisational changes. The White Paper suggested that four of the factors producing an inefficient service—overlap of provision, insufficient staff, inefficient use of existing staff, and difficulties in client access—could be corrected by organisational change in the personal social services at the local government level. It proposed the creation of a social work department in each local authority to provide community care and support for children, the handicapped, the mentally and physically ill and the aged within a single organisation. This organisation, it was proposed, should include virtually all the personal social services at local government level and since it was thought undesirable to separate the administration of support in the community from that of residential care the Social Work Department should be responsible for residential establishments as well. This Social Work Department should also, the White Paper proposed, include the whole of the probation service. It argued that since the main duty of the probation officer—personal social work with the offender and his family in the community—was basically the same as that of any other social worker (namely the assessment and meeting of need albeit manifest in a variety of ways) there was no clear reason for maintaining a separate organisation for this service. This represented a simple extension of Kilbrandon's assumptions to probationers over, as well as under, sixteen years old. The whole proposal represented a major reorganisation of the structure of Scottish social work and the White Paper's expectations for the new department were correspondingly ambitious. Apart from correcting the defects that I have already discussed, the new structure would, it was argued, facilitate movement of staff between institutional and community social work, encourage the recruitment of psychiatric and medical social workers who did not usually enter local authority employment, allow for continuity of care, facilitate communication and consultation between staff and simplify communication between social work and other local government departments. Overall, individuals would be provided with a better and more economical service aimed at meeting their needs.

The fifth factor, which, it was argued, had produced a service of poor quality—the inadequate provision of compulsory measures for children in need of care—could not be corrected simply by reorganising social work. To correct this defect a reorganisation of the system of juvenile justice was proposed. Normally, the White Paper explained, social work service with children would be provided by voluntary measures, accepted by the family concerned. Sometimes, however, compulsory powers would be required. The White Paper implied (although did not say so explicitly) that the juvenile courts could not provide the social work services with powers that were adequate for use in cases of this kind. It therefore accepted Kilbrandon's suggestion for a system of Children's Panels.

The paper commented that it did not intend to outline in detail the Panel's powers and procedures but it did explain that the Panel would be a body of lay people set up in each county or city and that a Reporter would be appointed for each Panel to arrange the hearings and ensure that the decisions were carried out. Some suggestions were also made on appeal and review procedures and on the principles to be applied in selecting members to serve.

The important point I want to note here is that sufficient detail is provided to make it clear that in the White Paper's view a major objective of the Panel system should be that of providing the new Social Work Departments with those compulsory powers over children and their families which they would otherwise lack. In the White Paper's eyes a Panel has very little to do with enforcing the law as an end in itself. Indeed there were deliberate attempts to rid the panel of any vestiges of the court. Throughout the proceedings the needs of the child should be the criterion of action to be employed. The whole enterprise should be in close accord with the development of social work practice within the new departments.

This concluded the White Paper's proposals for improving the quality of service in order to meet social needs. So far as the reorganisation of social work was concerned the basic assumptions adopted in the White Paper and the major recommendations which followed from these assumptions were common to Kilbrandon and the White Paper and closely paralleled those of the Seebohm Report. I have mentioned some differences. The Kilbrandon proposals for reorganisation were framed largely in terms of a social education department. The White Paper rejected this proposal (although the reasons for this decision were not fully explained). A Social Work Department was proposed instead but the objectives of this agency differed little from Kilbrandon's suggestions save only that, as in Seebohm, it became an independent organisation under the direction of someone who in most cases was expected to be a senior member of the social work profession. The White Paper, too, was not restricted to the needs of children and young persons and was therefore able to extend Kilbrandon's suggestions to recommend the inclusion within the Social Work Departments of the probation service as a whole. This, however, as I noted, was in line with the logic of Kilbrandon's own position. Indeed it is one of the most significant features of the whole debate that while Seebohm, Kilbrandon and the White Paper began with rather different terms of reference all three held important basic assumptions in common and strained, as it were, at their terms of reference to produce recommendations for a change in social work administration which in essentials bore close resemblance to one another.

A signpost

In this chapter I have looked at the way in which the idea of social need has been managed in one area of social policy. I have tried to make explicit the model of service provision underpinning the policy debate upon which major changes in the administration of social work services in Scotland and in England and Wales were based. This model consisted of a set of empirical assertions which advanced the organisational structure of the services as a major independent variable to account for what were seen as serious defects in service provision. At the heart of this model lay a particularly important assumption about social need. It was believed that views of social need centred on the existing categories of social work and social need were simply unrealistic. They merely served to perpetuate 'rigid' and 'artificial' distinctions. Such obsolete views had persisted, it was thought, only because the organisational structure within which social workers had previously functioned prohibited the operational adoption of an alternative body of ideas. It was presumed that the promotion of a new organisational structure would promote the adoption and practical application of new and more accurate notions of the nature of real need. It is this assumption which I want to examine empirically.

Before embarking on such an examination, however, I should recall one further point that I have made throughout this discussion of the idea of social need in the context of a policy debate. The point is this. Although criticism of existing services was based upon their embodiment of artificial notions of need, what would count as a more appropriate set of categories was not clearly indicated. The concept of need was not defined. Contributors to the policy debate did not spell out what they meant by real need nor explain how such needs might be identified or assessed. While it was assumed that the reorganisation and integration of welfare services which were proposed would promote operational notions of need closer to reality, no specification of the criteria for determining what that reality might be was offered. This policy debate as it stands does not offer a concept of need that could serve to guide the processes of collecting and analysing research material.

It might be objected, of course, that there is no reason why it should—that the criteria of validity and clarity and the rationality of social science are not appropriate criteria to use in reviewing a policy debate. I took time out during this chapter to consider that objection. I argued that since we want to understand the consequences of making important assumptions about the nature of social need when these assumptions may or may not be true, and since much debate has taken place in what we may term a context of assertion, then the criteria of social science are very relevant indeed to discussions in the arena of social policy.

In Part two of this book I shall therefore turn to the research literature on social need. I shall examine several major empirical studies of social service provision in Britain in which the concept of social need is assigned an important role. I shall look at how the idea is employed, some conceptual and methodological difficulties stemming from particular uses and some of the proposed solutions to these problems. Then, hopefully armed with a notion of need that might serve the purposes of my own research, I shall return in Part three of the book to examine empirically the policy questions that I have spelled out in this chapter.

Part Two

'Need' in research

Chapter three

Studying need

A preliminary survey of the research literature on social need yields two broad conclusions. These are my starting points. First, the idea of need is used extensively in discussions of, and researches on, almost all aspects of the provision of social work services. This is only to be expected. If, as most practitioners, policy-makers and researchers agree, social work services are, in some sense or other, about meeting social need, then it is diffficult to see how any serious discussion of these services could avoid the idea. Certainly this is the conclusion of both many standard texts and many research reports in the field (Wareham, 1970; Holman, 1970).

The second general conclusion that rapidly emerges from a survey of the literature is that in spite of its widespread occurrence, the notion of need has received scant and unsystematic theoretical treatment. My review is likely, therefore, to be a critical one. The confusions surrounding the idea of need in research have, of course, been noted before. Bradshaw's (1972) review article has described the plethora and imprecision of usages. In her survey of the social welfare services in Buckinghamshire, Jeffreys (1965) said: 'In the absence of generally agreed definitions on precise concepts of need, the requirements of a county like Bucks in 1961 for social welfare services cannot be reliably estimated, and can only be described in the most general terms' (p. 17). Certain measurement techniques may have been improved since that was written but the position on agreed definitions or precise concepts has not changed. All too often, however, the strategy is to note the problems of definition and usage but continue nevertheless regardless of them. As Noel and Rita Timms (1977, p. 141) note, 'Considerations of "needs" usually acknowledge the existence of complexity, even though, as far as social work is concerned, discussion is often launched in the absence of any deep sense of puzzlement about the concept.' It is this practice which invariably leads to substantial confusion in conducting and reporting the subsequent researches. Rein (1969) summed up his feelings about most of the work in the 'needs-research' framework thus:

> This type of research attempted to identify the disparity between needs and resources where resources were defined with reference to the established pattern of professional services and community facilities. Not surprisingly, with unfailing regularity these studies concluded that there was a need for . . . whatever community service was the focus of the inquiry. Such studies were mired in a conceptual confusion from which they could not be rescued (p. 174).

In this chapter I am going to try to detail more closely the nature and source of this confusion. Given that what I am looking for is a concept of need for use in research I have decided that a wide ranging and general survey of the literature will be less useful than a rather particular examination of a smaller number of major empirical research reports. The crucial advantage of this latter course is that we can examine in some detail the practical management of the idea of need in the actual working out of a research project. We can look not only at the possible conceptual confusion but also at the impact of this confusion on the research methodology and techniques of data analysis employed.

The studies I have chosen for review have been selected as major examples of several quite different types of research on the topic of social need. First, there are those studies which focus on variations by agency in the official rates of the provision of services. The central problem underlying this type of study is whether or not the different rates reflect different levels of need in the areas covered or whether they can be explained in some other way. I shall discuss two studies, Packman (1968) and Davies (1968), both of which have had an important effect upon subsequent re-searches. (Also, both the work of Packman and Davies was closely related to the investigations of the Seebohm Committee.)

Second, there are those studies which base their conclusions upon interview or questionnaire surveys of population samples including both respondents who are and who are not in receipt of the services under review. Typically the problem underlying this type of work is whether or not those who are eligible for the services are getting them and whether or not the services that are provided are in a form that meets the needs of the population. One of the best known studies of this type of research is Townsend and Wedderburn (1965).

Third, there are studies which are conducted from a specifically planning perspective. The particular concern here is with the problems of senior welfare professionals and administrators as they seek to design the future development of services in a way that will allow them to meet forthcoming levels and types of social need. Such studies must not only assess existing needs for services but must also estimate levels of future needs and the resources required to meet these needs. Sumner and Smith (1969) is a study which examines the planning activities of a sample of health and welfare authorities in Scotland as well as England and Wales.

Finally, there are experimental studies in the field of social work practice. This type of study seeks to evaluate service delivery by measuring the effectiveness of one or more closely controlled 'input' treatment measures. Levels of client need before and after intervention are recorded and a judgment on the effectiveness of particular treatment strategies is based upon the differences (if any) between the before and after measures. The major British example of this type of research is Goldberg's study *Helping the Aged: A Field Experiment in Social Work* (1970).

So, the studies I shall examine, to see how the concept of need is managed in research, all deal explicitly with the idea. All are empirical research reports. All are studies of the social services in Britain. All have influenced subsequent researches, are regarded as major studies and are widely quoted throughout the literature. Taken together they cover several different services as well as a range of different types of research strategy and data collection techniques. Throughout the chapter I shall have two questions in particular in mind: (1) What notions of need are the researchers using and what problems do they encounter in formulating these ideas? (2) Methodologically what relationship do these notions bear to the data collection strategies used and what difficulties are encountered in managing these strategies within the research project?

Studying agency rates

Needs and numbers in child care

Packman's study *Child Care: Needs and Numbers* (1968) sets out to explain why rates of children in care should vary by local authority area. Several factors are suggested but the one that is particularly relevant here is the suggestion that variations may reflect 'need'.

Early on Packman states clearly the problem that has troubled many researchers seeking to compare agency performance with some non-agency notion of need. She explains:

In the first place it is necessary to know what need is, and second to be able to measure it so that its incidence in each local

authority area can be compared with numbers in care to see
how closely they are related. The immediate difficulty is that need
cannot be defined and measured (p. 33).

The reason for this difficulty is that:

> It is difficult to find any yardstick of need which is independent
> of the decisions of child care staff. Nevertheless an independent
> measure is essential to see whether these decisions are
> themselves variable or whether the numbers in care are an
> accurate reflection of the needs in each area (p. 25).

So to succeed the study must define need, use measures of it
independent of the service agency to assess levels of need in each
area, and then compare these assessments with numbers of children
officially 'in care'.

Packman's management of the concept of need in pursuit of these
objectives has some important weaknesses that we ought to avoid if
at all possible. No definition of need is in fact ever presented and the
study slips through to the task of measuring need without acknowledging that a definition has not been produced. In practice need is
defined in terms of the way in which it is measured. The weakness in
this strategy is that it is difficult to know whether the measurements
are good ones or not. In order to decide how successfully the idea of
need is managed we must therefore depend largely upon the criteria
of the study's internal consistency.

Packman goes about the measurement of need in the following
way. In order for the researchers to remain independent of the
decisions of child care staff, they measure the need for care by
measuring the incidence of those circumstances that give rise to the
need for care. That is, measurement is performed on factors
considered to be empirically related to need. But in order to do this
it must first be established which circumstances *are* associated with
need. And to do this, of course, some measure of need is required.
The measure of need selected is that of 'applications for admission
to care' and to establish the causes of this variable Packman sent a
questionnaire based on the current Home Office classification of
reasons for care, to a sample of Children's Departments where it was
completed by Child Care Officers. On this basis six groups of factors
'which seemed likely to give rise to need' were identified. Thus need
for care is measured in terms of social workers' perceptions (using
Home Office categories) of those factors that tend to give rise to
applications for admission to care.

There are some odd features about this methodology. First, it is
not at all clear why the questionnaire exercise was necessary. If we
are prepared to assume that rates of application for admission to

care are indexical of need then a direct comparison of rates of application with rates of care would seem to suffice. Certainly given the importance of defining and measuring need independent of the attitudes of child care staff it seems unwise to rely on the opinion of professional staff in isolating factors deemed to be associated with social need. Second, Packman herself explained that the category 'application for admission' was itself unreliable since the Home Office nowhere defined it and Children's Officers clearly differed in their interpretations. It seems likely that variations in agency classifications do intrude at this point into the operation of measuring need. Although agency policy on accepting children into care has been excluded from the definition of need, agency policy on accepting enquiries as applications for admission to care has not. We cannot be sure that the population deemed to be in need has been extended beyond an administratively defined one. And third, it is odd that, given the importance of measuring need independent of the services, the Home Office classification of reasons for care should have been used in the questionnaire. One point that clearly emerges from the first part of this book is the importance of evaluating not only service-based estimates of the numbers in particular categories of need but also the appropriateness of those very categories.

Nevertheless the study concludes that a set of 'factors producing "need" ' has been identified, allowing for an approximate guide to the expected amount of need in each area to be compared with the actual numbers in care. This comparative exercise is reported in a chapter entitled 'Measuring Need' and is based upon a table of correlation coefficients (Table XVIII, p. 66) for numbers in care, in fifty-three industrial towns, with thirty-four 'independent variables'. What is surprising about this part of the study is that these variables are not confined to those validated as measures of need in previous sections of the research. Other factors 'thought *likely* [sic] to be relevant' are added. 'Need', previously defined in terms of quite precise measurement operations, is now used, at least in part, as a commonsense category, indicators of which are taken as self-evident. Indeed it is not clear that it is useful to invoke the idea of need at all since the calculation of correlation coefficients of numbers in care with as many factors as possible selected because of their potential relevance, entails no necessary recourse to the notion.

In any case the correlation coefficients yield few significant results, an outcome which, the study concludes, means that the number of children in care in an authority bears no relation to the real need of the locality. However, Packman adds: 'But the obvious difficulties of defining "need" and of subjecting it to accurate measurement suggested that this viewpoint ought to be treated with caution.' The reader never knows whether the measures of need adopted are good ones or not and the precise import of this part of the study's findings remains ambiguous.

Now this rather critical summary of this study has highlighted several important weaknesses in the management of the concept of social need for research purposes. There is throughout the report a rather serious lack of definitional clarity about just what is meant by 'social need'. As the result of a generally atheoretical approach no conceptual framework is advanced within which the concept could be defined. The study seems over concerned with problems of measurement before deciding clearly just what it is that is being measured. And in spite of the study's insistence on both definition and measurement of 'need' independent of the official categories employed by professionals, such categories *are* used at crucial phases in the argument. Finally, there is a circularity to the study's argument. To establish a measure of need a set of measurable social conditions that produce social need are identified. But in order to do this, a measure of need is required. That is why the index 'applications for admission into care' is introduced.

Social needs and resources

In *Social Needs and Resources in Local Services*, Bleddyn Davies (1968) approaches the analysis of the provision of social services at the local authority level by assuming that resources should be distributed according to the 'needs' of the population resident in a particular area. This is the principle of 'territorial justice' which is defined thus:

> The statistical definition of territorial justice is a high correlation
> between indices of resource use, or standards of provision
> [A note explains that 'standards of provision and the allocation of
> resources are here treated as synonymous'] and an index
> measuring the relative needs of an area's population for the
> service, the relative inequality of the standards indices being the
> same as that of the need index (p. 16).

The study is concerned to establish whether or not this principle is upheld in a number of local authority services.

The first problem is that, like Packman, Davies does not define what he means by 'need'. At times the meaning of the term is assumed to be self-evident. At other times difficulties are acknowledged—by admitting, for instance, that local authorities might have different policies about what constitutes need—but then glossed over or dismissed by referring to 'distorted' or 'inappropriate' criteria without explaining what accurate or appropriate criteria would be. In fact the study moves rather confusingly between discussions of 'need', 'apparent need', 'perception of these needs', 'judgements about need', 'the needs of individuals', 'the needs of areas', 'need creating circumstances' and 'clients' interests'.

Like Packman, Davies devotes most of his consideration of the concept of need to the problems of measurement. The task of identifying need is seen as the task of identifying measurable factors producing need. In effect 'need' is defined in terms of the measurement operations employed so that as the measures change through the study so do the operative notions of social need. Davies's basic strategy is that of establishing a performance index for each service and then a needs index, by locating factors deemed to be causally related to needs and measuring these as measures of need. The basis for assuming some factors rather than others to be significant is 'studies of the needs of individual persons for services and the factors that create or accompany individual needs' (p. 16). Finally a calculation is made of the correlation between performance and needs indices.

There are several difficulties here. There is the problem of translating measures of individual needs to measures of a given population's need without performing the operation of addition upon ordinal data. There is the fact that the empirical studies from which Davies draws evidence are themselves using the idea of need in different ways. The fact that they use the same term does not mean, of course, that the data relate to the same phenomena although Davies tends to assume they do. There is the limitation of the fact that most of the material in the needs index comes from studying the supposed needs of people who are already in receipt of services. Very large assumptions have to be made about those groups in need who have not gained service access. And there is an important circularity which resembles that in Packman's study. The population in receipt of services is deemed to be 'in need' for the purpose of discovering correlates of 'need' to construct a 'needs index' which is then used to compare standards of provision with levels of 'need'.

Social Needs and Resources in Local Services is a substantial and complex study. It is beyond the scope of this chapter to discuss the text in great detail although I have commented on the construction of the indices of need in relation to services for the elderly and child care services elsewhere (Smith, 1973). I want here only to make some general points in order to indicate that the limitations exhibited by Packman's study in managing the concept of need as a research tool are by no means idiosyncratic. Indeed they are rather widespread in needs research based on agency rates.

First of all Davies's approach is almost entirely atheoretical. Because the concept of need is not placed within the context of any broader theoretical treatment of the provision of social services difficulties which arise throughout the study must be solved in an *ad hoc* manner. There is no broad schema of ideas to which reference can be made. The study is often therefore prematurely concerned with the problems of measurement. Constantly the task of formulating procedures for constructing indices of 'territorial justice' or 'provision' or 'need' is viewed as synonymous with that of defining the phenomena, so that the meaning of the concepts is confined to that given them by their statistical definitions.

The lack of conceptual clarity is associated with an important circularity in the study's reasoning. Basically measures of need are obtained in this study by identifying a population 'in need' and establishing correlates (which are sometimes assumed to be causal factors) of this population. Since a notion of 'need' independent of service provision is not available, populations in receipt of services are generally taken as being 'in need'. But the question of 'territorial justice' which this study explores implies that this may not be so. Thus, in effect a proposition under investigation is built into the measurements.

I have already mentioned that Davies's use of other research on 'need' is not always valid because it tends to be quoted as if it were all examining the same phenomena. In selecting some secondary data to use, rather than others, there is an important value component to the debate which is often obscured because the questions are posed as technical questions of measurement. In particular there is an insensitivity to the problems involved in using official statistics which are produced by government departments and local authority service agencies. Although Davies comments several times upon the 'arbitrary' actions and policies of officials and organisations in administering the services he does not take seriously the possibility that some of the statistics which he uses are likely the outcome of very similar administrative activities, affected by similar vagaries.

Finally, this piece of research is restricted since it is conceptualised and carried out almost entirely within the confines of the existing structure of service provision. At the root of the research lies a notion of need *for existing services in their current form*. The meaning of the correlations between 'need' indices and 'services' indices are thus ambiguous. For instance, an area with both a comparatively low needs and service index could indicate a genuinely low level of 'need' (defined independently of the form of services offered) but it could also mean a very high level of 'need' that was taking a form for which the existing services were completely inappropriate. As Rein (1969), in a more general comment on this type of research, explains:

> to start with the intervention and to neglect the problem left the research with a self-contained framework, a circular logic which failed to separate the task from its solutions. Means and ends became blurred, as the service itself came to be regarded as the social aim (p. 174).

Population sample studies

Townsend and Wedderburn's study *The Aged in the Welfare State* (1965) is a very well-known piece of 'needs research' based upon data collected from interviews with a sample of respondents drawn from the population at large. It is also a good example of research *pre-eminently* concerned with matters of social policy. The question of 'effectiveness' is of primary concern and effectiveness is defined in terms of meeting need.

The report is set out in two sections, the first, by Townsend, headed 'Community Care' and the second, by Wedderburn, dealing with the financial aspects of social need.

Community care of need

Initially Townsend manages to avoid some of the problems of using the idea of need in research which seem to be associated with studies of agency rates. First, a sample for the study is drawn from both those who are and those who are not using the services. A distinction is therefore maintained between 'use' and 'need'. Second, Townsend uses his own independent measure of that factor, personal incapacity, which is considered *a priori* most likely to lead people to make use of services for the elderly. By comparing incapacity scores and other characteristics of users and non-users, Townsend concludes that services for the aged function in part to serve the relatively severely incapacitated but also as a substitute for the extended family networks which would otherwise provide the services. And, third, a limited notion of need is avoided since Townsend envisages the *possibility* of forms of service provision which are quite different from those currently operative. It is when the study then uses the concept of need to make policy prescriptions that difficulties arise. Townsend asks: 'Is there any evidence (i) that more people need to receive certain services; (ii) that present recipients need more of the same services, and (iii) that people have a need for services that have yet to be decided?' (p. 44), and adds, 'The concept of need is not easy to explore'.

Two separate ways of providing 'rational criteria' for assessing need are suggested. The requests of a potential client population for a particular form of service may be taken as evidence of need. This approach is objected to because requests are likely to be made in terms of the *existing* provisions (since few potential clients possess the information that would enable them to do otherwise), and because some people may plead for support when in fact they can manage for themselves while others who cannot manage may not ask for help. Townsend has a notion of what *really* counts as need and tends to reject clients' (or potential clients') accounts if they are not in line with this independent assessment.

But the independent assessment of need also poses difficulties, Townsend explains. Any general criteria must take into account individual variations in circumstances and must also be influenced by a comparison of the individual's conditions and circumstances with those he might previously have enjoyed and with those currently enjoyed by groups with whom he now compares himself. Townsend sees 'need' as closely related to the ideas of 'reference group' and 'referred experience' and adds that whatever 'rational criteria' may be established any policy recommendations about need must also be politically realistic (which seems to mean that in practice radically new forms of service provision will not be pursued).

The puzzling feature of this discussion is that the outcome is ambiguous. Two separate notions of need are outlined but in effect each is stated as an objection to the other. The discussion is also confusing because the analysis has *already* relied quite heavily upon independent assessments of clients. The apparent 'obviousness' of the 'personal incapacity score' should not be allowed to obscure the basic methodology which depends upon an unexplicated judgment by the researcher about what normal domestic activity should entail without reference to the respondent's own notions of what would count as 'incapacity'—all of which leads to confusion in the later sections of the analysis in which evidence is presented for the expansion of services.

Each of the existing range of services for old people is taken in turn and throughout (1) the movement between the use of 'need' as 'felt need' and 'assessed need', (2) the absence of a justification for the criteria of assessment where 'assessed need' is used, and (3) the movement between a concern for those who are eligible for services in their existing form and those who are deemed to be in need but ineligible, allows for the data to be manipulated in rather confusing ways. In a discussion of the home help service, for example, a contradiction between 'felt' and 'assessed' needs is evaded by suggesting that some respondents may be 'stubborn'. Similarly the proposal for an extended chiropody service is supported by the fact that the 6.1 per cent of those who said they did not require regular foot treatment, who were unable to care for their own feet, might benefit from a service, 'if they could be persuaded to have treatment'.

That is, the evidence that urges a dramatic expansion in the welfare state services to the elderly in Britain is produced by invoking alternately the criteria 'felt need', 'assessed need' and 'eligibility'. I should stress that I am not here doubting the general desirability of Townsend's policy recommendations. What I am questioning is the way in which the concept of social need is managed as a research tool in supporting these proposals. For although some of the problems that seem endemic to studies of agency rates are avoided in a study based on a questionnaire to a sample of the population, there remain some features of the analysis which a research design featuring 'need' should preferably avoid.

The apparent objectivity of the independent assessments of need is in some respects spurious since the measures used depend upon a set of value assumptions about normal domestic activity which, data in the study itself suggests, are not shared by many of the respondents. Also, assessments are presented as 'hard' data although they were invariably based upon replies to interview questions. The distinction between ability to care for one's feet and *reported* ability may seem trivial. But the concept of need is such a slippery one that it is crucial to be clear at every stage about the precise status of the data that are being used to support particular claims. When we realise that the reported 'reluctance' or 'stubbornness' of the elderly reflects an apparent inconsistency of replies to interview questions, we can see that the data may also be interpreted as casting doubt upon the validity of the measurement instruments. Perhaps the elderly do not share the researchers' views on what are important capacities.

As is so often the case, 'need' is ill-defined. At points in the study Townsend deals with one or more of seven variables: (1) access to existing services, (2) eligibility for existing services, (3) felt need for existing services, (4) assessed need for existing services, (5) felt need for non-existent services, (6) assessed need for non-existent services, and (7) demand for existing services. The study's lack of an adequate theoretical framework makes for difficulties in handling the variables without confusion. Indeed the lack of conceptual rigour allows for presentations of the data in misleading ways.

The point can be illustrated by cross tabulating just the first four uses of 'need' listed above ('access', 'eligibility', 'felt need' and 'assessed need', all in relation to existing services). Survey respondents fall into sixteen cells (see Figure 3). But Townsend does not present the data thus.

Sometimes one cell is referred to, sometimes another, sometimes cells are collapsed to support the case. Much is made, for example, of the population in cell 7 while others are largely ignored—for instance cells 9-12. Perhaps the numbers in these cells are not significant and I repeat that I do not want to deny that a major expansion of the services may be required. The point is that some of the cells not considered are theoretically interesting and an examination of these data might highlight some of the conceptual difficulties involved in working with a notion of social need that can be defined in a number of different ways. Townsend's overriding interest in questions of immediate policy distracts him from such an approach.

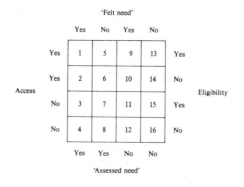

Figure 3

It is perhaps this interest in immediate policy which also accounts for the fact that, in the outcome, the potential of this study for proposing new forms of service provision is not realised. The evidence for the expansion of services is presented under the headings of existing services. It is ironical that a very close identification with matters of policy seems to have led to a set of proposals which, radical though they are, fall somewhat short of the set of far-reaching recommendations that might have emerged. The most useful service research could perform in the field of social policy about 'need' would be a rigorous clarification of the notion outside of the structure of existing services.

Financial aspects of social need

Whereas Townsend was concerned with the extent to which the personal social services were meeting the needs of the elderly in the context of the health and welfare services, Wedderburn is more concerned with the study of financial provision for old age in Britain. This second part of *The Aged in the Welfare State* is particularly about the operation of the (then) National Assistance Board and touches upon some of the central problems involved in using the notion of social need in relation to services dispensing cash.

Wedderburn begins by making two potentially far reaching comments on the idea of 'need', both of which I shall be taking up in later chapters. She suggests that the relationship between 'need' and services designed to meet need is complex partly because there is a sense in which the services themselves actually generate the 'needs' they purport to meet, and she quotes Galbraith (1958): 'Wants are increasingly created by the process by which they are satisfied.'

Wedderburn also questions the objectivity of need by pointing to the way in which some politicians have employed the notion as a means of limiting the rising bill for social security benefits. By focusing additional help only upon those who are deemed to 'need' it the scope of the problem of poverty is considerably reduced. This comment is important as the first reference we have encountered in this review to the way which the notion of need *is actually employed* for specific purposes by policy-makers, administrators or welfare professionals in the context of the services under review. I shall argue at greater length in later chapters that the way in which the concept is used for particular purposes should constitute an aspect of any theoretical formulation of the notion.

Neither of these themes, however, is pursued by Wedderburn at an early stage. In common with the other authors that I have reviewed, she views empirical matters as more pressing. The conceptual problems associated with the idea of need are viewed as an aspect of the policy recommendations rather than as a part of the design and data collection phases of the research.

Wedderburn's problem initially is that she seeks simply to describe the level of financial resources available to the elderly. Such a description, however, is of little practical importance unless it also entails judgments about the adequacy of these resources. That is, as the study progresses, it becomes necessary to establish some criteria of 'poverty' or 'financial need'. The research report is detailed and at times complex and I am not proposing to summarise it here. (Smith, 1973, contains a more specific review.) I intend to make only some general comments to indicate that some difficulties I have described in managing 'need' in research are not confined to studies of the personal social services but are apparent also when the object of the services is a cash benefit.

Wedderburn's analysis also lacks a theoretical framework. This is

important because without it there is no underlying research rationale for the study to which reference can be made in formulating
definitions, making methodological choices and so on. Political
expediency is inclined to influence the movement between definitions as the analysis proceeds. The notion of 'need' that
Wedderburn offers, although it is central to the analysis, is no
clearer than that in the other examples of research I have reviewed.

On the general level, two separate tasks seem to be confused. On
the one hand there is the task of deciding what is to be meant by
'need'. On the other hand, if what is to be meant by 'need' is the
achievement by an individual or group of a rather extreme score on
some measurement standard, there is then the task of determining
the 'cut-off' point on this standard below or above which 'need' shall
be deemed to have arisen. Some definitions of need—for example,
'felt need' as used by Townsend—do not entail this second task. In
at least parts of Wedderburn's analysis, she proceeds directly to the
second task (as do the agencies whose activities she was examining)
and this pre-empts a broader discussion and possible alternative
usages of the term.

More specifically, Wedderburn's use of 'need' is not consistent.
Important parts of the research are based on a supposedly objective
measure of need, arrived at by assessing the level of financial
resources required to purchase the 'necessities' of life. Those whose
income and assets fall below this level are 'in need'. Elsewhere 'need'
is viewed as akin to 'felt need'. Wedderburn speaks of the importance of the 'priorities' of the aged themselves and in conclusion
refers to the 'psychological "need" for economic independence'.
Wedderburn also suggests that 'need' can be defined by studying
how the aged receiving National Assistance Board benefits spend
their financial resources (although if this procedure is intended to
presume *a priori* that those in benefit are also in need it is open to
the criticism, that I have already discussed, of being a circular
argument). And 'need' is also used in this report to designate those
who are *comparatively* deprived in relation to some other group. But
the discussion is further complicated here by the fact that the
comparative group varies.

Sometimes the resources of the aged are compared with those of
the population in general and on this standard the entire aged
population seems to be deemed to be in need. Sometimes the comparative standard is the mean of the aged population itself, in which
case no matter how deprived the aged are as a group only those with
resources so much below the mean of the group would be in need.
And sometimes the resources of a given individual are compared
with the mean level of resources of those of the individual's type of
income unit in terms of sex and marital status. On this standard

those within the lowest group *of each type of income unit amongst the aged* would be 'in need'. These different standards are not only of theoretical interest for if the implications of different definitions were fully spelled out the policy implications derived from each would be substantially different. Thus the study's objectivity is in parts an illusion because the definitions of need and comparative standards for determining financial need are themselves matters of policy and value judgment.

The dilemma which Townsend faced—on the one hand wishing to reject completely the terms in which the services are provided yet, on the other, wishing to produce recommendations judged to be politically acceptable—is also apparent in Wedderburn's report. She is very critical of the National Assistance Board but for much of the analysis engages in an exercise that closely resembles that undertaken by the NAB itself—namely the construction of a supposedly objective measure of the necessities of life to serve as a scale measure for the alleviation of need. When it comes to substituting replacement policies Wedderburn adopts a notion of need quite similar to the official account and follows closely the official format of service provision which sometimes limits the potential scope of the research.

Finally in commenting on this study, and to return to a point I made earlier, it does not fully capitalise upon an important lead offered by Wedderburn's own comments. In several places Wedderburn points to the impact upon the service the clients receive, of the attitudes and activities of welfare officials. The designation of a client 'in need' is the outcome of these activities. If we are fully to understand the phenomena of 'need' amongst the elderly the way in which officials administer the system should come under close scrutiny. In practice, however, Wedderburn focuses primarily upon a sample of potential clients and the data analysed constitute statements about the properties of this potential clientele. The methodology adopted constrains the way in which 'need' is conceptualised. It is viewed as a relatively static and measurable property of particular individuals. In spite of the fact that the study points *en passant* to the importance, for the definition of need, of the social processes actually operative in the workings of welfare organisations, data on these processes are not a part of the analysis. The study implicitly adopts an official view in implying that the phenomena of need can be grasped by studying samples, if not of those who are actually in receipt of services, at least of those deemed to be 'at risk'.

The planning perspective

In *Planning Local Authority Services for the Elderly*, Sumner and

Smith (1969) are initially concerned with a problem which resembles that of much 'needs research'. They state: 'The two major issues which face local authorities are the assessment of needs for the services and the mobilisation of resources to meet those needs' (p. 15). But, as they go on to explain, they are particularly interested in questions of planning *from the planners' point of view*. They accept Townsend's findings that provision falls short of needs. They also accept Davies's view that the highest levels of provision are not necessarily in the areas in which one would expect the greatest needs but they regard this as understandable since although local authorities are responsible for assessing the need for services in their areas, there is no general agreement as to how this should be done. It is precisely the way in which it is or might be done that Sumner and Smith seek to explore. Initially this study offers the potential for an account of the way in which 'need' is actually employed within official agencies.

By drawing on data collected mainly in interviews with officials in a sample of the health and welfare authorities that they visited, Sumner and Smith begin their analysis of the assessment of 'levels of need' by reporting those factors which officials themselves considered to be related to demands for residential accommodation for the aged. Four factors are mentioned as generating 'need': replacement of old accommodation, creation of new forms or expansion of old attractive forms of provision, developments in related services (for example, in sheltered housing), and the increasing age and infirmity of applicants, itself a function of the move away from institutionalisation towards community care.

Now the important aspect of this list for our discussion is that the characteristics of those deemed to be in 'need' was only one of several factors in terms of which welfare officials viewed the phenomena of need, and even an apparent increase in the age and infirmity levels of applicants was seen in part as a function of the kind of services offered. Sumner and Smith's data also show that officials clearly evidenced considerable confusion on any precise definition of social 'need' and encountered major problems in its measurement. However, it is not simply a measurement problem. According to the data, officials appear to operate with no notion of need that is independent of the existing services. Thus, conceptually, the task of discussing 'need' on the one hand and 'services' on the other, is inappropriate. In the official's view 'need' is largely a function of the services. For everyday purposes officials use notions such as the form of existing services, the numbers in receipt of those services, and the numbers not receiving them but requesting them in various ways. It is only planners and researchers who require officials to consider concepts of 'need' separate from those operative notions.

It is hardly surprising then, that when asked to compile a ten-year plan and forecast 'need' levels, most authorities 'thought that planning was a useless exercise'.

Sumner and Smith are implicitly highly critical of the welfare officials and authorities involved in their research. They lack, they argue, an adequate notion of 'need' and they fail to adopt anything more than the crudest of approaches in planning services for future 'need'. Repeatedly the authors stress the essentially pragmatic approach taken by practising officials to questions of current and future need. But what they do not explain is why we *should* expect welfare professionals to be very concerned about problems other than those which they encounter in practical form from day to day. The overall planning task which Sumner and Smith, together with central government planners, seek to impose upon the officials is apparently one which the officials themselves see as largely irrelevant to the routine management of the services for meeting 'need' with which they are concerned.

Sumner and Smith press upon the authorities what Braybrooke and Lindblom (1970) call the classical decision-making approach to planning strategy. They urge officials to hold a notion of 'need' clearly defined and independent of the structure of the existing services. Meeting those 'needs' is the service goal. They urge them to develop data sources to serve as reliable measures of the 'need' clearly distinct from merely 'expressed demand'. These measures, they suggest, should then be employed to review the quality of existing services, estimate levels of 'unmet need' and formulate reliable projections as to levels of 'future need'. But in practice, Sumner and Smith report, the officials do none of these things. Rather they adopt a strategy which, again to use the terminology of Lindblom (1964), closely resembles what he calls 'the science of muddling through'. They hold no independent notion of 'need', acknowledge the deficiencies of the available data but continue to use them, when required to do so by central planners or in response to some practical task within their authority, in highly routinised ways and with the help of a set of fairly arbitrary correction factors.

This raises, of course, the question as to why it is that authorities and officials do not conform to Sumner and Smith's ideal model for meeting need. Sumner and Smith presume that the form of administration they promote is sociologically realistic and that with better information, improved techniques, greater determination on the part of local planners, or whatever, it could be achieved. But there are good reasons for believing that this is not so. It may be not simply that a number of administrative and other changes would allow authorities to approach the means-ends ideal, but that this model is fundamentally alien to the social processes under review.

This suggestion seems worth pursuing on a number of counts. I have already referred to Braybrooke and Lindblom's suggestion that it is neither practical nor desirable for welfare services to pursue the classical ideals of rational planning. On observing the actual practices of policy formation and evaluation they propose a model in which means-ends analysis is replaced by a 'strategy of disjointed incrementalism' as both a realistic and desirable alternative. Such a stance also gains considerable support from the recent literature on the nature of organisations which heavily criticises their treatment as 'planned, deliberately structured, constantly and self-consciously reviewing their performances and restructuring themselves accordingly' (Etzioni, 1965). Albrow (1968) adds that such a view does not present a picture of real organisation but is only an ideological account of some hypothetical state of affairs.

There is also evidence from *within* Sumner and Smith's report that suggests that their criticisms of welfare officials are inappropriate. Although their criticisms centre on the concept of 'need' they themselves provide no clear statement of what they mean by the 'needs' of the elderly. Certainly they do not tackle the problem of formulating a concept of 'need' *apart* from expressions of requirements for particular forms of service by potential clientele. Neither do they approach a solution to the problems of measurement that they criticise the welfare professionals for failing to solve. And the same is true of the problems involved in producing estimates of future levels of 'need'.

The point is that had the researchers formulated, in theoretical terms, the functioning of the concept of 'need' *as employed by the welfare officials*, it might well have emerged that the measurement strategies they were urging upon *them* were actually quite inappropriate. The author's own data suggest that the notions they are employing are quite alien to their research subjects. But given this, what is required is not a set of moral exhortations about pursuing some, probably unrealistic, planning ideal but rather more detailed information about the strategies that such officials currently do pursue and the notions and measures of 'need' that they actually do employ when faced with the practical day-to-day tasks of administering the welfare services.

I noted initially that Sumner and Smith's approach held promise because it sought to explore how the welfare professionals themselves defined and used 'social need'. In outcome this promise is not realised mainly because the researchers refuse, as it were, to take their own findings seriously. Because the welfare officials do not use 'need' as Sumner and Smith expected them to (or at least thought they should) the activities of the research subjects tend to be dismissed as 'unreliable', 'haphazard', 'inefficient' and the like. The researchers' attempt to employ a notion of 'need' that will serve the practitioner's purposes in fact results in a notion that does not seem to serve these purposes at all well. Evidently, for maximum practical utility the researcher must not only know how the practitioner defines social need but also the purposes for, and the manner in which the notion is used. These cannot be taken for granted but rather constitute objects of empirical research in their own right.

The experimental approach

The research that I have described so far in this chapter has relied mainly on the traditional kinds of data of questionnaire survey, research interview and secondary analysis of official records and statistics. It has often been said in social work that we could escape from some of the limitations of these data if we could experiment. The highly controlled experiment poses obvious problems for the social sciences but there are some instances of this approach to social work research (Reid and Shyne, 1969). In Britain the major example is Goldberg's study *Helping the Aged* (1970) which reports upon an experiment designed to measure the effectiveness of professional social work activity.

Goldberg quickly explains that one of the main difficulties facing studies seeking to evaluate methods of meeting need is that of deciding upon the criteria of evaluation. This is difficult because social workers' own accounts of what they do are 'often somewhat partial and misleading' and conflict with the findings of research. Social workers' ideal notions of social work practice seem to be quite different from the practical realities and even within the domain of ideology there is considerable dissensus within the social work community. Three important questions about the study's design are therefore raised:

1 What role in the design is to be assigned to professional ideals on the one hand and actual practices on the other?

2 How is the study to cope with ideological variation within social work?

3 How can criteria of evaluation be derived from vague and ambiguous statements of aims?

The fact that these questions are not clearly answered at an early stage poses problems for the successful management of the idea of 'need' as the research progresses.

Goldberg's strategy is this. Two samples of clients as similar as possible are to be selected. Then the treatment to be evaluated must be specified and a distinctly different treatment administered to the control group. The fourth point that Goldberg mentions is that

'It is essential to spell out what is meant by a "successful" result, i.e. what the criteria of success are we wish to measure', and finally,

> Those criteria will have to be measured in both groups in as unbiased a fashion as possible *before* and *after* treatment; that is to say the assessors carrying out these measurements should be unaware of who is in the experimental and the control groups and be independent and separate from the workers engaged in treatment (1970, p. 27).

The questions I listed above are not answered, because the study proceeds directly and prematurely to questions of measurement. What is problematic in the appointment of 'independent' assessors is that it leaves ambiguous just what it is that is being assessed and precisely how these judges are estimating the clients' needs.

It is true that Goldberg does specify some evaluative criteria that may be employed but there are several and they are very wide ranging. It is not at all difficult to think of ways with which to measure changes over time in social workers' clients. The crucial problem is that of deciding which of these criteria are appropriately applied to the evaluation of social work practice. The point is that the use of professional assessors to judge upon the extent and nature of 'needs' simply bypasses many issues raised elsewhere in the design.

In fact difficulties do emerge as the concept of 'need' is used in the practicalities of the research. As the 'baseline' for the experiment 300 clients already referred to a welfare department for social work help were divided, randomly, into two groups—a 'special' and 'comparison' group. The comparison group was served by the regular welfare workers in the agency while the 'special' group was assigned to the caseloads of a small number of workers specially employed on the project. Both before and after treatment the 'needs' of clients were measured with a view to relating differences between the groups in the changes in clients' 'needs' to the different social work treatments offered. Clients were visited by a 'medical assessor' and 'we also examined the needs of the whole group for social support and services of various kinds *as they appeared to the social work assessors'* (Goldberg, 1970, p. 73) (italics mine). While a good deal of attention is paid to the *reliability* of these measures their *validity* is largely neglected for we are given little information about just how assessors coded clients in terms of particular 'needs'. In practice 'need' is used here simply to mean 'that which the professional assessors term "need"'.

Data are also presented on the clients' perception of their own 'needs'. When these perceptions are in accord with the assessors' view they are quoted with approval. Often, however the clients' perceptions and assessors' opinions do not agree. Sometimes assessors rate needs that clients do not acknowledge. For example, 'a considerable proportion' of old people judged as living in 'unsuitable housing', 'appeared to be quite satisfied with their environment'. Sometimes the opposite is the case. 'About a third' of the clients said they found it difficult to meet some particular expense but a much smaller proportion were classed by the assessors as 'in need' of 'financial help'. The interpretation of apparently contradictory results is problematic because the study uses multiple criteria in assessing client need but without a clear theoretical rationale to link quite different kinds of measures.

This difficulty is accentuated at the next stage of the research in which measures are taken of the differences in the 'input' of social work treatments to the two groups. The first difference is relatively simple. Social workers in the special group spent more time with their clients. But these social workers also had rather different perceptions of their clients' problems and need for social work help as compared with the 'comparison' groups' social workers. The framework of the study cannot handle these data. Goldberg asks:

> Does this mean that the social workers in the special group
> recognised more problems which really did exist or that they
> 'found' more problems, whether they existed or not? This is a
> very difficult question which cannot be answered definitively.

Why not, is not clear. There is a sense in which Goldberg, like Sumner and Smith, seems reluctant to take her own data seriously. Certainly there is a reluctance in this study to accept that there are important differences between assessors' and social workers' accounts of client need. But if the assessments are to be abandoned as the established baseline of accounts of real 'needs' it is by no means clear why they should have been obtained at all.

Throughout the measurement stages of the research Goldberg is really trying to have the argument both ways. On the one hand the strict model of a clinical trial is adopted together with an objective 'diagnosis' of the disease ('need'). On the other hand, as the data begin to indicate that 'social need' may be a quite different kind of phenomenon from that of a precisely defined medical condition, this model is abandoned in favour of one focusing on a range of perceptions and interpretations of client 'need'. There is juxtaposition in unspecified ways of the views of assessors, project workers, regular welfare workers, clients and the researchers themselves.

So, in spite of a research design which emulates the strict 'scientific method' of the clinical trial, precise measures and rigorous conclusions do not in fact emerge. The study fails to provide an unambiguous account of the 'needs' of the client sample at the start of the experiment and again at the end. Measures of social work input also proved more difficult to formulate than was originally anticipated.

Goldberg's concluding comment is particularly revealing:

> What we do wish to convey is our belief that if social workers
> were prepared to define their middle-range goals in more
> precise operational terms, to describe and where appropriate to
> categorise and measure their social work activities [and] to
> tolerate independent assessments . . . then we could take a great
> leap ahead in any sphere of social work we cared to study
> (p. 200).

It is a somewhat ironical comment for the counts on which social workers are criticised here are precisely those counts on which this research study fails to achieve the objectives it sets itself. It is not only that social workers apparently have no clearly defined objectives but also that the research does not produce any clearer ones to serve as evaluative criteria. Similarly what is important for our assessment of this approach to managing need in research is not that social workers do not describe and categorise their own activity but that the research, in important areas, has not produced any more systematic an account. Again it is not that social workers will not tolerate independent assessments. Rather the research failed to produce valid assessments or to put those that were obtained to significant effect. When the data begin to suggest quite strongly that the model of 'social need' that is being used is inappropriate to the phenomena under review it is not enough to urge the research subjects to change.

I am suggesting then that the way in which 'need' is managed in this study may benefit from revision. First, I have mentioned that there is material in this study itself to indicate that the methodological paradigm of a clinical trial may not be a relevant one for a study seeking to evaluate the effectiveness of different strategies for meeting social need. Prerequisites of this methodology are (1) precise measures of client need both before *and* after treatment, (2) an unambiguous criterion of effectiveness on which to compare these measures, and (3) precise measures of the type of treatment that is being evaluated. But we cannot automatically assume that 'social need' is the type of phenomena that allows for these conditions to be met. The equation of client 'need' with a medical condition is particularly doubtful when, as in this study, 'need' itself is not clearly defined. There is no reason to suppose *a priori* that data, for instance, on clients' accounts of their 'need' and the views of professional social workers on 'need' are data of the same order. Different kinds of data must be handled in different ways and a theoretical model of the 'needs meeting process' should provide the rationale for this methodology.

Second, any revised notion of need must cope with the fact that the air of objectivity and independence conveyed in this study is somewhat misleading. The assessments of client need in the Goldberg study frequently restrict the potential for negative evaluation by making use of the categories of the existing services — a point that I have discussed earlier. Also, although the assessors of 'need' which the study employs are independent of the particular treatment given to these particular clients, they do not in general bring to the study an independent perspective for the purposes of evaluating the forms of social service that are being offered. Indeed the assessors were chosen specifically for their close identification with the perspective of professional social work practice. Their skill and experience in welfare work is stressed throughout and 'the social work assessors . . . used their knowledge and insight to assess the old people's needs'. But it is the validity of this knowledge and insight which is one of the questions to be investigated in the research. It is in this sense that the objectivity and independence of some of the measures may be more apparent than real. It is in this sense too that there is a certain circularity to parts of the argument. Goldberg frequently takes as both given and good those aspects of social work practice both the empirical existence and virtues of which the study purports to explore.

Finally, as I have argued at several points in discussing *Helping the Aged*, 'need' is managed in a way that shows over-concern with the reliability of its measures but insufficient concern with their validity. Very considerable care was taken, for instance, to ensure that assessors avoided contact with the social workers, piloted the interviews for assessor agreement, made the initial and second assessments independently and so on. This does not compensate for the fact that the validity of a professional assessment of 'need' as the basis for a study seeking to evaluate the professional treatment of 'need' remains in doubt.

Conclusion

In this chapter I have reviewed major examples of several different types of research into the functioning of social work and welfare agencies in Britain, which have assigned an important role to the concept of social need. I have been looking at the way in which the notion of need has been managed in the context of social research.

I have made a number of specific and sometimes rather detailed criticisms. Some of these may be applicable only to particular studies and some may be applicable only to particular types of study.

It is also important to bear in mind that there are sections of some of the studies discussed in this chapter which are not relevant to a discussion of the concept of 'need'. So far as this topic is concerned, however, one general conclusion is very clear. In general the way in which 'need' is managed in the context of research exhibits some important weaknesses. Taking the discussion overall several points emerge as characteristic of research which seeks to examine how the welfare services function to meet need. In particular the following features are apparent:

1 Typically the research approach is atheoretical. I am certainly not promoting 'theory' for its own sake but if we mean by 'theory', minimally, a clarification of the basic definitions, concepts and principles of a research design then it is something which neither theorists nor so-called empiricists can avoid. Yet seldom is the idea of need placed systematically within the context of a broader set of concepts or within any overall theory of the functioning of welfare services. Decisions on the collection and analysis of data are frequently made arbitrarily without reference to a research problem formulated in theoretical terms.

2 In consequence circular arguments are often apparent, particularly in relation to the measurement of need.

3 There is a serious lack of definitional clarity, generally accompanied by the notion of need being used inconsistently. Typically researchers note the difficulty of defining 'need' and proceed not to do so. Thus often need is defined only in terms of the measurement operations performed (the process called 'measurement by fiat' (Torgerson, 1958)).

4 There is an overdependence upon official administrative and practitioner categories, in spite of the fact that it is often the appropriateness of these categories which is being evaluated.

5 There is an overconcern with questions of measurement and data reliability to the neglect of questions of the validity of the research material.

6 Typically the objectivity of the research is more apparent than real. Generally the value bias remains unexplicated.

7 There is a notable lack of observational data on the actual practices involved in the operation of social work and welfare services which purportedly function to meet social need.

In the next chapter I shall suggest that these defects spring from an implicit model of social need that in fundamentals is common to the majority of British studies in the field of 'needs research'. I shall call this model the 'traditional' notion of need and argue that important revisions are required if several major difficulties in managing the idea of social need in research are to be avoided.

Chapter four

A different approach

In the last chapter I discussed several quite different types of research on social work and related services in order to study how different approaches to managing the concept of 'need' in research actually did work out in the practical conduct of the investigations. Several major theoretical and methodological deficiencies emerged which seem to be rather widespread in the field of 'needs research'. Such defects, from a research point of view, are apparent too often to be dismissed as the errors of any particular enquiry. In this chapter I shall therefore ask why it is that such confusion should occur with such consistency. I shall suggest that it is rooted in the attempt to seek out universal criteria of need. I shall then suggest an alternative to this traditional approach which may avoid some of the difficulties that I have discussed.

The traditional notion of need

What I wish to suggest then, as the first stage in my argument in this chapter, is that the studies I have discussed embody a notion of need which in fundamentals is common to each and which I believe typifies the dominant tradition of research into the functioning of British social work and social welfare agencies. The hallmark of this tradition is that it has undertaken the search for universal criteria of need, criteria to be used commonly by professional practitioners, administrators, clients and researchers alike. The criteria are intended to be applicable at all times in all situations and to serve several functions. For clients they are the indices of eligibility for service provision. For administrators they serve to guide the design and planning of future services. For professional social workers they direct the day-to-day functions of service provision and for both professionals and researchers they serve as measures of the effectiveness of particular services. I call the notion of social need embodied

65

in this universal approach, the 'traditional' notion of need and it is characterised by four particular features.

1 Need is viewed as an unambiguous and objective phenomenon. True, it is admitted, there may be definitional difficulties but a solution here is thought to rest with the skills of the researchers, practitioners and administrators. The lack of definitional clarity is not viewed as symptomatic of the nature of the phenomenon itself. It is true, too, that subjectively perceived needs receive attention in passing from time to time. They are viewed, however, as minor phenomena, perhaps an interesting research diversion but one that must remain subservient to the central task of exploring 'real' (objective) need. Typically 'need' is viewed as independent of the percepts, concepts and theoretical models of social workers and others who are professionally employed in the business of 'meeting need'.

2 Need is viewed as an attribute of the client or potential client as an individual or collectively. Typically it is taken for granted that, with very few exceptions, those who are already clients of welfare organisations are 'in need', but that in addition there are an unspecified number of potential clients who, because they too possess attributes indicative of their 'need', are also eligible for service provision from 'needs meeting' agencies. Often a substantial portion of the research is devoted to the identification of this latter group (or at least an estimate of their number) with a view to service provision designed to meet their need. Just as need is viewed as independent of the concepts of professional practitioners so too it is viewed as independent of the organisational milieu within which interaction between professionals and clients or potential clients occurs. That is, the contextual dimension of social need is largely ignored.

3 Since need is viewed as the property of an individual or collective (what Lazarsfeld and Menzel (1961) call an 'analytic' property) a measure of need is obtained by performing some measurement operation upon the members of the client or potential client population. The collection of data on the professional activities of welfare personnel is seen as appropriate to the study of the meeting of social need but not to the prior task of measuring need itself.

4 Need is viewed as an essentially static phenomenon. What I mean by this is that although changes in need levels may be charted over time such changes are viewed as a sequence of static states. Such a notion is qualitatively different from a view of need as itself a social process. It is revealing that Goldberg's study which comes closest to charting the dynamics of need nevertheless says very little about the actual social processes involved in the period between the

assessments of need. More generally, in 'needs research' little attention is actually given either to the process of 'becoming needy' or to the process of 'meeting need'.

This, then, is what I shall call the 'traditional' notion of need. Universal criteria are sought for need viewed as a static, objective and measurable property of the individual client (or potential client) of the service agency. And at the heart of studies based upon a traditional notion of need three central questions guide the analysis. My argument is that problems arise in managing 'need' in research as a result of the failure to answer these questions which are endemic to the traditional approach.

First, there is the question of definition. Given the traditional notion of need and given the view that welfare agencies function to meet need thus conceived, it is incumbent upon the researchers to produce a specific, unambiguous and objective definition of social need. Yet repeatedly they fail to do so. Second, there is the question of measurement. Given the traditional notion of need, it is also incumbent upon researchers to specify a set of operations for measuring need. This is generally accomplished but seldom is there evidence of the validity of these measures and, as I have argued, frequently need is just defined in terms of the measurement operations, a procedure that is not open to separate validation. Third, there is the question of independence (or evaluation). Again given the traditional notion of need and the view that welfare agencies function to meet need thus conceived, researchers see themselves as having to produce their measures of need in such a way as to remain independent of the existing categories of service provision and existing functioning of the welfare agencies. Yet again, in spite of the emphasis placed upon the significance of evaluation, seldom is a sound basis for evaluation in practice achieved.

Now what is particularly disturbing about this tradition of needs research is that time and again the problems I have mentioned are noted, yet time and again the traditional notion of need is employed to similar confused and confusing effect. I conclude that neither minor modifications to the traditional approach nor further research investigation along similar lines is likely to resolve those problems which are endemic to that tradition of research. What is required is a theoretical *reformulation* of these central problems. In this chapter therefore I am going to outline proposals for a rather different approach to the research study of the phenomena of 'social need' which involves a rather different approach to the management of 'social need' as a concept in research. Part three of the book is going to describe some empirical research which was conducted within this alternative framework.

An alternative approach

The alternative approach to the study of social need that I propose to outline differs from the traditional notion on each significant count. In outline this alternative has a fourfold base. I will list the points briefly together before going on to comment more fully on each in turn.

1 Need is viewed as socially constructed reality; as the objectification of subjective phenomena. As such it is closely dependent upon the concepts of professional practitioners.

2 The central topic of enquiry is therefore the ways in which need, thus viewed, is practically managed or accomplished. Need is viewed as closely dependent upon those organised professional practices that routinely establish its fact and nature.

3 Need is viewed as situated. Attention focuses upon the context of need.

4 A distinction is drawn between 'topic' and 'resource'. Need is viewed as a research 'topic' and as a welfare professional's 'resource'.

But before elaborating on these features of 'need' I should make one further point very clear. The alternative that I am suggesting emerges from a loose group of theoretical and empirical literature, some of which has been written within the ethnomethodological approach to sociological enquiry. However, I am making no pretence to contribute to the body of ethnomethodology *per se*. I have simply drawn on a number of insights in the literature in attempting to tackle the problems that I have encountered in trying to do research on social need. I shall highlight certain features of a particular research stance and indicate their potential relevance to the study of social need. But there are many general issues related to this stance which I shall not consider, particularly where very full discussion can be found elsewhere (e.g. Garfinkel, 1967; Douglas, 1970; Dreitzel, 1970; Douglas, 1971; Filmer et al., 1972; Turner, 1974).

In general form, the approach I shall follow stems from Berger and Luckmann's (1967) discussion of the nature of social reality. The existing research literature on social need has not taken seriously their argument that reality is socially and in important respects subjectively constructed. They summarise the point thus:

> The central question for sociological theory can then be put as follows: How is it possible that subjective meanings *become* objective facticities. Or ... How is it possible that human activity (*Handeln*) should produce a world of things (*choses*)? In other words, an adequate understanding of 'the reality *sui generis*' of society requires an enquiry into the manner in which this reality is constructed (p. 30).

This enquiry they view as the task of the sociology of knowledge, so they project that sub-discipline into a central position within sociological analysis. (That is why I see this study of social need as being an empirical study within the sociology of knowledge.) So in terms of our particular interests here the first feature of my approach will be that social need will be viewed as the objectification of a set of subjective phenomena. As Berger and Luckmann explain:

> It is important to keep in mind that the objectivity of the institutional world, however massive it may appear to the individual, is a humanly produced, constructed objectivity. The process by which the externalised products of human activity attain the character of objectivity is objectivation . . . In other words, despite the objectivity that marks the social world in human experience, it does not thereby acquire an ontological status apart from the human activity that produced it. The paradox [is] that man is capable of producing a world that he then experiences as something other than a human product (p. 78).

Zimmerman and Pollner (1971) have put the point another way:

> The distinctive features of the alternative perspective, which we offer here, reside in the proposal that the objective structures of social activities are to be regarded as the situated, practical accomplishments of the work through and by which the appearance-of-objective-structures is displayed and detected (p. 103).

So I am suggesting initially that social need may be viewed as consisting in substantial part of the concepts and precepts of professional practitioners and others who are concerned with the process of 'meeting need'. I am not suggesting that need consists solely of such phenomena. It consists in substantial part too of those practical actions which give such concepts the appearance of objective reality to those who use them. As Zimmerman and Weider (1971) stress: 'that such accounts [of 'need' or whatever] display the property that they are accounts of independent events is a feature of the phenomenon of members' accounting practices of critical interest' (p. 293).

The second feature of an alternative approach is that it is the *ways* in which this objectification of need is practically accomplished by welfare professionals that fruitfully constitutes a topic for sociological study. Just as need is not viewed here as independent of the concepts and models of professional social workers so it is not viewed either as independent of the routine practices employed by social workers to establish the fact and nature of need in each case. Again

Zimmerman and Pollner argue that: 'The topic then would consist not in the social order as ordinarily conceived, but rather in the ways in which members assemble particular scenes so as to provide for one another evidence of a social order as-ordinarily-conceived' (1971, p. 83). They add: 'What we are proposing is that common-sense methods for making features of the social world observable must be subject to investigation as phenomena in their own right' (p. 87n).

One example of a study which has tried to explore the ways in which this process of objectification actually does occur is Emerson's (1970) study of the strategies used by medical practitioners for constructing and sustaining the 'fact' that ' "this is a gynaecological examination going right" '. Another example is Berger and Kellner's (1970) essay 'Marriage and the construction of reality'. Of particular relevance to the study of social work and welfare agencies is Voysey's (1975) research on the way in which both professionals and parents handle the 'fact' of a severely 'disabled' child within the context of family life. Also particularly relevant is Scott's (1970) review of 'The construction of concepts of stigma by professional experts', in which he draws upon his study of institutions for the 'blind' (1969), to conclude:

> expert meanings are not constructed in advance and by the
> ordinary rules of logic and scientific reasoning; rather, they
> evolve, often unconsciously as the expert 'muddles through' the
> day-to-day problems of running a welfare organisation. This in
> turn implies that one can only speak of 'constructed' meanings
> of stigma in the sense that they are genuinely man-made and
> do not inhere in nature or in the stigmatising conditions to
> which they are applied (p. 287).

In line with these studies and following Sudnow's (1967) analysis of 'death' (which I shall examine further later) I shall not seek to study 'need' as I define it but shall rather seek to give an account of social need based upon the empirical study of those practices which give 'need' and need-related categories their concrete organisational foundations.

The third feature of an alternative approach to the study of need takes up the point that this process of objectification occurs in particular situations. It is an error to view need out of context of those situations. The point has been stated in general form by Douglas (1971) as the principle of the 'contextual determination of meaning': 'The basic idea of which is that the context within which a given statement or action occurs is of fundamental importance in determining the meanings imputed to it by the members of society' (p. 37). And amongst the most important kinds of contexts (and that which I shall be looking at most closely) is that called 'the practical (use) context'. Douglas explains: 'The practical or use context consists primarily of such things as the time and place in which they occur and the knowledge that is taken for granted about the persons involved' (p. 38).

Zimmerman (1969a) adds that this context consists too, and most importantly, of those tasks, the satisfactory completion of which serves to display for organisational members an adequate performance of their role. In concluding a study of the establishment of client 'eligibility' for welfare aid (a second study that I shall discuss in greater detail below), he notes that meanings 'are provided by members' practices dealing with the practicalities of action in the setting'. Zimmerman, in the tradition of an early paper by C. Wright Mills (1940), stresses that notions of 'eligibility', 'need' or whatever must serve for the professional as 'adequate for all practical purposes'. The point is that we are unlikely to grasp the significance of such practical purposes without detailed attention to the situational features of professionals' meanings. That is why the contextual dimension of need must be given a more prominent role.

Now it is true that social workers' and other professionals' own notions of 'need' do generally purport to be accounts of social phenomena (such as the characteristics of clients) independent of the particular situations in which they are employed. What I am suggesting, however, is that if we reject this convention in formulating a notion of need for research purposes then important features of the functioning of welfare agencies are thrown open to examination. In particular we are led to ask how the practical tasks that a social worker must perform at any particular time constrain the notion of social need that actually gains effect.

Fourth, and finally, the approach to the idea of social need that I am electing to pursue suggests that, throughout, a distinction must be made between need as a research *topic* and need as a *resource* for research enquiry. Again a quotation from Zimmerman and Pollner's article, 'The everyday world as a phenomenon' (1971), explains:

> [Traditional enquiry] is addressed to phenomena recognised and described in commonsense ways . . . while at the same time such commonsense recognitions and descriptions are pressed into service as fundamentally unquestioned resources for analysing the phenomena thus made available for study. Thus [traditional enquiry] is characterised by a confounding of topic and resource (p. 81).

The traditional approach to need, guilty of this confusion, has treated need both as a subject of investigation and as a tool of analysis. In consequence it has left unexplicated the methods which social workers and other members of an organisation may use to 'produce', 'accomplish', or 'manage' social need.

This distinction between topic and resource is closely related to an early discussion by Schutz (1967) of the nature of the constructs of commonsense and scientific thinking. Initially Schutz makes the general point about the subjectively constructed nature of reality later taken up by Berger and Luckmann. Schutz then stresses that the processes of 'construction' are common to scientific research as well as the everyday world of the research subjects:

> All our knowledge of the world, in common-sense as well as in scientific thinking, involves constructs . . . Strictly speaking, there are no such things as facts, pure and simple. All facts are from the onset facts selected from a universal context by the activities of our mind . . . This does not mean that, in daily life or in science, we are unable to grasp the reality of the world. It just means that we grasp merely certain aspects of it, namely those which are relevant to us either for carrying on our business of living or from the point of view of a body of accepted rules of procedure of thinking called the method of science (1967, p. 5).

Moreover, Schutz notes, it is a distinctive feature of the social sciences that the constructs which are used as resources in this research enterprise are often the same commonsense constructs as those used by the subjects of the research for their own purposes. Schutz explains:

> The thought objects constructed by the social scientists refer to and are founded upon the thought objects constructed by the commonsense thought of man having his everyday life among his fellow-men. Thus, the constructs used by the social scientist are, so to speak, constructs of the second degree, namely constructs of the constructs made by the actors on the social scene, whose behaviour the scientist observes and tries to explain (ibid. p. 6).

Schutz concludes that it is therefore most important to undertake a very close examination of the nature of those 'thought constructs' (and 'social need' is one of them) which are taken for granted in the everyday world for it is upon them that the tools of social scientific investigation are based.

What Zimmerman and Pollner are suggesting, however, is that in so much traditional enquiry such an examination is in fact not undertaken. Concepts in everyday use are 'pressed into service' as 'unquestioned' resources for use in the research enterprise whereas rightly, at least initially, their everyday use should be viewed as a topic of enquiry in its own right. Only then can researchers decide whether or not a particular concept may well serve the purposes of the research. In the area of 'needs research' I have given several examples of studies which have assumed the notion of social need to be an unproblematic research tool. This has both led to confusion and has precluded important areas of investigation from review.

The point is that, whereas need has been treated as the topic of professional activity and a resource for research investigation, an alternative approach suggests just the opposite strategy; namely that we should focus attention on the way in which professional social workers employ need as a *resource* and that need, as constituted by such activities of welfare personnel, should constitute the *topic* of needs research. I have explained throughout this second part of the book that my objective is to seek out a notion of need that will serve our research purposes; that is, a notion that helps us to study social need in a way which is clear about exactly what it is we are studying. The approach that I have advocated implies that this is best achieved by viewing need solely as the topic of research activity (at least for the time being). Interest in need as a *research* resource should be suspended. Research must first focus on need as a practitioner resource.

It is this point which I anticipated when I said in Chapter 1 that social scientists interested in researching social need might be well advised to look elsewhere for the tools of their trade. That is not to say that 'need', defined with a good deal more conceptual rigour than is currently apparent in most of the literature, should *never* be used as a research instrument. I take that to be an open question. But we are certainly not in that position at the moment. My argument is that knowledge in this field will be advanced (1) by acknowledging that fact and (2) by collecting material of the kind I shall go on to discuss through the rest of this book.

There has emerged from this discussion, then, an approach to the study of social work and welfare services that is an alternative to that based upon what may be called the traditonal notion of need. This alternative promises to resolve, or more simply avoid, some of the main difficulties otherwise encountered. Of central importance is the fact that in attempting to follow through this alternative approach we should not undertake the search for universal criteria of need. I assume it more likely that the notion of social need is employed in different ways, in different situations and by different personnel to different effect. These differences will constitute the central topic of investigation.

So, rather than viewing need as an objective and unambiguous phenomenon, I shall view it as typically highly ambiguous and closely dependent upon the concepts and theoretical models of professional social workers. Rather than viewing it solely as an attribute of the individual, I shall view need as a property of the organisational milieu in which the professional interacts with the client in the course of service provision. Rather than viewing need as measurable by performing some operation upon the individual or collectively of clients or potential clients, I shall view it as measurable through fieldwork observation of the processes involved in service delivery within an organisational context. And rather than viewing need as a static phenomenon, I shall view it as a dynamic social process in itself. From this perspective questions of the administrative procedures of agency functioning and professional activity with respect to the client constitute essential components of the definition and measurement of social need.

I am arguing that by viewing need in this way problems encountered in pursuit of the traditional notion of need are avoided. Rather than formulating some spuriously precise definition of need, I shall abandon this pretence in favour of the principle of meaning and use. That is, by studying empirically how need is actually employed I shall try to arrive at some meaningful account of the term. I shall not attempt to specify my own measures of need but rather examine the operational measures used by social workers and other welfare practitioners who themselves routinely accomplish this task. Neither shall I attempt to evaluate these practices from some supposedly independent stance although this should not be taken to mean that my observations can have no policy significance. As Bloor (undated), in another context, has explained:

> If there is no standard outside the practice of a group to which appeal can be made doesn't this imply that social practices can never be deemed incorrect? Fortunately the theory does not have this conclusion. Social practices can be readily criticised by appeal to another set of social practices. The possibility of criticism resides in diversity.

There already exists plenty of evidence (I have mentioned some of it in Chapter 3) to indicate that there is very wide diversity in the way in which need is defined. From the perspective of the traditional notion of need such diversity, complexity and ambiguity is an embarrassment. Much of it must be dismissed as 'ignorance', 'error', 'confusion' or 'inefficiency'. I shall pursue an approach which tries to cope with such features of social need. In many respects this approach is less ambitious than the research investigations of more traditional studies. It makes no pretence to an objectified definition, precise measures of levels of need or the formation of independent evaluative criteria. Ironically, however, as I shall try to show, by apparently moving away from what have been

assumed to be central practical and policy concerns of the administrator and practitioner the approach in fact gains substantial
potential for radical policy and practical initiatives.

Some examples

So far I have outlined an alternative approach to the study of need in
rather general terms. In this section I am going to examine the
potential of this approach as demonstrated in two empirical studies:
Zimmerman (1966, 1969a, 1969b, 1971) on 'eligibility' for welfare
aid and Sudnow (1967) on 'death' in the hospital setting. As in
Chapter 3, I shall take quite a detailed look at these studies because
that is the way to see how the theoretical starting points of the
research influence the projects as they go along. I have chosen these
two studies, first, because both, especially Sudnow, are well known
and have had influence upon subsequent work and, second, because
both, especially Zimmerman, are closely related to the interests of
this book in health and welfare organisations. However, neither of
these studies, nor the type of research of which they are examples,
has so far been taken very seriously in social work research.

Don Zimmerman's study, initially titled *Paper Work and People
Work: A Study of a Public Assistance Agency* (1966) is a study of the
intake system in a welfare department in America. It was designed
to examine the way in which clients' 'eligibility' for welfare aid is
established by the welfare workers. Theoretically it closely parallels
the alternative approach to the study of 'social need' proposed here.
By viewing 'eligibility' as a professional accomplishment the concept
is rendered problematic (Garfinkel, 1964) from the research point of
view.

I noted in the introduction to this book that the traditional
treatment of concepts at work in organisations (such as 'need',
'death' or 'eligibility') was closely related to a view of organisations
as functioning basically rationally in pursuit of agency goals, more
or less in accord with formal rules and policy dictates. Zimmerman,
too, takes this alliance of perspectives as his theoretical starting
point. He notes that investigators have repeatedly taken as *their*
starting point *their* understanding of what the formal policies dictate
and have then reported substantial divergence between this standard
and organisational practices. This they explain by recourse to the
construct 'informal rules', which are deemed either 'functional' or
'dysfunctional' to the formal objectives. Zimmerman objects to this
mode of analysis on two counts:

1 This view slights the question of *what it takes* to warrant the
   application of any rule . . . in concrete situations . . .

2 Invoking one set of rules to account for the interpretation of another set dodges the issue (1971, p. 223) (italics in original).

He adds:

It is typically the case that the issue of what such rules mean to and how they are used by personnel on *actual* occasions of bureaucratic work is ignored as an empirical issue (ibid.) (italics in original).

Zimmerman therefore states his alternative approach:

The issue of what rules, policies and goals mean for the bureaucratic actor upon the concrete occasion of their use . . . must be treated as problematic . . . i.e. the major assumption guiding the present endeavour is that the relationship of such idealisations to conduct may be found only by investigating the the features of the circumstances in which they are deemed relevant and used by members (ibid. p. 225).

and adds, as a more general statement:

Behind this tack is the assumption that *the* problematic topic of sociological inquiry is the member of society's 'socially organised common practices' for detecting, describing, warranting, and accounting for the sensible features of everyday activities. Any socially organised setting, precisely in the way it organises itself, provides an occasion for the study of these practices (ibid. p. 225n.) (italics in original).

From this it is apparent that Zimmerman, too, proposes to focus on the subjective, contextual and processual dimensions of 'eligibility'. And dictates for 'measuring' the chosen phenomena follow from this stance.

The aims of this study dictated that an attempt be made to observe and record ongoing activities in the setting, in their natural sequence, as they were placed according to the relevancies guiding the timely accomplishment of tasks, and as they were phased in terms of the organisational conditions for co-ordinating such activities (1969b, p. 247).

Given this stance: *'Nothing short of an attempt to observe these activities "in motion" would suffice'* (ibid. p. 248) (italics mine).

So, a substantial bulk of Zimmerman's report is a very detailed ethnography; in this instance of reception and intake practices in a welfare department. In the main this description is based upon field observations, notes on conversations made in the field and transcripts of conversations tape recorded *in situ*. Zimmerman also conducted a small number of unstructured interviews. I cannot, of course, adequately summarise the description of the professional construction of 'eligibility' here. However, it is instructive to mention the *kind* of observations to which Zimmerman is sensitised as a result of his theoretical starting point.

Zimmerman suggests first that, as an approximation, two alternative approaches to the work of the agency may be detected, the 'caseload oriented' approach which 'accords first priority to the practical problem of managing a caseload' and the 'applicant-oriented' approach which 'accords first priority to dealing with what is conceived to be the applicant's problems'. He notes that although the latter stance is broadly in line with what many welfare workers vaguely view as their 'social work' functions, to understand which gains operational expression in the actual construction of client 'eligibility' we must examine the particular tasks and situations encountered by these workers in the day-to-day course of their practical work.

Zimmerman describes the events of client reception, intake interview and final assignment to the caseload of an approved worker and stresses three features of these events. The first is their processual character. At each 'step' in the performance client management is based upon professional accomplishments at the previous stages:

> As the approved worker's caseload is assembled by virtue of the prior performance of the intake worker in certifying eligibility, so the intake worker's investigation is preceded by the work of receptionists in pre-processing new applicants for public assistance (ibid. p. 243).

In this way:

> The applicant approaching the reception counter seeking public funds to assist in the management of her personal affairs is at the threshold of a process. This process makes of her affairs a 'case', and of her, a 'client' (ibid. pp. 325-6).

The second feature of the 'eligibility' events that Zimmerman describes is their highly routinised character. The professionals have the task of ensuring the smooth transfer of clients both in and out of their sphere of influence. And this must be done in a way that demonstrates competent performance to their supervisors and to other welfare workers at prior and subsequent stages. Receptionists must 'move applicants through the process in a smooth and orderly manner' while for the intake worker 'the chief concern is the assembly of information sufficient to insure the rapid processing of the case' by the assigned worker. Both at reception and intake all must function under the constraints of temporal co-ordination, the attempt to even out an uneven work flow, the maintenance of satisfactory caseload levels, and the requirement to provide adequate documentary evidence of both client eligibility (or ineligibility) and the worker's own organisational performance. These tasks are not managed by treating client 'eligibility' in a highly individualised way. On the contrary:

> The routine character of the process will be seen to be one of its most salient features, one to which receptionists orient and, by their management of work activities, seek to preserve. That is, receptionists (and other personnel as well) orient to the management of the day's work so as to provide for the defensible claim that it was accomplished in sufficient-for-all-practical-purposes accord with rule and policy (1971, p. 227).

Third, the routines surrounding client eligibility are characterised throughout by the inspection, collection and generation of documentary records which all go to establish the 'facts' of the case. 'What is required is some means for "objectively" deciding for all practical organisational purposes, the factual character of the applicant's story' (1969b). And, as with other matters, 'The process of assembling a case record proceeds over a series of steps, each one informing the preceding.' Zimmerman states the general point thus:

> While perhaps obvious, it is worth observing that record-keeping activities such as these are crucial to the maintenance of an organisational 'routine', that is, in the present case, facilitating the matter of course processing of applications . . . The generation of records of various sorts permits . . . the identification of the person reported on as one who has been 'run through' the usual procedures, and hence as one to whom the typical organisational constraints and opportunities may pertain (1971, pp. 226-7n).

He adds:

> The point to be stressed here is that, whatever the uses to which records may be put, it appears crucial that records of some sort be produced. For however in fact they are generated, the use of records to chronicle (or more likely reconstruct) a given person's fate at the hands of some organisational process seems indispensible for the typical claim of organisations that (at least most of the time) they handle their affairs in a routinised, rational, and responsible fashion (ibid. p. 227n).

Thus the records serve not only to make details of the case 'available for reconstruction in terms of eligibility factors' but also to make the process through which the welfare workers accomplish this task itself available for reconstruction in terms of adequate organisational performance.

Now let us return to Zimmerman's initial description of the alternative approaches available to the task of establishing 'eligibility'. He suggests that the above observations are important since in practice these features of agency procedures make the 'applicant oriented' approach quite unworkable 'in the setting as constituted'. He explains:

> The problem of temporal co-ordination and allocation, taken together with the enforced requirement for detailed documentation of the applicant's circumstances focuses practical concern on those elements of the task which are within the worker's manipulative control (1969b, p. 263).

And this control is maximised if the worker sees the 'eligibility' of the client 'as potentially employable by her as an instrumental means to control the investigation in accordance with her interests' (ibid.).

, This, then, is one example of a study in line with the research approach that would view 'social need' as a professional accomplishment. Zimmerman views 'eligibility' in a similar way. As such it is dependent upon the welfare workers' categories and concepts but used as a resource to solve the practical tasks posed by a particular situation. In the process of objectification, agency records and documents play a particularly significant role. So far as the actual conduct of the research is concerned, since 'eligibility' is viewed as a property of the organisational milieu it is researched through direct observational methods.

A second piece of empirical research in line with an alternative theoretical approach to 'need' is Sudnow's study of 'death'. Although *Passing On: The Social Organisation of Dying* (1967), was conducted largely within the setting of medical organisations, by implication we may learn a good deal from this research about the study of social work organisations.

At the start of Sudnow's report the research problem is set out thus:

> My central effort has been to locate 'death' and 'dying' as organisationally relevant events, conceive of their handling as governed by the practically organised work considerations of hospital personnel and ward social organisation, and sketch out certain themes which appear to bring together a set of observed facts about social practices relating to 'dying' and 'death' (ibid). p. 3).

It will by now be clear that this formulation is rooted in a particular theoretical stance and Sudnow's account of that stance is worth quoting quite fully. He explains:

> That perspective says that the categories of hospital life . . . are to be seen as *constituted by the practices of hospital personnel* as they engage in their daily routinised interactions within an organisational milieu. This perspective implies a special concern with the form a definition should take, that concern involving a search for the *procedural basis* of events. By this I mean that a search is made, via the ethnographic description of hospital social structure and activities, for those practices which give 'death related categories' their concrete organisational foundations (ibid. p. 8) (italics in original).

It is particularly clear from this statement how the stumbling block of the definitional problem, traditionally posed, is here reformulated in manageable and *empirical* form. As Sudnow adds:

> Rather than entering the hospital to investigate 'death' and 'dying' *as I conceived them* [italics mine], I sought to develop 'definitions' of such phenomena based on actions involved in their recognition, treatment and consequences. 'Death' and 'dying' *are* [italics in original] from this perspective, the set of practices enforced when staff employ these terms in the course of their workday on the hospital ward . . . Taken together I refer to these practices as what 'death' and 'dying' *are* [italics in original], not as the 'ways dying and dead people are treated', or such a formulation . . . My emphasis is on the 'production of dying and death' (ibid. p. 8).

The methodological implications of this approach are also very clear in this study. Sudnow regrets the absence of many very detailed descriptive accounts of the practices of patient care in hospitals and himself spent the bulk of his research time collecting direct observational data, simply 'watching and listening'. The number of formal structured interviews conducted was very small although throughout he talked to many of the hospital personnel, some patients and bereaved relatives, and incorporates extracts from these conversations into the analysis. They do not, however, *substitute* for observational material.

The bulk of Sudnow's study, then, like Zimmerman's research, consists of a very detailed case study account of 'death related practices' and the 'production' of death in an American hospital. I am not going to summarise this description here but again it is instructive to note the kinds of phenomena to which attention is drawn.

Throughout close attention is paid to death routines, for 'death' as a whole is described as highly routinised. Death is not described as a distinctly individualised matter. The morgue, for instance, has official opening times and there are separate, but nevertheless standardised arrangements for dealing with 'death' when the morgue is closed. Wards maintain a regular supply of 'morgue bundles', sets of materials, labels, strings and pads for preparing the body. Names of patients predicted as 'terminally ill' are placed on a 'posted list', routinely inspected by, amongst others, the chaplain, who administers the last rites to those of the Catholic faith. Patients on this list are then eligible for revised visiting hours. Described also in considerable detail are the routines for body management, the closing of the eyes, the removal of a body from a crowded ward—the construction through all such practices of a 'social category of death', bearing only partial relation to death as 'the cessation of cellular activity' or some other such 'clinical' 'definition'. Sudnow reports that there are standardised ways for accomplishing these tasks.

Also given attention throughout the account are the documentation and record-keeping systems of the agency, for an important feature of the professional accomplishment of 'death' is the recording of times, causes, sequences of events and other matters which serve to establish the 'facts' of the case. Indeed there are so many forms to be completed that 'death packages' are assembled ready 'for instant use as it were . . . [providing] an indication of the way the occurrence of deaths is regarded, namely as events in a class along with all those matters that are the recurrent daily happenings of ward life'.

Sudnow also draws attention to those unusual happenings that serve to disrupt the death routines and thus highlight their normal character. He describes for example, the occasion on which a secretary was shot in the hospital, causing considerable disorder in the emergency ward. The point was that while this was a death, 'it was not a death-in-an-order'. It was not a 'hospital death' but simply a death 'in the hospital'. The importance of this 'order' of death is highlighted too by the occasions on which the procedures of death are instigated but the patient does not 'die' in the 'right' place in the sequence of events. Sudnow describes relatives calling to pay a last visit only to return next day to find the patient 'still' alive. Alternatively some patients 'died' too early, at times when, for example, the removal of the body was inconvenient or relatives had not been called. But these are exceptions.

To be 'dead' or 'dying' is from our sociological perspective to be so regarded by those who routinely and rightfully engage in assessing those states and premising courses of action . . . on the basis of these assessments (ibid. p. 62).

And normally this occurs in a routine and orderly fashion.

In a concluding overview of the study Sudnow returns to his opening remarks. He says: 'It has been a predominant theme of the report that what "death" and "dying" *are* cannot be decided *a priori* but must be formulated as a problematic topic of research' (ibid. p. 169) (italics original).

And he generalises the conclusions:

> I have sought indirectly to provide empirical warrant for the general proposition that the categories of social life derive their sense, first and foremost, from the *procedures* which members of the society engage in when dealing with the phenomena of their environment (ibid. p. 169) (italics orginal).

To refer back to what I called the traditional approach to the study of social need we can now see that Sudnow treats death in a way substantially at variance with this approach. Death is viewed as closely dependent upon the precepts of medical personnel. It is viewed as a property of the organisational milieu and is 'measured' through the observation of the ongoing day-to-day features of this milieu. Moreover these observations reveal 'death', not as static, but as that process through which professionals accomplish their tasks. Again to refer back to social need, what I am suggesting is that need may be seen similarly as a category which is problematic. Similarly need may be viewed as consisting in substantial part of the agency procedures which social workers engage in when dealing with what they consider to be the object of their professional practice.

These reports by Zimmerman and Sudnow are not, of course, the only examples of published work stemming from the kind of theoretical stance I have discussed. Another study by Sudnow (1965) on 'normal crimes', Cicourel's (1968) research on juvenile justice, Blum (1970) on mental illness, Silverman and Jones (1976) on grading in organisations and the studies by Berger and Kellner (1970), Emerson (1970), Scott (1970) and Voysey (1975) that I have referred to, are further examples. However, the course of research in the field of social work has remained largely unaffected by their findings. The studies of 'eligibility' and 'death' that I have discussed briefly serve to indicate the kind of research strategy, data collection techniques and modes of analysis that may usefully be adopted in the study of social need.

Some limitations

So far in the chapter I have stressed the positive advantages of a particular research approach. However, perhaps in reaction to the fact that this approach has been given so little attention within social work, I may well have overstated the case. Before presenting empirical material in Chapters 5 and 6 I should make some comments of reservation.

In suggesting that social need may be viewed as the practical accomplishment of welfare professionals operating within the context of social work agencies I have pointed to the importance of 'need' as a specifically organisational construct. In part this simply reflects the general fact that the majority of social work and welfare services in Britain, and certainly those offered directly by the local authorities, are provided within the context of formal organisations. Thus so far as the research here is an examination of existing forms of service provision it is an organisational study. More specifically my approach reflects the fact that matters of the internal structure of social service organisations are central to the policy question that lies at the heart of this book. It is also true that much of the literature upon which I have drawn in formulating an alternative to the traditional approach is based upon research conducted within the confines of an organisation; a medical hospital, a doctor's surgery, a welfare department, an institution for the blind, or whatever.

However, none of this should be taken to imply that 'need' is *exclusively* an organisational phenomenon. 'Social need' is undoubtedly constructed, by both lay and professional publics, with different purposes and to varying effect in a range of settings throughout the social structure. Voysey's (1975) study of 'disabled' children, for example, focuses on the family context. Sudnow (1967) also makes the point well. Although his study is based in the hospital he does try to examine 'death' in settings beyond the confines of that institution. In conclusion to the study he notes:

> It is to be made very clear that the categories 'dying' and 'death' have very broad currency, being variously used in many settings throughout the society. I have examined only one setting; only one locus of meanings and associated activities. The sense of the categories (i.e. their use) in the hospital, is to be regarded as hospital specific; and while in other domains their usages may share features in common with those found in the hospital, many non-hospital-based uses can be noticed (p. 172).

I wish to express a similar reservation with respect to the study of 'need'. A *total* examination of the phenomenon of social need in British society would be required to review its meaning and use in institutional and non-institutional settings alike. However, should such an analysis be undertaken, I would argue that a theoretical approach similar to that which has been advanced here for the analysis of 'need' as an organisational construct would be appropriate.

I have also stressed the importance of 'need' as a specifically professional construct and particularly a construct of professional social workers. Again, however, that should not be taken to imply that it is exclusively so. A full account of the phenomenon of 'need' in a social work organisation would also be required to examine the activities of lay members based upon the meanings that they assigned to the nature of social need. Such lay persons include not only clients and potential clients but also other constituents of a local authority department in Britain such as members of the Social Work or Social Services Committee. Moreover the 'need constructs' of other professional groups, particularly those acting as referral agents to the social work agency, are likely to be significant in particular situations. Examples of such groups are justices of the peace, sheriffs, doctors, health visitors and reporters to the Children's Panels.

Now at points through the remaining chapters of this book I shall indeed be concerned with such phenomena, and in particular with concepts of social need offered by clients themselves and by those who refer clients to social work agencies. I shall explore the role that social workers assign to such concepts and thus explore, in part, the reflexive relationship between social need as a construct of professional social workers on the one hand and lay and other professional notions of need on the other. However, I do not focus upon clients' (or referral agents') concepts *per se*. They enter the analysis only in so far as they are deemed significant by social workers and employed by them in the day-to-day management of agency affairs.

In adopting this focus I have borne two considerations in mind. First, I should reiterate the policy question that lies at the heart of this report. It was assumed that the reorganisation of social work would bring about a reconceptualisation of the notion of need on the part of professionals responsible for providing social work services. That is why I am particularly interested in 'need' as a professional construct.

More generally, there are grounds for believing that so far as the forms and structure of service provision are concerned the nature of the needs and problems of clients as depicted by those claiming professional skills in the field is particularly influential. Scott (1970) concludes: 'More and more the character of stigma in industrialised societies is changed to fit professional experts' conceptions' (p. 257). And in support of this view he notes, quoting Zald

(1965), (1) that most clients do not buy the services they receive, (2) that the general societal status of the client is low in comparison with the professional and (3) that genuine service alternatives seldom exist. Meyer and Timms (1970) add that the structurally isolated position of social work clients in particular, further minimises the potential for the embodiment of lay notions of social need within the forms of service provision which they receive. No part of this discussion, however, denies the significance of research into lay and other professional notions of need and the relationship that these bear to welfare workers' concepts and practices. But again I would suggest a theoretical approach to the study of 'need' similar to that which has been advanced here for the study of need as a construct of professional social workers.

Finally I should make it clear that the research approach that I am pursuing makes no pretence to explain the causes of the occurrence or distribution of those primary social conditions, psychological states, or whatever, that may subsequently be construed by laymen or professionals, as constituents of 'social need'. What I am suggesting is that in so far as studies of such causes purport to be studies of the causes of social need (in some sense or other) then research along the lines suggested in this chapter is a prerequisite to studies of that kind. That is, a most fruitful topic of 'needs research' is the way in which accounts of the social needs of clients are constructed as an intrinsic part of the management of social work organisations. Much subsequent research must be based on an adequate understanding of the way in which both the fact and nature of social need are regularly established by social work professionals as a matter of organisational routine.

Part Three

'Need' in practice

Chapter five

Exploratory study and methods

On the basis of discussion in the first two parts of this book I have suggested that an important aspect of social work awaiting investigation is the way in which professional social workers actually do use the idea of social need in the day-to-day conduct of their practice, and the relationship that this usage bears to the organisational and administrative contexts within which they function. In this third part of the book I am going to describe the results of an empirical study of social work agencies which was undertaken with this focus.

The data were collected in Social Work Departments in Scotland during a period which began around six months after the formal creation of these agencies and extended in all over a period of some two and a half years. My conclusions reflect wide discussion with social workers throughout Scotland but are particularly based upon more detailed research in the Social Work Departments of a more limited number of local authorities.

The process of data collection fell into two phases. I first of all undertook a series of preliminary studies in four of the smaller Social Work Departments and these data, together with other material that I shall mention, formed the basis of an exploratory phase in which I was particularly concerned with working out the best methods to use in studying 'social need' in practice. This chapter describes that work. I then conducted a rather detailed case study of one of the larger departments, and this second phase of the project is described in Chapter 6.

Defining the problem

Clearly my research interest, stated in general terms—namely, the way in which 'social need' finds expression within the administrative context of social work agencies— required more severe delineation if it was to serve as a research problem to guide fieldwork and data

89

collection. That very feature of the concept of need, its ubiquitousness, which initially enticed me to study it, now proved an embarrassment. I had no criterion of data exclusion because almost all that happened in a social work agency was potentially relevant to the problem stated in such a general way.

At an early stage in the exploratory work I therefore decided to limit the general approach by focusing in particular upon the intake and allocation routines adopted in the new Social Work Departments. I shall give reasons for this choice but first I should explain what exactly I mean by an agency's intake and allocation routines.

Although 'intake' and 'allocation' are sometimes discussed separately, in practice they are not distinctly separate functions. I apply the term jointly to the continuous sequence of events I observed that constitute in social work agencies the process of the client becoming a 'case'. Studies which take the caseload of an agency as the basic population for analysis often assume that it is unproblematic so far as it serves as an index of the population in contact with that organisation. In reality this is not so for typically the process of becoming 'a case' is a rather complex one (see e.g. A. S. Hall, 1974) which seems worth investigating in its own right. For the caseload of a welfare organisation is the *outcome* of the intake and allocation routines. I noted that in general only when (1) some classification of 'client need', albeit purportedly provisional, had occurred, (2) this need was accepted as a legitimate focus for the activity of this particular agency, (3) the client had been assigned to the caseload of a particular social worker, and (4) a 'file' on the client had been opened and absorbed into the organisation's records system, did the casual enquirer or potential client become a full agency 'case'. Routinely these tasks were accomplished during the practices of intake and allocation. I decided therefore to focus on the arrangement of events between (a) a client's initial contact with the social work agency either personally or as a 'referral' (either verbally or in documentary form) and (b) the assignment of clients to the caseloads of particular professional social workers in the agency.

There were several reasons for this choice. First, intake and allocation routines are important organisational features common to all Social Work and Social Services Departments. All these organisations are faced with a central division of labour problem which is solved by and large by constructing 'caseloads'. Once a case is assigned it is usual for future contacts with the client to be made by the professional concerned, a practice which allows for the smooth management of the organisation as a whole by confining the scope of any crisis—the emergency admission of a child to care, the unexpected appearance of a probationer in court, or whatever—to an individual worker and his or her immediate supervisors. Unless a case is allocated or otherwise disposed of, it is a threat to the smooth running of the agency. Zimmerman (1966) captured the point in his study:

> A normal first question addressed to a 'stray' client is, 'Who is your worker?' The answer opens a 'line of action'. A worker is called, responsibility assigned, the applicant eased into an interview booth, control restored, the incident recorded, the applicant admonished and the routine re-established (p. 135).

An unassigned client is termed by Zimmerman 'a structurally ambiguous object'.

The second reason for deciding to focus on intake and allocation was the relationship these phenomena clearly bear to the general theoretical interest of this book in 'social need'. I saw in exploratory work how it is part of the conventional wisdom of social work in Britain that clients of social work organisations are 'in need', that social workers possess skills appropriate to meet these needs, that the needs are infinitely variable and demand individual assessment and that intake and allocation consist of the attempt to assess these needs and match them to the skills of professionals best able to meet them. Given this view, intake and allocation become complex tasks for the activities become, to a large extent, the activities of establishing the fact and nature of social need.

Third, the policy significance of intake and allocation routines is clear. I have discussed the view that the promotion of a new organisational structure in social work would promote a new set of codings for client need. Exploratory research showed how it is within the domain of affairs associated with allocation and intake that agency need codings emerge and are most clearly visible. It is, of course, always possible that the need code assigned to any particular client may be changed during the course of his or her contact with the agency. However, the coding framework itself—the set of categories in terms of which the 'needs' of all particular clients of an agency are described—is not amenable to change in this way. The framework generated at the point of intake and allocation establishes the limits within which subsequent individual redesignations may occur. Moreover the literature on 'labelling theory' (e.g. Rubington and Weinberg, 1968, 1977; Matza, 1969) suggests that redesignation is in any case unlikely since a set of social processes are operative with a progressively reinforcing effect.

The policy relevance of focusing on intake and allocation was also apparent when I saw that discussions amongst social workers of the needs of clients were discussions also about the type of professional skills the social workers themselves expected to exercise. The policy debate about need upon which reorganisation was based was also a debate about the nature of social workers' claimed specialist skills. Not only were new needs expected to emerge but new skills also to meet these needs. The two expectations were two facets of the same underlying assumption. If intake and allocation is the process of matching professional skills and client need, then as intake and allocation consist of establishing the fact and nature of need, they consist too of establishing the fact and nature of professional skills—a theme at the heart of the reorganisation debate.

Fourth, the topic of intake and allocation had important advantages in terms of the practicalities of the research. The topic could be clearly delineated and, for each client, most of the events in which I was interested took place within quite a short time span and within the department's central or area offices. One of the difficulties of research in social work has always been that practice often extends over a lengthy period of time, even years, and may be geographically widely dispersed. This has encouraged reliance upon recall interviews and case records. But the approach I was adopting dictated the importance of observational data. A short time span and confined locations were therefore important in a project with limited resources.

For these several reasons, then, I decided to focus upon intake and allocation procedures in Social Work Departments as being one area in which professionals routinely employ the construct of social need. I shall now describe how I collected exploratory data with this more closely defined problem in mind.

Collecting data

The exploratory phase of the research was an evolving process rather than the application of an inflexible research instrument. The theoretical stance I had adopted gave broad guidelines as to how the data should be collected but in matters of detail I did not adopt a rigid research design. I often abandoned lines of enquiry that had seemed promising, in favour of new lines which suggested themselves. I also experimented with various research instruments, However, within this flexible approach I pursued specific objectives which I felt to be particularly important at the exploratory phase of the project.

Establishing rapport

The literature on research methods, particularly on interviewing and participant observation, has been much concerned with researcher-research subject 'rapport' (e.g. Miller, 1952; Goode and Hatt, 1952; Junker, 1960). Definitions are usually quite similar:

A state of rapport exists between interviewer and respondent when the latter has accepted the research goal of the interviewer, and actively asks to help him in obtaining the necessary information (Goode and Hatt, p. 190).

[Achieving rapport] is a useful shorthand taken from the French by psychology, for a very complex social process in which the fieldworker enters into relationships with those he observes—relationships he selects, or creates in order to get the information he seeks (Junker p. 32).

The use of a relationship for research work is stressed and most often the task of establishing rapport is perceived as dependent upon the emotional attitudes of the researcher and his use of interaction techniques in order to manipulate a satisfactory relationship between himself and the research subject.

Johnson, in a more than usually frank account of what is involved in *Doing Field Research* (1975), offers a more complex account of what he calls 'developing trust' and questions the view that 'developing trusting relations is like a technical skill'. Certainly I assumed that in order to 'get by' in the field I would have to be 'well briefed' on the issues which formed the day-to-day talking points in any particular department. Although I planned to use the 'daft laddie' stance a good deal during the fieldwork, the successful use of this approach depends on the fact that it really is only a play.

Selecting data

Some issues of data collection can, of course, be decided *a priori*. I have already explained doubts about the wisdom of relying very heavily upon one data source. I have also discussed the problems of using official documents and interview data that reflect pre-eminently the subjective perceptions of professional social workers. However, some issues of data selection must be explored empirically.

I did not know, for instance, in what ways conclusions based upon different types of data might differ and how I should interpret these differences. I did not know if direct observation would prove possible and if so what situations I should try to observe. I was not sure how the presence of an observer might affect the situation. I did not know exactly what records were kept in each Social Work Department and how these might differ between agencies. I did not know how familiar workers would be with areas of work that did not directly concern them (e.g. court work) and indeed I could not even be sure who would count as a 'social worker' in each agency. (Consider, for example, the roles of 'community worker', 'administrator' or 'home help organiser'.) These are some of the topics I studied with a view to adequate data selection subsequently.

Conceptual refinement

Although I had what I hoped was a clear theoretical approach to the study of social need I did not suppose that it could persist unmodified throughout the research. I planned during exploratory work to begin as early as possible that process which in practice is usually rather muddled in research: the movement from theory to data, from data to theory, and back again.

This relationship between theory and data has, of course, received extended treatment in the philosophy of social science and research methodology literature. (See Sjoberg and Nett, 1968, pp. 33-8.) Glaser and Strauss (1967) for example, have dealt with this theme in their promotion of 'grounded theory' and Denzin (1970), following Glaser and Strauss, comments:

> Sampling does not end until a completely grounded theory is constructed. A logic of ongoing inclusion . . . that dictates progressive sampling from relevant events must be employed. If such logic is absent, the investigator runs the risk of prematurely ending his observations. *A fluid interaction relationship must exist between theory and sampling* (p. 83) (italics mine).

Certainly it seems that one of the reasons why so many research projects are not completed and written up successfully is that procedures for systematically revising the ideas that guide the research are not built into the phases of data collection. The problem with Denzin's comments is that they do not catch the sense of chaos and disjunction actually experienced by those empirical researchers with theoretical aspirations who attempt to marry the two in *practising* research. Few have described their experiences, but I am sure that even fewer have achieved a *fluid* relationship between theory and data. Probably the position is more accurately summed up by Sjoberg and Nett:

> The split between those scientists who stress theory over those who emphasise observation (or data) reflects to some degree the cleavage between scholars who are committed to a logicodeductive approach in science and those who are oriented towards discovery . . . More generally Merton [the reference is to Merton (1957)] among others, has, in an effort to build a bridge between the theoreticians and the empiricists, argued at some length that theory and data are in constant interaction.

Such a position is widely acclaimed today. But the idea of such interaction has become almost a cliché in some circles. We can readily concur that it is inherent within the scientific method, but in reality we know little about the specific content and form of this interplay between theory and data (p. 35).

I can add little to this. I simply hoped that if I examined some data early on the theoretical framework might be revised, permitting the collection of more adequate data, so allowing for a more thorough examination of the theoretical starting point.

Research management

Finally, I wanted to solve as early as possible the practical problems concerned with organising and managing the research. The use of tape recorders in particular situations, the transcription of recordings, timing of the fieldwork, the ease with which interview appointments could be made, gaining information about the time and place of meetings and arranging to be present—all are examples of things which bothered me at the time. In retrospect they seem mundane but if, as I shall argue, the practicalities of professional practice have significance beyond that with which they are normally credited, there is no particular reason to suppose that the practical tasks of professional research are any the less significant.

So, with these objectives in mind I undertook a period of participant observation in four specific departments and in more general locations, which I shall describe. I chose participant observation as a basic method since it clearly fitted my research problem. Becker (1970) describes what the participant observer does:

[He] gathers data by participating in the daily life of the group or organization he studies. He watches the people he is studying and sees what situations they ordinarily meet and how they behave in them. He enters into conversations with some or all of the participants in these situations and observes their interpretation of the events he has observed (p. 25).

And Denzin comes to the heart of the matter when he says; 'Participant observation is a commitment to adopt the perspective of those studied by sharing in their day-to-day experience' (1970, p. 185). Denzin continues:

In participant observation . . . observation of ongoing events is typically less concerned with recording the frequency and distribution of events than it is with linking interaction patterns with the symbols and meanings believed to underly that behaviour . . . The method, when appropriately employed,

entails a continuous movement between emerging
conceptualization of reality and empirical observations. Theory
and method combine to allow the simultaneous generation and
verification of theory (1970, p. 186).

Although Sjoberg and Nett (1968) have argued that the term
'participant observer' is a misnomer since the research worker
'must always be able to take the role of his subjects, to participate
symbolically, if he is to interpret or impute meanings to the actions
of others', they do contrast the 'casual marginal observer' with 'one
who strives to maximise acceptance of the system he is studying'.
Generally the term would be used in relation to this latter stance.

In an attempt to describe the method more precisely Denzin has
recalled Gold's (1958) typology of the four observer roles: complete
participation, participant as observer, observer as participant and
complete observer. My own view is that these are not distinctly
separate research positions but that there is a continuum of
approaches ranging from the total participant, who actually is a
practising doctor, social worker, or whatever, and who would not
normally be thought to be doing research upon his own activities, to
the total observer who typically has little knowledge of or sympathy
with his research subjects beyond the strict confines of a specific
research problem and avoids personal contact with them. Moreover
this continuum is a shifting one as different stances are adopted at
different stages in the research project. Indeed in doing fieldwork I
found that there were even changes from moment to moment as I
took up varying roles in the attempt to control patterns of interaction between myself and the research subjects.

The general problem of selecting the right point along this
continuum was that of permitting the imputation of meaning while
avoiding the dangers of 'going native'. Denzin (1970) warns the
research worker;

Learning and sharing the meanings inherent in another
person's symbolic world poses problems for the participant
observer, for he may cease to think entirely as a sociologist
(or anthropologist) and instead, begin to adopt the perspective
of those he is studying. This 'going native' can inhibit the
development of hypotheses, for the observer finds himself
defending the values of those studied, rather than actually
studying them (p. 188).

Sjoberg and Nett (1968) also warn that 'the researcher may become
the captive of the group he is studying'. Lang and Lang (1960) report
an extreme example in which participant observers at a Billy

Graham religious crusade themselves 'decided for Christ'. In the field of social work the phenomenon is sometimes seen in the research work of those who themselves have a personal history of practical social work. With this dilemma in mind I adopted a flexible position at first quite close to the participant end of the continuum but moving a little in the observer direction as the research progressed.

Initially I took part in a number of general activities that brought me into contact with social workers throughout Scotland. Hey and Rowbottom (1971) have shown the utility, for example, of data collected in conference discussions and, although we must be aware of the limitations of inferring operational practices from semi-public accounts in such situations, I regard them as useful in highlighting issues at the early stages of research. I then collected some detailed fieldwork material in four separate Social Work Departments. All were relatively small agencies, none having a professional fieldwork staff of over twenty social workers, headed by a Director of Social Work. They had basically similar structures with four tiers in the formal organisation chart although they differed somewhat in the structure and use of area teams. They differed too in size and density of the population they served and the kind of geographical area they covered.

The four departments were chosen on largely pragmatic grounds. I chose small agencies because at this stage in the project I wanted to visit as many departments as possible within the available time and resources. Had I chosen larger agencies there would have been fewer in the sample. I did consider the possibility of visiting larger departments but focusing on the activities of one or two area teams rather than the agency as a whole. However, early data quickly suggested important disadvantages. The actual functioning of area teams within the work of a department is usually more complex than the formal accounts offered to researchers by senior staff suggest. Typically there are many exceptions to almost every planned arrangement. Few area teams are the self-contained units of service provision that they sometimes purport to be. So much takes place within and between area teams. There are the processes of allocation *to* the teams and transfer of cases from one team to another. Court work, residential services, home helps, financial loans (under Section 12 of the Scottish Act) and aids to the handicapped are usually arranged centrally. It would have been difficult to study these features of allocation with a remit confined to one team. There is a danger that by focusing research work on area teams excessive attention is given to casework practice which, since it involves few resources apart from the time of the field social worker and his senior, is amenable to routine management in this way. By taking the area team as the basic sampling unit for analysis I would have been accepting a model of the functioning of the organisation which I should have been investigating. That is why I preferred to take the organisation as a whole as the basic unit.

Typically, fieldwork in these departments lasted for a period of between one and two weeks full time, with subsequent individual visits lasting a day or two. In no case was the request for research access refused. In two of the departments contact extended over two to three months and in the other two it was shorter and more intensive. In general throughout the fieldwork I tried to fit in with existing agency routines and cause as little disturbance as possible but, as I have mentioned, the research activities differed somewhat between the agencies.

In the first department I held a loosely structured interview with each social worker. These varied in length but focused on a set of prepared topics covering the underlying rationale and objectives of social work reorganisation, the relationship between the Children's Panels and Social Work Departments, the defects of the old system necessitating change, the emerging structure and procedures of the organisation and anticipated forthcoming difficulties and problems from the professionals' points of view. These interviews were tape recorded and subsequently transcribed. I also attended the daily morning meeting at which cases were allocated and which, once a week, was attended by the Director and extended to cover topics of departmental business.

In the second department similar meetings were attended and were recorded and subsequently transcribed. Data were also collected here in semi-structured tape-recorded interviews which began to dwell more closely on topics that seemed likely to provide a focus for the research. Data collected here also included an overview of the record and filing systems used in the department.

In the other two departments fieldwork became increasingly systematic. Interviews were progressively more focused, reviews of the records and record-keeping systems were more thorough and the emphasis I placed on observation work increased throughout. Samples of documents completed over the three-month period preceding fieldwork were taken. I examined financial accounts and monthly department reports, attended various kinds of meetings of professional staff and began to document my observations more systematically. I was now 'observing' not only while 'participating' in a meeting, casually while taking coffee, waiting for an appointment or whatever, but also more self-consciously in planned periods of time spent, for example, sitting in the waiting room or reception area of the department's offices. I took scribbled field notes throughout the day and carried too a pocket dictaphone, putting impressions, quotations and observations onto tape during the midday lunch period and each evening.

This sharpening focus to the fieldwork was possible as I came to see the agencies' intake and allocation arrangements as an area of social work practice which provided an operational context for studying the general theoretical and policy questions that I had in mind. In the next section of this chapter I shall describe the use I made of the exploratory material as I began to map out the different notions of need that social workers actually employ and the relationship between these notions and an agency's administrative routines. I shall try to describe how social work agencies are organised to accomplish the routine task of designating 'need'.

Ideologies of need

During the exploratory work I soon realised that the failure of the policy debate, and much of the research literature, to specify precisely what was meant by social need was but a reflection of the fact that at different times, in different places and in different situations in social work practice several quite different notions of need are actually employed. Clearly 'need' is not managed in practice as a single simple concept but is a rather more complex social phenomenon. This was hardly surprising. It was an observation to which I had been sensitised both by the theoretical approach I had adopted and by the secondary data available. But although I had expected to locate dissensions and variation in the use of the notion of need no previous study had indicated in any systematic way what these differences might be. The first requirement was for a descriptive framework, a conceptual map, as it were, upon which it would be possible to chart these differences.

In beginning to unravel the complexities of the concept of social need, I organised some of the exploratory material around a model in which the notion of 'professional ideology' played an important part. It is a notion which gained sway in the study of welfare, psychiatric and other non-industrial organisations in reaction to the stance which had examined such structures as if they pursued a set of clearly and objectively defined corporate goals in a rational and co-ordinated way. Studies, particularly in hospital settings, by Perrow (1963) and earlier work by Gilbert and Levinson (1956) and Wessen (1958) for example, had paid more attention to organisational members' own subjective ideas and had shown variation not only in accounts of the goals of different types of hospitals but also in the underlying rationale and purposes of the medical profession. These differences were described as reflecting different professional ideologies.

Strauss *et al*. (1964) and Marx (1969) have suggested important refinements to the idea. In their major empirical study, *Psychiatric Ideologies and Institutions*, Strauss and his colleagues confine the use of ideology to relatively *abstract* ideas and attitudes in which the elements are bound together with quite a high degree of interrelatedness or functional interdependence. They point out that it is helpful to draw a distinction between such abstract ideas on the one hand and the operational application of these ideas to specific tasks in concrete situations on the other. These applications are termed 'operational philosophies' and defined as 'systems of ideas and procedures for implementing therapeutic ideologies under specific institutional conditions'. Our attention is thus brought back to the contextual dimensions of professional practice and we return to the point that notions of 'need', 'illness' or whatever are practically employed by professionals for the competent performance of specific tasks as well as for the abstract portrayal of general service objectives.

Marx, too, suggests a refinement to the concept of ideology. He argues that the nature and structure of these belief systems has been oversimplified because distinctions have been made only on a uni-dimensional basis. He explains;

> Ideologies in professional arenas . . . have a multi-dimensional structure. More specifically, ideologies encompass several dimensions, each of which represents and is defined by a range of specific orientations and commitments to a particular referent or substantive focus of ideological concern. These are the specific ideological orientations and commitments to diverse referents which constitute the actual substantive components of ideologies (1969, p. 80).

He argues that although 'it is impossible to be certain that all of the ideological dimensions which are significant to ideology-bearing subjects have been specified in advance, and, hence, included in any particular investigation' (p. 82), during the very early stages of the research, 'the investigator must be able to select and specify the major dimensions of ideological concern to members of the particular subcultural arena that is being studied' (p. 81).

Geertz (1964) refers to ideologies as 'systems of interacting symbols as patterns of interworking meanings . . . [which operate] . . . . . to render otherwise incomprehensible social situations meaningful, to so construe them as to make it possible to act purposefully within them'. I shall use the term in a similar way but bearing in mind (1) that such belief systems are multi-dimensional in character and that a specification of the major relevant dimensions is a prerequisite to further research and (2) that a distinction must be drawn between abstract portrayals of an ideological stance, on the one hand, and operational specifications within the constraints of particular tasks and situations on the other. I also use the term without pejorative connotation for I view ideologies as a general and necessary feature of the administrative patterns of day-to-day decision-making in all types of organisation.

Certainly such a view helped me to disentangle some of the exploratory research material. I was able to chart some of the major dimensions of 'ideologies of need' in professional social work and explore the relationship between these ideologies, in their operational form, and the intake and allocation procedures of the reorganised Social Work Departments. I could distinguish between ideologies about the nature of social need along at least three dimensions which I shall describe. First, I shall examine concepts about the appropriate *unit* of need, second, different views about the *causes* of need, and third, varying definitions of the appropriate *assessor* of need.

There were three quite clearly separate accounts of the *unit* in terms of how it was believed social workers should conceptualise social need. In most of the agencies studied the generally dominant view was that which regarded the individual client as the basic unit of social work thought. Social workers explained:

'There are people with particular needs and I think they need people who are specially qualified or knowledgeable about these needs.'
'Just because you happen to be working with a family that does not mean to say that you are automatically the best one to help a *particular member* of that family' (emphasis original).

But although an individualistic ideology abounded, the exploratory material also evidenced alternative views. Expressions of a need-ideology were apparent in some areas of practice which posited the community subculture as the basic unit of need. This was explained quite fully by one worker:

'There are parts of the area covered by the department that definitely have a subcultural pattern—where you hate the police and everyone's out to get you and you have a gang and the gang's your life and everybody is against the gang as the enemy and so on and the people who are in the area are maybe well adjusted to the subculture, but they're not adjusted to society and so they come into conflict. It's like two different tribes, one within the other.'

A further ideology focused upon the family as the basic unit of need. One worker explained:

'I think it right that the departments should come together, that they should be able to co-operate and regard problems in a wider basis than they did before . . . so that more work can be done with families and preventing the break up of families and, you know, making family life better . . . we began to see how an awful lot of children could be prevented from coming into care by working with the family as a whole.'

And another social worker adhering to this ideology and clearly attempting to implement it, saw it as important to claim: 'we do everything. And it's mostly on a family casework basis. I have various families with each member in it involved with us in some way or another.' And another, when given a complicated hypothetical case and asked to define the type of case, replied: 'Must you define it? I mean . . . how do you mean define it? It's just a family needing help, a family requiring help, isn't it?'

The importance of this dimension so far as the task in which I am particularly interested—the intake and allocation of cases—is organised is that each position has different operational implications. The individualistic stance implies that the development of specialist and highly individualised skills in social work is a most important feature of the service to clients. Social workers gave many examples, of which the skills involved in dealing with aged clients was one: 'I think it's different from working with children. And with ordinary adults—younger adults. I would think you need more understanding and more patience maybe. Or of a different kind.' An individualistic need-ideology implies also that the criterion to be employed in allocating a client to the caseload of a worker is that of matching the individual client's needs to the social worker's particular skills or characteristics. For example: 'If somebody came in and said, "I'd like to adopt children or I'd like to foster children", well automatically I'd give that to [the name of another worker] because he is the one who deals solely with these kinds of problems.' A further example of the individualistic need-ideology in operation in this respect was the transfer of a girl probationer from the caseload of a female to a male worker because she 'obviously needed a father figure'. An error of allocation was considered to have risen because the individual needs of the client were not met by the individual characteristic (the sex) of the particular social worker.

An individualistic ideology also has implications for the way in which the filing arrangements are made in a social work agency to house the case records and other documents of the organisation relevant to intake and allocation. The documentary presentation of social need, the reduction of the 'facts' of the case to a written, often standardised form, plays an important part in intake and allocation routines. Where an individualistic ideology was in evidence each file related to just one client; it was classified in the system under one of a relatively small number of headings relating to 'type' of need and, while the client was in contact with the agency, professionals saw no reason why this file should not be retained by the worker dealing with the case and even housed in his room. This reflected the fact that dealings with the case were conceived of on an individualistic basis and were not thought to relate to the needs of any other of the agency clients. By and large the recording and filing systems in the agencies I visited during exploratory research were in accord with the operational philosophy which posited (1) the assignment of particular skill labels to individual social workers, (2) a filing system which categorised clients as isolated cases in terms of a relatively small number of single needs, and (3) a set of administrative procedures in which the matching of self-evident needs and skills was the operational criterion employed.

A community ideology, on the other hand, has operational implications which differ radically from those of an individualistic view. The geographical area or subcultural unit would be the basic unit of the department's recording and filing system. Workers would be encouraged to become specialists, not by developing a skill to meet a type of individual need but by becoming familiar with the needs and problems of one particular area. Clients would be allocated to workers on an area basis and workers would, of course, have ready access to the records of clients resident in the same area since each client would be considered a manifestation of an area need.

In the departments I visited some attempt was made to implement this view in some sectors of the intake and allocation practices. In one department a community worker operated from a building situated in a perceived 'problem area', a local housing estate. In this department too, the geographical area served by the agency was divided into two with separate small teams serving areas with quite different social and demographic characteristics. This allowed workers to become familiar with the problems of one area, although several workers complained that this imbalanced the type of cases on their caseloads. Nevertheless the division persisted since it served an eminently practical purpose in providing a rationale for the division of two teams of professionals each responsible to a senior social worker.

Thus in some respects it was convenient in practice for departments to adhere to the operational dictates of a community view of the basic unit of social need. However, attempts to implement this kind of operational philosophy consistently throughout intake and allocation would encounter difficulties in most agencies. Seldom

were all the records for one area in fact readily available, for a filing
system based upon the client as an individual unit is very much
simpler. Often where area divisions were constructed there were so
many practical constraints that in outcome there was little evidence
to suggest that the boundaries of these sections actually correlated
with perceived problem areas. In one department, area boundaries
did exist but were used only for the purpose of some particular types
of case, 'probation' for instance. Thus while the community ideology
of need is useful in providing a rationale for the division of
departments into area teams, so far as simplifying the intake and
allocation arrangements was concerned its utility seemed somewhat
restricted.

The implications of taking the family as the basic unit of need are
again at variance with an individualistic view. Clients would be
allocated to workers by family, workers would become specialised in
dealing with types of need associated with particular types of family
structure and the family would be the primary unit of the department's recording and filing system.

Now this view too has many practical advantages so far as
allocating clients is concerned. In most departments a client new to
the agency was almost automatically assigned to the caseload of a
professional if another member of that client's family was already
assigned to that worker. This was usually discovered by a declar-
ation to that effect by a worker in the allocation meeting and many
cases were readily disposed of in this way. In spite of its advantages,
however, such a view also involves difficulties at the operational
level. Seldom, for instance, was the system of filing records based
upon the family unit:

Interviewer: How are the families where you see nearly
every member, classified in the filing system
of this office?

Social Worker: I don't think that the filing system is very
good at the moment and the one family I am
thinking about will be under three different
headings . . . there'd be three different files.
We haven't got one file on the family but
various files on the different members of the
family.

This was typical. The point is that while a particular ideological
position may simplify matters of intake and allocation at one phase
of the procedures it may, if operationally applied throughout, serve
only to complicate matters at some other point. Most departments

found the individual rather than the family the simplest unit for the documentation of client need. Some workers, it is true, were able to circumvent the constraints of a record and filing system imposed upon them by retaining a copy of their reports and arranging these in their own way but, so far as intake and allocation are concerned the areas in which a professional can reject an individualistic ideology and adopt measures of an operational philosophy at variance with the institutionalised procedures, are very limited. For in general the arrangements for intake and allocation could be described as (1) a set of institutionalised routines in which the client was initially depicted in terms of an individualist need-ideology, for instance at reception, and in the generation of a 'case' file and other records but (2) alternative operational philosophies adopted in other situations at other stages of the routines in line with a collectivistic view of need. The point is that when we examine the contextual dimension of 'need' distinct variation as between situations is apparent (at least as far as the unit dimension is concerned).

The second dimension that called for attention was that which referred to the professionals' beliefs about the *causes* of social need. Three distinct positions are apparent. The first, the material ideology of need, points to the distinct material, and particularly, but not exclusively, economic situation of the client as the root cause of his problem:

Interviewer: Can you tell me what constitutes social need?

Social Worker: Overcrowding . . . unsuitable housing for a person who is disabled . . . if they are housed on a first or second floor and require ground floor tenancy . . . things like that.

or again:

Social Worker: Illness strikes, husband goes off work, wages are stopped. Most of these people are in unskilled jobs, they're not on a salary which would be kept on. Their wages are stopped when they stop and this results in them . . . just everything has to go on as normal, but no money coming in to pay for it.

The operational philosophy through which such an ideology about the cause of social need is mediated stresses the *relief* functions of a social work agency. The amelioration of poverty and inconvenience is seen as the primary focus of social work practice. The major implication for the way in which clients are allocated to workers is that here social need is seen as substantially self-evident. Complex assessment procedures are entirely redundant since the need is viewed as clearly visible and well documented. There were substantial areas of the work in the departments I studied in which this ideology was dominant at the operational level. Several categories of specialisation related to the provision of types of material or financial benefits or to accommodation, and clients were assigned to workers on the basis of their material needs. For example, one member of one department dealt almost entirely with welfare foods, another dealt with admissions of old people to residential accommodation and in several departments one worker made arrangements for all home help services. However, the effective implementation of this ideology encountered an important restriction.

An adequate level of material resources is a prerequisite to any operational philosophy through which the material ideology is to be mediated. However, the pattern of social services, of which social work is but a part, may constrict this particular operational philosophy since very few of the most important resources of material provision are under social workers' direct control. Social security benefits, housing provision (including ultimate decisions about the management of rent arrears), and gas and electricity supplies are examples of resources in terms of which the problems are perceived by social workers but over the provision of which they exercise very little control. A dilemma confronts social workers if they define need materially but cannot control the resources with which need, thus defined, may be met.

A second ideology locates the causes of need within the characteristics of the client. Indeed, that need should have arisen at all was seen by some of the social workers interviewed as an indication of the client's deficiencies. Need was here conceptualised in psychodynamic terms, the concept of 'inadequacy' recurring often:

'One can see that the wife, perhaps, through her inadequacy in managing budgeting has allowed the situation to get out of hand.'

'You find certain families who have certain basic inadequacies, they just can't cope with life.'

A psychodynamic ideology also tended to entail a denial of alternative points of view, for example:

'people say it's a problem of poverty—I don't really agree with this . . . it's not a question of poverty but mismanagement or emotional difficulties which make them spend the money the wrong way—you can manage on it [Social Security payments] but it's not the kind of thing an inadequate person can do.'

Whereas the material ideology stresses the *relief* functions of social work the psychodynamic view highlights the *treatment* functions of the agency. The professional conceives of his work, not in terms of making particular arrangements for the alleviation of poverty and distress but in terms of forming a satisfying therapeutic relationship with his client. This is a device for enabling the client to overcome his deficiencies and thus, subsequently, to solve his own problems independent of professional help.

Now so far as the establishment of simple and smooth running intake and allocation procedures, is concerned an operational philosophy derived from this stance has both advantages and disadvantages. Initially such a view does seem to render complex the procedures for allocating cases to the caseloads of social workers. In contrast to the materialistic view, needs are no longer seen as self-evident. On the contrary, one social worker explained:

'The usual thing is that the social worker at reception must
decide is this a presenting problem, is there more to it? If it's
an apparently material visit . . . it may well be that there is a
lot more behind this.'

In spelling out a psychodynamic ideology at the operational level the concept of the 'presenting problem' was prominently featured. The needs encountered when the client first contacted the agency were not regarded as the 'true' needs but only as pointers to the possible necessity for intervention.

It was also this philosophy which found its expression in the establishment of allocation procedures which allowed for the detailed and expert assessment of the 'real' nature of the problem. The case was discussed at the morning allocation meeting or the social worker on reception duty might consult with his colleagues if they were available or, in some departments, the assessment and subsequent allocation decision would be entrusted to a senior member of staff who, by virtue of training and experience, was deemed to possess a superior competence. It was this philosophy, too, which accounted in part for the transfer of cases from one social worker to another. It may be, it was thought, that only in the course of a developing casework relationship was the professional worker able to assess the fundamental needs of his client and decide that these would best be met by a worker with alternative skills or characteristics.

However the implications were by no means unambiguous. I have explained that in general the stability of a social work agency rests upon a delimited locale of responsibility for each case. Constant transfer of cases from one worker to another represents a threat to this order. The psychodynamic ideology, stressing as it does the importance of the 'helping relationship' between client and worker was generally taken to point to the importance of a permanent allocation arangement. Thus although in certain instances this stance was taken to justify a transfer of cases from one worker to another, more routinely an operational philosophy was applied dictating that, provided a reasonably satisfactory allocation had initially occurred, further 'structural ambiguity' should be avoided.

The psychodynamic ideology also has dramatic and again partially ambiguous implications in escalating the total volume of work in a welfare agency. Since the discovery of *any* problem might be seen as but an indicator of further and, in terms of the social worker's time, more demanding need (since casework is a relatively time-consuming activity) there is potentially no limit to the amount of attention that any given client might require. Indeed at first sight this position seems to render almost inevitable a permanent perception of inadequate resources in terms of the number of professional social workers available. On the other hand it is apparent that, in certain operational forms, this ideology can be used both to limit the total volume of social work and considerably simplify intake and allocation routines. Because a distinction is drawn between the 'presenting problem' on the one hand and the 'real' underlying problem on the other, so that almost any problem can be seen as indicative of an underlying need, it is also the case that an apparent problem can be dismissed as merely a superficial difficulty, not requiring continuous professional attention.

In some of the departments this philosophy found expression in the appointment of an administrative assistant. In one department clients visiting weekly in order to deposit a regular sum of money with which to clear off their rent arrears or debts were dealt with by the assistant. In another an administrative assistant was responsible for the financial affairs of residents of the old people's homes and dealt too with any problem that they raised with him on his weekly visits. It was felt that this procedure of allocating clients who could be dealt with in terms of what was seen as routine financial accounting, to the administrative assistants, allowed the other social workers to concentrate their efforts upon more important problems. In terms of the psychodynamic ideology of the causes of need the mere incursion of debt, or whatever, was not seen as a problem in itself. Although many members of these departments referred to the assistants as 'social workers' they were not expected to engage in casework practice outside of the prescribed routine duties. If, during the course of these duties, they did 'uncover' a more fundamental problem, they were expected to refer that case to a colleague.

The third ideology about the causes of social need, apparent in the exploratory material, also functions to provide social workers with a rationale for considerably reducing their workload. Social need is here described in moral terms. Such an ideology has much in common with the Poor Law conception of the undeserving poor. One social worker said: 'We've got to be able somehow or other to separate the needy from the chancers—God knows there are plenty of chancers around.' Reference was made to similar moral concepts: to clients in rent arrears as 'offenders' for example, and to 'alcohol or bingo' as 'social evils'. In terms of this ideology much of the need evidenced by demands for the service of a social work agency is seen as unreal because of the morally unjustifiable nature of the demands. Also, as with the psychodynamic view, a moral philosophy about the causes of social need renders allocation procedures complex since need cannot be regarded as self-evident. Only the prior establishment of a morally justifiable claim on the part of the client renders his allocation necessary at all. In departments I visited, establishing this claim might take the form of checking the client's statements with his doctor, the Social Security Office or other agency with whom he claimed contact. It might also require the examination of a pension book or other documentary evidence. In this way the operational philosophy through which the moral ideology of the causes of social need is mediated promotes the 'investigative stance' (Zimmerman, 1969a) as a prominent feature of the procedures for caseload allocation. Whereas ideologies mentioned above stress the relief or treatment functions of social work a moral ideology presents a social work organisation as an agency of *social control* and *moral reform*.

This philosophy did gain a degree of institutionalised acceptance in the departments studied. Although its consistent application complicated intake and allocation by introducing sets of 'checking' procedures into the routines, in some contexts, especially in situations in which the resources, particularly manpower resources, were regarded as being very scarce, the philosophy functioned with two overriding advantages. First it facilitated disengagement from some groups of clients. Only in cases of 'genuine need' was a social worker allocated to the case at all. 'Scroungers' were dismissed immediately and a rationale was provided for transferring other groups of clients outside the field of social work. 'If the circumstances', for instance, 'are such that it's . . . just sheer bloody mindedness, then of course you've got to use the big stick of the law to weal them'. And second, this philosophy facilitated, in sharp contrast to a psychodynamic view, the economical management of some clients who were taken into regular contact with the departments. In one agency, for instance, some clients called at the office and were not visited at home, 'because we can make life too easy for these people'. An adequate framework for mapping social work ideologies must, then, distinguish between different views about the causes of need. So far as the tasks of intake and allocation are concerned my exploratory material suggested that operational philosophies pertaining to psychodynamic, material and moral factors as causes of need, in turn both complicate and simplify management routines. The point I am making is that when we examine the contextual dimension of need we note not only varitions in usage but the emergence of a pattern to this usage related to the practical day-to-day problems faced by agency personnel in accomplishing the tasks of client management.

Finally, in drawing distinctions between the different need-ideologies held by professional social workers, the early material suggested that a third dimension is also important—that of perceptions about the appropriate assessor of social need. The crucial distinction here is that between the expert ideology which regards need as a subject of definition largely independent of the views of the client himself and the client ideology where the prime reference is to the client himself. Of the expert ideology two variants are apparent.

First, there is the view that the professionally qualified social worker is best designated the ultimate assessor of need. The implications of this position for the allocation of cases to the social workers are complex. Principally it is taken to mean that client need cannot be viewed as self-evident but only determined through a process of assessment. In several departments this position found expression in the holding of the morning allocation meeting attended only by the professionally qualified social workers (sometimes together with trainees). Ancillary workers such as the administrative assistant or the home help organiser did not usually attend these meetings. This operational stance was also expressed in the conduct of sometimes quite lengthy intake interviews in which a professional social worker questioned the client with a view (1) to noting the client's own account of his need but (2) forming an expert assessment of what the need 'really' was. In forming this assessment the client's account was only one piece of evidence, amongst others, upon which the professional based his judgment.

Second, there is the view that although the assessment of need is a skilled task it is one which can be delegated to the referral agent, principally but not exclusively, the general practitioner, the courts, or, in Scotland, the Children's Panels. For example in most departments professionals agreed with the social worker who explained: 'A probation case comes to us through the courts.' Another example is found in the case of a client potentially needing the home help service: 'The agency I mentioned, the family doctor, the health visitor, the district nurse, the midwife, the medical social worker or the psychiatric social worker, has already made the decision.' And again: 'The informant has already made the decision that this person cannot return or continue to stay at their home [without help]. This is the "need".'

Where it gained operational effect in the departments I explored this view considerably simplified intake and allocation procedures. Categories of specialisation adopted in some parts of intake and allocation in the departments simply reflected those employed by the referral agent. No re-assessment was involved since it was considered that the task of the social work agency was that of making efficient arrangements for the meeting of a *predetermined* need.

The third ideology about the assessment of need posits the client himself as the appropriate assessor. Here need is not seen as a matter for expert diagnosis but as a matter of subjective evaluation on the part of the client. One social worker gave an example of this ideology in practice: 'Often when we find out the person's feelings on residential accommodation we find that the person is not prepared to go, because they wouldn't go near an old folk's home.' This ideology may have profound implications for the organisation of allocation procedures in a department for it is this ideology which appears most likely to generate novel categories of professional specialisation in social work.

Which of these three views about the appropriate assessor of need is likely to be implemented in particular facets of the intake and allocation routines again, my initial data suggested, depends upon the degree to which tasks are accomplished or troubles created in the agency (Zimmerman, 1969a). From the point of view of the routine day-to-day administration of a department it is often simplest to accept the referral agent's definition of need. In particular, this eliminates the necessity for assessment by the social work staff. Indeed if need has been predefined by the referral agent an alternative definition might only serve to endanger inter-agency co-operation.

However, since this view challenges the social worker's definition of himself as the possessor of distinct assessment skills, the status of the referral agent in the eyes of a social work department is also important. For example in most departments I studied, the definition of need for a client referred to a social work department by a neighbour was questioned, whereas this was less likely if the referral agent was a psychiatrist or general practitioner. Yet however high the status of a referral agent, by delegating its assessment function, a social work agency does lose some control of the level of demand for services to meet particular kinds of need. And if the resources available to meet this demand are limited the department itself has to cope with the problems that result. By accepting the client's definition of his need, however, demand for services may sometimes be restricted. In one department for example, there was a serious shortage of ground-floor residential accommodation for old people. Clients referred by their doctors as being in need of this accommodation were asked if in fact they wished to enter a home. Some declined and these cases were not approached for a further six months. Home help services, on the other hand, were not in short supply. Clients referred by their doctors as being in need of this service were encouraged to accept it, even though some were reluctant to do so and were required to make some financial payment.

Thus a full account of need ideologies and allocation procedures in social work seems to require some consideration of a dimension referring to the assessment of need. In general, in the departments I first studied, the view that the social worker is the most appropriate assessor certainly did predominate but other ideologies found expression as well in particular situations. Again the conclusion must be that we should pay much closer attention to those particular situations.

In trying to decide how to collect data and organise this empirical material around the themes raised earlier in the book, I have introduced the notion of professional ideology as a resource to supplement the theoretical discussion of Chapter 4. A phase of exploratory work which I have described indicated the following:

1 'Need' as used by welfare professionals, is not simply a single concept but rather a set of interrelated notions and assumptions about what is to be viewed as the proper object of social work activity.

2 It is helpful to view this body of ideas in terms of a professional 'ideology' about the nature of need.

3 In social work, ideologies of need are multi-dimensional, referring at least to the unit, cause, and appropriate assessor of need.

4 In social work agencies considerable variation in the operational use of need can be observed in different situations and at different phases of the routines concerned with client management as professionals and other staff encounter different tasks in the day-to-day management of agency affairs.

In view of these suggestions I decided that the second phase of my research (the subject of Chapter 6) should take the form of a very detailed and rather more systematic case study of the intake and allocation routines of a larger and organisationally more complex social agency. Within the conceptual framework that I have outlined I hoped it would be possible to study in more detail the way in which different notions of social need are used operationally at different points in the management routines of a social work organisation and thus be able to suggest, at a more general level, the nature of the relationship between notions of need and patterns of administration —the question at the heart of this book.

However, before moving to the case study of 'City' Social Work Department I undertook a review of my methods of selecting and collecting data, for experience gained during the exploratory phase of the research pointed to the relevance of several issues discussed in the research methodology literature. In the rest of this chapter I shall recall that review. Although my research strategy did not change fundamentally in the second stage of the fieldwork, I did modify the data collection process in some particular ways.

Triangulating methods

During the exploratory phase of the research, under the general guise of 'participant observation', I collected, as I have described, material of several different kinds. I perused records and files, interviewed staff and, to a limited extent, I watched them at work. Although much research in the field of social work is heavily dependent upon a single data source, there emerged from my experience as well as from the methodology literature reservations about each of these methods, taken singly.

A very great deal of research on the service activities of welfare professionals takes as its primary source the records and statistics produced by those organisations as a part of their regular day-to-day functioning. In work of this kind the researcher has to assume a more or less direct correspondence between the content of these records and the phenomena that are the real focus of his enquiry. It is this assumption which has led to a rather concerted attack on the research use of official records and statistics, particularly from within the field of criminology. Kitsuse and Cicourel (1963), for example, conclude that: 'criminal statistics clearly cannot be assumed to reflect a system of criminal justice as ideally conceived, and labels assigned convicted defendents are not to be viewed as "the statutory equivalents of their actual conduct" ' (p. 137). Rather, it is argued, such statistics should be viewed as indicative of the 'rate producing processes'. To give a simple example, while the size of a social worker's 'caseload' is sometimes taken as indicative of the number of clients with whom he is working, in one department I visited many workers knew of no way in which they could 'officially' close a case with the result that their 'caseload' totals were very high. Thus: 'the question to be asked is . . . about the definitions incorporated in the categories applied by the personnel of the rate-producing social system to identify, classify, and record behaviour as deviant' (or 'needy' or whatever) (p. 136).

Now although such a comment should thwart the intentions of a

113

researcher intent upon treating professional documents as un-problematic indices of the properties and events they purport to represent, the implications of the point are for my purposes more constructive. For we are sensitised to the documentation procedures and the categories of social phenomena embodied in these procedures as indexical of agency practices as well as client characteristics, workload totals or whatever. However, the collection of documentary material as an isolated method remains inadequate. In my example it was only also by interviewing the social workers that I learned the reason for their high caseload totals, and through the exploratory phase of the project I had relied quite heavily upon interview material.

The interview, too, however, as an isolated research tool, has also come under sustained methodological attack (e.g. Benny and Hughes, 1956; Weiss and Dawis, 1960; Cicourel, 1964; Manning, 1967; Sjoberg and Nett, 1968) in spite of the fact that it remains a major instrument of data collection used by students of social work as well as in other areas of social science. Webb (*et al.,* 1966) concludes that its very versatility and apparent utility has encouraged the misuse of the interview as a technique. Exploratory work on my research raised doubts about the status of interview data when I noticed that responses tended constantly to evidence a high level of abstraction and idealisation. In spite of several devices aimed at posing questions in terms of specifics, respondents in the interviews remained essentially removed from any situational constraints but those of the interview. I concluded that whereas the interview was a valuable source of information on professional ideologies of need, it was relatively ineffective in yielding data on particular operational philosophies. The interview is a relatively poor source of data if we are to take seriously the contextual dimension of need. Webb notes:

> When the interview or questionnaire is viewed as the only method, the researcher is doomed to either frustration or a studied avoidance of thoughts on external validity. Peace of mind will come if the investigator breaks the single method mold and examines the extent to which other measurement classes can substitute for verbal reports (ibid. p. 180).

As my interest increasingly focused on the operational use of philosophies of need for practical tasks in particular situations, I placed less and less emphasis on interviews and more upon direct observation as a data gathering technique.

As I have already mentioned, observational methods have seldom been used in published studies of social work in Britain. There appear to be two most obvious reasons for this: (1) the practical difficulties involved and (2) the assumed 'confidential' nature of the professional-client relationship, but during exploratory work I found that both of these objections were surmountable to a considerable extent.

From the practical point of view two lessons were especially helpful. As the research progressed I spent an increasing amount of time in the secretarial and general office areas of the departments. Not only were records often housed, telephone calls taken, and personal callers to the office met there but it was also there that social workers meeting by chance discussed cases, arranged meetings and the like. I initially underrated the significance of this location but later learned that a period of time each day spent there not only allowed for the collection of significant data but eased the practical problems by keeping me in touch with the time and place of consultations, where different people were likely to be for the day and so on. The use of a tape recorder for fieldnotes also eased the practical problems of recording observations. As well as carrying a note pad on which I constantly scribbled and a small tape recorder for dictating notes directly during the day, I also dictated onto tape each evening notes, recollections and observations for the day. The use of a recorder eased the problem of research fatigue and encouraged me to keep a very full account of my material.

Confidentiality proved in many aspects to be much less of a problem than I had anticipated. Much material both in written and verbal form that I thought might be restricted was in the outcome readily observable. Given that social workers and secretarial staff need constant access to this material at unpredictable times and given that there is a constant flow of information between agency personnel, it is most difficult to organise the offices of a social work agency in any other way. Any material that must be treated as strictly 'confidential' nearly always disrupts agency routines and is only with reluctance coded thus. Where such material was encountered research access seemed to rest largely on my personal credibility as a research worker sympathetic towards social work and I have already explained that during the early stages of the project I was at pains to establish this credibility.

Again there are extended discussions in the literature on the merits and de-merits of observational data, particularly in relation to the problem of establishing validity (see especially Becker, 1970). I am not going to supplement this discussion here, except on one particular point. It is sometimes assumed that although there may be problems in the researcher convincing his readers of the validity of his account, given observational data the researcher can at least arrive at an account that he finds satisfactory himself. In my experience this was not always so. Even when I was physically

115

present as an observer there were some situations in which I felt I could not grasp 'what was going on' because so much occurred that was not readily visible. In these situations I had to ask respondents to explain to me either at the time or as soon as possible after the event just what had been happening from their point of view.

To give two examples: in most departments at some point in the intake and allocation routines a secretary extracted, from some version of an intake form on which a social worker had described the client's 'need', a shortened account to be entered onto small index cards. Although I could note that this took place, the times and occasions and sequence of events, and could watch the secretary sort the forms and type the cards I could not tell simply from observation how she decided what information to exclude or select, or how to describe the 'need' in ways that were sometimes different from the professional's emphasis. Again, in several departments there were, with varying frequency, allocation meetings in which discussion of the case was followed by an offer from a social worker to accept it onto his caseload. Frequently such an offer was preceded by a period of silence (described by one respondent as 'Quaker Bingo; eyes down and pray that it doesn't come to you'). I required more than my own observations to understand what happened during this period. Observational data were not entirely adequate alone.

I have described then, the three types of data that I used during the exploratory phase of the research: agency records, interview material and observations in the field. There have emerged, however, both from a review of my own material and comment upon these kinds of data in the methodology texts, reservations about each type so far as the study of social need is concerned. Denzin (1970) has suggested that indeed such a conclusion is likely with respect to *any* particular investigation so long as methods of data collection are treated separately. He believes it most unlikely that a sole data source could prove adequate to the satisfactory resolution of a research enquiry. As Webb (*et al.*, 1966) notes: 'As long as the research strategy is based on a single measurement class some flanks will be exposed . . . Findings from this . . . approach must always be subject to the suspicion that they are method-bound' (pp. 173-4). But, Webb adds: 'If no single measurement class is perfect, neither is any scientifically useless' (p. 174).

Denzin takes up the point and argues that if several research strategies are used together they may then be employed to compensate for the weaknesses of any one alone. Denzin terms this approach the strategy of methodological triangulation. He explains:

As methods are adapted to the special problems at hand, their relative strengths and weaknesses must again be assessed . . . It must also be remembered that each method has unique strengths and weaknesses . . . In designing triangulated investigations, the methods that are combined should reduce as much as possible all threats to internal and external validity (pp. 308-9).

Denzin describes two forms of methodological triangulation. One is within method triangulation in which, for example, two measurement scales may be constructed from questionnaire data as separate indices for the same variable. But, second:

A much more satisfactory form of method triangulation combines dissimilar methods to measure the same unit, what I call between or across-method triangulation. The rationale for this strategy is that the flaws of one method are often the strengths of another, and by combining methods, observers can achieve the best of each, while overcoming their unique deficiencies (p. 308).

Denzin adds that in any particular study it is likely that one method will be dominant but that the conclusions deduced will be supported by data collected in one or more other ways. Much will depend upon the particular problem to hand. In conclusion he stresses the flexible nature of the approach:

To summarize, methodological triangulation involves a complex process of playing each method off against the other so as to maximize the validity of field efforts. Assessment cannot be solely derived from principles given in research manuals—it is an emergent process contingent on the investigator, his research setting, and his theoretical perspective (p. 310).

The relevance of a discussion of methodological triangulation for research on the management of social need in professional practice is that as this study progressed I tried to organise the data in line with Denzin's suggestions. I tried to relate the different types of data. A shift in focus from one dominant data source to another also occurred. Thus, as the study entered its second phase:

1 I attempted more systematically to use different types of data in complementary ways. For example, a review of agency records would be complemented by observations of record-keeping activities and interviews with the staff who made and kept the records. Likewise if agency records were taken as indicative of organisational procedures, a review of the record-keeping system could be used to complement observational material on intake and allocation routines.

2 In comparison with the earlier exploratory work the role of

interview data declined and I came to rely more heavily upon my observations as I worked out ways of collecting more, and more systematic material. This was the methodological basis of the case study that forms the bulk of the next chapter.

Summary

I have described in this chapter the first stage of a project designed to bring empirical data to bear upon a question of social policy and welfare practice outlined in Part one of this book. I have begun to examine, as a proposition amenable to research, the belief that a reorganised administrative structure for the provision of personal social services would bring about new and more realistic operational categories of social need. In the absence of a specification of what was meant by 'real need' I started to explore just how, in practice, social workers do designate clients as being 'in need' and the relationship of such designations to the administrative structure within which the professionals practise. I limited the scope of this enquiry to intake and allocation routines and I have described how I went about fieldwork during an exploratory phase of data collection. I have introduced the concept of professional ideology as a resource to supplement the theoretical approach to the study of 'need' proposed in Chapter 4, and in this chapter I have been particularly concerned with some of the methodological issues involved in studying social need in this way.

Several points of both theoretical and policy significance have emerged during the course of this chapter. The exploratory material shows how 'social need', as made use of by social workers, is not a single simple concept but rather a set of interrelated notions and assumptions which may be viewed as professional ideologies with variations on several dimensions. These ideologies gain operational expression in the context of the routines of client management. But no single consistent stance is apparent. Rather a range of meanings of social need is managed by professionals and others as a resource to accomplish those mundane tasks that constitute the practical basis of everyday social work. In the next chapter I shall present a rather detailed ethnography of those organisational processes as I report a case study of client intake and allocation procedures in a larger and more complex social work agency.

Chapter six

Managing 'need'

In this chapter I shall report the second stage of a project designed as an empirical examination of the way in which the construct of social need is employed by social workers within the administrative context of social work agencies. The majority of the chapter is a detailed ethnography of one agency's intake and caseload allocation procedures. I adopted the single case study method both because it allowed me to examine an agency that was somewhat larger than the majority of those I had visited previously and because it allowed me to fill out in more specific detail some of the general suggestions of the earlier part of this research. The description presented here is thus an illustrative account of the way in which both the fact and nature of social need is accomplished by welfare workers as a matter of organisational routine.

I shall refer to the agency described in this chapter as 'City' Social Work Department. It was a local authority Social Work Department in Scotland established as a result of the Social Work (Scotland) Act, responsible for duties, under the Act, in a compact geographical area with a population of a little under 200,000. Within the reorganisation of local government in Scotland, City has now become the centre of one of the mainland regional authorities. The department occupied suites of offices in a large modern block in the centre of the town and was generally known amongst social workers, certainly within Scotland, as a 'good' agency. It had relatively little difficulty in attracting professionally trained staff, was in high demand as a student placement location by social work teachers and had on its staff a number of well known figures active at a national level in the field of social work. A total professional staff of over fifty was headed by the Director, Depute and three Assistants. The fieldworkers were divided into three groups, with two teams, each headed by a senior social worker, within each group. Also employed at the central office of City department were a senior administrator

119

and assistant, a home help organiser and assistant and around twenty-five secretarial and clerical staff.

In the first section of this chapter I shall describe how I collected the material for my account, which is presented under the three headings of 'reception', 'intake' and 'allocation'. I shall then describe how the fact and nature of need in a number of particular cases was established in line with these routines. At times I shall focus on patterns of events that sometimes pass as mundane. A concluding discussion will spell out the significance of these detailed materials so far as the more general themes of this book are concerned. Although some of the details may have changed since I completed my fieldwork I shall use the present tense a good deal. It will go some way to preserving the sense of my original field notes. More importantly, wider observations both before and since have indicated clearly that the basic conclusions that can be drawn from this case study of City are generalisable to a considerable degree.

Fieldwork

The most important general issues about the methodology of this research project have already been discussed in Chapter 5. Here I intend simply to indicate how I collected the particular materials upon which the description in this chapter is based.

Fieldwork in the City department extended over a period of several months, with particularly intensive involvement covering a period of some six weeks in the early summer of 1972. I also returned to the department on numerous occasions while preparing the research report. Several methods of data collection were employed. First, I discussed the topics of interest to me with each social worker in the agency and with members of the secretarial and administrative staff. While I shall not depend extensively upon interview materials, they were invaluable in several ways. They ensured that my account was not over-influenced by the perspective and interests of any particular sector of the agency and that it did not neglect factors that might be important to only a small number of staff. The interview materials were also used to provide a provisional working model for understanding 'what was going on' in particular settings; a framework within which my own observations could then be performed. Many of those subsequent observations were made in pursuit of 'leads' of enquiry which derived initially from the interviews and conversations.

The second source of data was fieldnotes made on the basis of first-hand observations of agency practices. Rough notes made openly on the spot were dictated and transcribed soon afterwards. I also carried a pocket tape recorder and when the occasion allowed I put observations and memoranda directly onto tape for subsequent transcription. Notes of this kind were made in a number of settings. I spent time in the corridors and waiting areas and coffee rooms of the agency. A considerable amount of time was also spent sitting at a table in the department's central reception room, a particularly good location for my purposes since much connected with intake and allocation took place here. Telephone calls were answered here. A central card index on all agency clients together with other documents and records were housed, and regularly consulted by social workers and clerical staff, in this room. And clients calling at the office enquired at a reception window which opened on to this area. In this reception area it was often possible, too, to ask members to explain their actions while observation took place. For instance, I might ask why a particular record was being consulted and how the information thus obtained would be used.

I observed, too, numerous meetings of social work staff in the agency, particularly the allocation meetings that were held each day. Because I intended the data to reflect direct observations but within the framework of participants' accounts, I sometimes enquired further about particular happenings at the allocation meetings in subsequent discussions with those involved.

I also collected data of this observational kind by observing directly a limited number of intake interviews between a social worker acting as duty officer and clients calling personally at the agency. These observations were arranged in the following way. Senior staff were approached initially and they indicated field staff who, because they were considered competent and experienced, would not feel 'threatened' by observations of this kind. Observations were then conducted throughout an afternoon session in which one such social worker was on duty as an intake officer and agreed to co-operate in the research in this way. For the most part the social worker sat behind his desk while I occupied a chair at the side of the room. It was left to the social worker to introduce me as he wished. On one occasion a client was told, 'this is a colleague who is doing some cases today', but most often no introduction was deemed appropriate. Clients usually began to discuss their problems freely on entering the room and were apparently undisturbed by my presence. Evidence of this derives from the occasions on which the social worker had to leave the room to consult records connected with the case. I left clients to open the conversation, which they generally did by continuing to discuss their problems. It seemed quite acceptable to clients that some other person—perhaps 'student', 'trainee', 'official' or 'colleague' — should be present at these interviews.

I made a record of the conversation that occurred between client

121

and social worker by taking notes at the time and dictating these onto tape very soon afterwards so that limited additions from memory could be made. In general, however, the transcript was achieved by omitting repetitions rather than by paraphrasing or making additions afterwards. The transcripts of some interviews will be produced fully in this chapter as part of the description of the intake and allocation of some specific cases.

The third main type of data that I used was based on a review of the record-keeping systems of the organisation, with particular reference to all documents which form a part of the routines for allocating a case. As well as being interested in the content of the layout of the various documents I noted who completed them, the situations in which they were completed and the situations in which information they contained was subsequently utilised.

Finally, I collected some material by distributing an earlier and shorter draft of this chapter to members of the City department with a request for any comments that they might wish to make. These comments allowed me to correct a number of points of detail. They also allowed me to check the observation, outlined below, that because of the way in which, as in most social work agencies, intake and allocation procedures are routinised, segmented and documented, important features of the way in which client 'need' is constructed are obscured from the view of members of the organisation itself.

Agency routines

The work of the City department is arranged in a way that in broad outline resembles that of most social work agencies. The total volume of work is divided into 'caseloads' assigned to the professional workers. This arrangement promotes the smooth management of the organisation by restricting the disturbing effects of those unpredictable occurrences which are endemic to social work practice. Once this caseload is assigned, the professional social worker may be a highly autonomous work unit, but the activity of initially allocating that load to him is a distinctly corporate affair. It is therefore conditional to the smooth running of the organisation that (a) new cases should be allocated as rapidly as possible, (b) throughout this process the location of responsibility for the case should be clear and (c) the transfer of responsibility should occur in line with clearly established routines. These are the administrative constraints to be reconciled throughout with the fact that allocation is deemed also to entail the individualised assessment of client 'need' and the client's assignment to the caseload of a worker deemed to possess the skills to meet that need. I shall describe how the 'needs' of clients are constructed within these constraints by describing the three broad stages of reception, intake and allocation in turn.

Reception

Clients attending the office of the City department personally with a new enquiry first call at the reception desk. This is behind a big sliding glass window which opens onto a large office where three typists/receptionists work. The layout of rooms in the main office accommodation of the department is indicated in Figures 4a and b, showing in particular the arrangement of waiting room, reception office, home help offices, social worker's rooms and waiting areas in the upstairs corridors.

First floor

Figure 4a

The receptionists are responsible for answering two telephones, completing a range of typing duties, keeping a note of which social workers are out of the office and a number of other tasks apart from client reception. Although the level of activity fluctuates the receptionists are usually rather busy. Generally, however, clients are dealt with quite quickly by whoever is free at the time. They are asked for their name, where they live, whether they have been to the department before, and if so whom they saw. Clients are not usually asked about their problem, although some clients do indicate the nature of their enquiry. The information which receptionists specifically

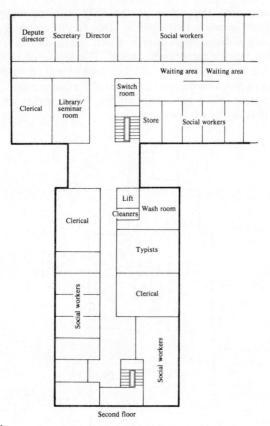

Figure 4b

request is required so that receptionists can classify clients as either 'not known' or 'known', if known as either 'no further action' (NFA) or 'allocated' and if 'allocated' as either 'ongoing case' or 'closed'. It is on the basis of the reception classification that the client's subsequent progress onto the next stage (intake) of becoming a 'case', in part, depends.

However, in performing this classification task receptionists encounter an important difficulty. The categories of this scheme are not readily shared by clients since the designations have precise administrative definitions which are only apparent to those who are a part of the agency routines—definitions which will emerge in the course of this description of agency practices. So the two questions 'Have you been here before?' and 'Who did you see?' elicit information which is 'unreliable' for the receptionists' purposes. A client may say, for example, that he *has* been to the department before when he may only have made an enquiry at the reception desk. For agency purposes if he has not been seen by a social worker in the particular setting of an intake interview he is 'not known'. Alternatively a client may say that he has *not* been before, and indeed may never have visited the social work department nor been visited by a social worker, yet nevertheless be 'well known' to the agency. Similarly, few clients know whether their case has been allocated or not and few know whether or not, within the department's administration, their case is formally 'closed'.

The information that the client provides must therefore be 'checked' against agency records, in case of dispute the records being taken to depict the 'true' state of affairs. In part this reflects an operational philosophy that casts doubt upon the client as the sole assessor of his need. In part it reflects the fact that in order to manage the client amongst a large number of other clients the case must be typified as rapidly as possible in terms of a set of administrative categories and existing agency routines. To do this the receptionist consults a central card index located in the main reception room. She actually needs only the name and address of the client for this task and if the office is particularly busy she may ask for no more than this.

The central card index is one of the most frequently used sections of the record system of the agency. It is consulted by clerical and social work staff on many occasions as well as by receptionists. Some 25,000 cards are arranged in alphabetical order (by surname) with details of the client's 'name', 'address', 'date of birth' (not always), 'children' (where applicable), 'referred by', 'date of referral' and 'assessment'. Sometimes there are several assessments on the same card relating to different visits, for example:

Lost suitcase while travelling. Requested financial help.
[*subsequent date*] Financial difficulties

or:

Accommodation wanted. Paying £9 weekly for furnished rooms.
[*subsequent date*] Has to find other accommodation due to birth of baby
[*subsequent date*] Accommodation. Advised to place name on housing list for G type [*a poor quality type of housing*]

125

[*subsequent date*] G.P. requesting background information on above named.

The index card also shows if a case is 'ceased' or if a case is of the 'no further action' type. Some index cards are also given a number in one corner and show the name of a social worker if the case was eventually allocated. If there is no number or name on the card the case is of the 'no further action' type.

Having classified the client on the basis of her record search, the receptionist then initiates one of several procedures. 'Ongoing' cases are taken (or directed if they know the way) to see 'their' social worker or, if he is not in his office, told when he will be available. This occurs regardless of the specifics of the client's current enquiry. Establishing the needs of these clients is not seen as a problem for the agency. Any request here is viewed as but a continuation of the 'ongoing' case, to be dealt with by the worker already assigned the case, under the supervision of his senior. The only rare exception to this practice is that if the case is deemed by the receptionists to be an 'emergency' the client might be seen by the duty officer.

Cases 'not known' are passed to the duty officer for an intake interview. If the duty officer is occupied clients wait until he is free, either in a waiting room near to the reception office or on seats in the broad corridors of the agency outside the social workers' offices.

'No further action' and 'ceased' cases are also passed to the duty officer for an intake interview. In these cases it is assumed that the client will have had previous personal contact with a social worker in the agency but such contact is regarded as qualitatively different from that of an 'allocated' case. The basic needs of an allocated case have been established and are not open to renegotiation. Further enquiries are treated as further manifestations of that need. But if a case has not been allocated (NFA) or allocated and subsequently closed and thus dropped from a worker's caseload, the need is seen as unestablished. The client must be passed through the intake and allocation routine again in order to reconstruct the existence and nature of need. Although I did not study in any detail in this research the way in which cases are 'closed' in City department, there is considerable variation between social workers in the agency in their closure practices and whether or not the needs of a client with previous contact are deemed 'new' is thus dependent upon these practices.

'Ceased' and 'no further action' cases are treated differently from those not known. Search procedures are initiated to produce those classifications of need made by the department at an earlier time. For all NFA cases referral sheets completed at the previous intake interviews are filed in alphabetical order by surname in the central reception office. There may be one or more of those sheets for each client. I found one case in which seven referral sheets were completed over a period of eighteen months, on each occasion but the last the case having been classified NFA. The receptionists extract the relevant sheets and pass them to the duty officer before the interview. 'Closed' files, however, are stored in a basement room and are not readily available, so the receptionist usually simply shows the index card on a client to the duty officer before he conducts the interview and then returns the card to the central file.

In general, then, clients are passed from reception to the duty officer. However, there are exceptions. One social worker, for instance, is responsible for liaison between the City Social Work Department and a local lodging house and between the department and an overnight shelter run by a group of voluntary workers. Enquirers who give one of those establishments as their address at reception are passed to this particular social worker if he is available. The same is true of some enquirers requesting accommodation, although it is not just *any* request for accommodation that falls in this class. It depends upon whether or not the enquirer is viewed as a 'down and out type of person' by the receptionists, and the history of previous contact with the agency as established in the existing records.

Exceptions to the general procedures described here are also the limited numbers of cases which are dealt with directly at reception and are not passed to a social worker at all. Enquirers are sometimes referred to other agencies if they have apparently called at the wrong office. These agencies include Social Security, chiropody, housing and health. Receptionists deal with some matters directly themselves. For instance, a list is maintained of registered child minders at the reception office. Enquirers who ask for information about child-minding facilities are simply given this list. Enquirers can also enter the name of their child on a waiting list for a nursery place at reception. There is a very long waiting list for these places and receptionists usually explain to the enquirers that they are unlikely to gain this service very quickly, except in exceptional circumstances. If the client does not mention at reception that she is merely seeking a nursery place, this is noted by the duty officer at the intake interview. If an enquirer whose child is already on the list wishes to know how progress is being made, she is referred to a clerk within the department who can inform her where she stands. The 'client' in these cases is taken to be the child. However, there is so little chance of a new request actually getting a nursery place in City that throughout the agency this type of case is known as 'nominal'. There is very little to be 'done' with the case.

Enquirers who request a home help at reception or indicate that they are making enquiries about the home help service are also exceptions to the general practice of passing clients from reception to a member of the professional staff. The organisation of home helps remains a largely separate activity within the City department. A home help organiser is responsible directly to an assistant director of social work and is in turn responsible for an assistant organiser and supervisors, the home helps themselves and clerical staff. The organisation of this sector of the department's affairs is an extremely complex matter administratively. Over 2000 clients are receiving home help and there are the equivalent of over 250 full-time home helps. The period of help varies from 3½ hours to 10 hours per week and the period worked by a home help from 20 to 40 hours per week. Some clients will not allow certain helps into their home and some home helps will not work with some clients. It is because of its administrative complexity that the home help section remains a separate entity.

'Home help' clients are directed by the receptionist down the corridor to the office of the home help organiser. He notes their request along with those received by telephone and by post. Clients are then visited by the assistant organiser to assess their 'need'. This need is described in terms of a specific number of 'sessions' of help and a request for home help is only deemed a 'need' for help if this assessment has been made. Social workers in City do not assign home helps directly, even to clients on their existing caseload. They make a referral to the home helps sector. The home help organiser may similarly refer cases to a social worker through the intake and allocation routines but in practice this seldom occurs. Thus a client coded 'home help' at reception is assessed as being 'in need' of home help (or not 'in need' at all). Records on the client are separately housed and throughout he is treated as a distinct type of case. The reconstruction of client 'need' is in general possible only if the client re-enters the allocation routines at the reception stage and also avoids re-classification as 'home-help'. Since the relevant index card which the receptionist will consult will already be coded 'home help' this may be difficult. The point I am making is that even at this early stage in the allocation routines we can see the impact of administrative factors upon the way in which constructs of social need are actually employed.

So from this description of reception in the City department several features of the process emerge which, I shall try to show, are of more general significance to the way in which needs are constructed in social work agencies.

1 The reception of clients is highly routinised. For clients wishing to see a social worker, reception consists of initiating one of a small number of standard procedures.

2 The choice of procedures depends upon a receptionist's classification of the client. This classification is an important initial constituent of client 'need'.

3 The scheme of classification employed is, in substantial part, an 'administrative' one, by which I mean that the terms of the scheme have meaning primarily as descriptions of specific agency procedures.

4 Reviewing agency records is an important part of the classification and these are themselves a product of the allocation routines.

Intake

Each day in the City department two social workers act as duty officers for the day. All fieldwork staff are eligible for this rota with the exception of senior social workers, trainee social workers, the home help organiser and assistant, one part-time social worker and two social workers who spend much of their time working at a psychiatric hospital nearby. It is the job of duty officers to deal with all enquiries from new and unallocated cases. They spend the day in the office receiving telephone calls, interviewing clients passed through to them from reception and perhaps completing reports or some other paperwork if there is any spare time. Most workers in this department have a room to themselves and in general they spend their time as duty officer in this room. However, one of the three groups of workers occupy rooms which are a little separate from the rest and duty officers from this group spend the day in an interview room near to the reception office.

The criteria for assigning clients to the duty officers are largely pragmatic. Clients are usually taken to see whichever officer happens to be free at the time. There is no attempt to match client and worker since the needs of the clients are viewed as unestablished at that stage. The number of clients seen in any one day varies a good deal but the duty officer has had a 'busy day' if he held more than nine or ten interviews. The interviews vary in length, lasting usually from around 15 to 45 minutes each.

In so far as I can generalise from the interviews I observed, expectations of the interview seem to differ between the client and the agency. The client expects 'something to be done' at the time. From the agency's perspective, however, the interview is not an 'action' location. It is primarily viewed as a data-gathering exercise. The task of the duty officer is that of collecting information upon which subsequent action will be based.

This operational procedure reflects three principles which are given widespread credence in this agency. First, there is the ideology of expert assessment. The needs of the client, it is felt, are not self-evident. They must be established. Only then can a client be assigned to a caseload and service provision commence. Second, it is thought, social workers should hold a caseload which consists of at least some cases of every 'type': the so-called 'generic caseload'. And third, it is felt that some attempt should be made to match the skills and experience of a particular worker with the type of problems with which he is asked to deal. But these principles can only be applied if the 'type' of each case is established at an early stage. Intake must thus function to reduce the case to a form which renders it amenable to subsequent allocation routines by arriving at some classification of need at an early stage of the client's career within the agency. In particular client need must be reduced to documentary form since many subsequent decisions are based upon written records and not upon direct observation or questioning of the client personally.

Duty officers perform this task of documenting need at the intake stage by completing a referral sheet (known in the agency as 'Form A'). This is shown in Figure 5. The duty officer conducts the interview with the object of completing this form and classifying need. Just as the central task of the receptionist is that of classifying clients in order to route them through to the intake phase, so the central task of the duty officer is that of classifying and documenting need as the basis for the client's passage to the allocation phase.

In completing this task, social workers in the department have several sources of categories for classifying social need. Amongst the most important are, first, those which reflect the requirements of some referral agency. The courts feature prominently here, offering a range of legally defined categories; for example, 'fine supervision orders', 'probation', or 'social enquiry report'. The categories 'mental health aftercare' and 'mentally handicapped' are also other-agency based. The Children's Panels, too, generate categories which are adopted by the Social Work Department. However, few clients calling personally at the department are coded in terms of this first set of categories. They are more usually applied to clients referred by the passage of documents of various kinds into the agency.

A second set of categories reflects the quite separate administrative arrangements that are made for some clients in City department. I have already mentioned that the home help service is organised quite separately. However else they may differ and however much they may resemble other cases in the agency, clients passed to this section of the department are classified 'home help'. I have already mentioned the special nursery places waiting list (NPA). Residential accommodation for the aged is also treated as a distinct organisational problem within the department. Applications for old people's homes (OPH) are documented in separate ways and after allocation processed through a filing system and decision-making process quite separate from the usual run of work in the agency. 'Financial problems' are also a separate category in City department. Any payment under Section 12 of the Social Work (Scotland) Act requires the specific approval of senior staff.

```
┌─────────────────────────────────────────────┐
│                                             │
│         REFERRAL SHEET            FORM A     │
│                                             │
│                                             │
│   NAME:               CHILDREN:  M............│
│   ADDRESS:                       F............│
│                                             │
│   REFERRED BY:                              │
│   PROBLEM:                                  │
│                                             │
│                                             │
│                                             │
│                                             │
│                                             │
│   ASSESSMENT:                               │
│                                             │
│                                             │
│   ACTION:                                   │
│                                             │
│                                             │
│                                             │
│                                             │
│                    SOCIAL WORKER: ..........│
│                         DATE: ..............│
│                                             │
└─────────────────────────────────────────────┘
```

Figure 5

A third set of categories draws upon the theoretical basis of social work, particularly casework theory. Clients categorised in these terms are invariably passed to allocation for assignment to a caseload. Examples are 'marital problems' and 'personal inadequacy'. Most frequently, however, such specific diagnoses are avoided. The very general category 'preventive' serves more often to indicate that 'general family casework' is required. The term 'preventive' has its origins in the principle that expenditure on casework is justified if it prevents children coming into care, but is now used more broadly than this in the City department, although retaining a connection with 'need situations' in which children are involved. In practice in this department 'preventive' is a residual category for cases in which 'general support' is deemed necessary but without specific legal or administrative procedures to further designate the case.

From my limited observations of the actual conduct of these interviews in the City department it seems that the duty officer arrives at an account of need by conducting the intake interview in the following way. Throughout, the social worker controls the flow of conversation. The professional asks questions and the client answers them. The social worker selects some material for specific attention while paying less attention to those facets of the case for which no categories are readily available. The interview resembles a moulding process in which the client and his situation are reconstructed to render them manageable within existing agency routines.

Initially in the interview, then, the social worker must obtain a statement of the 'presenting problem'. This, I was widely told, is a statement of the problem as the client himself presents the request for service. Thus early in the interview the client is given a cue by the social worker to 'tell me about things'. This is generally taken up by the client. However, the client's initial statement is often too long, given the agency procedures and modes of documentation, to constitute, as it stands, a statement of the problem. Even in constructing the 'presenting problem', the social worker must intervene, selecting, expanding, and reformulating where it seems necessary to facilitate the smooth management of the case.

Having stated the 'presenting problem' the duty officer then proceeds to establish whether or not there is some more fundamental 'underlying' need. He does this by questioning the client more closely on points of his opening statement, trying to pick up leads which will establish the relevance of some category and related procedures in the agency. The process resembles, in part, the enquiries of an examining lawyer. As lines of questioning appear fruitless they are abandoned in favour of others, more fruitful, hopefully.

When he has made his assessment the duty officer completes the 'action' section of the referral sheet. He makes one of three choices. A first choice is made if the assessment 'reveals an underlying need'. A home visit from a social worker is generally suggested. This suggestion is not taken as final in the department but, given that there is seldom another source of information, the duty officer's judgment is hard to refute. Seldom, however, is a recommendation for action made in very specific terms. 'Action' on the referral sheet may, for example, simply read 'for visit by social worker' or 'told Mrs A a social worker would be in touch'.

A second choice is made for those cases where 'no more' than the presenting problem is revealed but where the problem is categorised in terms of a distinct agency routine, for example OPH or NPA. Although such routines may involve (and may be expected to involve) no personal contact with the client, a social worker must be responsible for 'the case' while the routines are performed so it is passed for allocation to a caseload. In such cases, however, the 'action' section is often left blank. The coding of the case implies an automatic set of procedures and further comment is simply redundant.

A third choice is made for those cases classed by the duty officer as 'no further action required'. Here the 'action' section of the form is used in a different way. I mentioned earlier that intake is not viewed as a location for service provision itself. This *is* true if the duty officer expects the case to be allocated to another member of staff. If, however, during the course of the interview he concludes that this is not likely to happen, he may 'deal with it' at the time himself. He can do this by giving advice directly in the interview, by telephoning another agency on the client's behalf or by referring the client to another agency which might be the office of a lawyer, voluntary organisation, lodging house, the Housing Department, the Department of Employment, or Social Security. On the other hand, he may feel that neither he nor any other sector of the agency can offer any kind of help at all.

Beside his comment 'no further action required' the duty officer will generally describe briefly the action, if any, which he has taken. However, this is not necessarily so. For given the NFA coding any further entry would have no immediate impact upon the completion of any specific task within the department. A duty officer would make an entry only in order to justify his recommendation, although since most social workers in the department reported that they were very busy this recommendation was in fact seldom challenged. The point I am making here is related to my earlier comments about the use of agency records in research. The NFA code is a case in point. Its meaning in terms of the service provision a client receives is ambiguous. Only as an administrative construct is the meaning clear.

Some examples of completed referral sheets will serve to illustrate my account of how personal callers are handled. In all cases the name and address of the client is given together with the dated signature of the duty officer. Frequently no break is made between the 'problem', 'assessment' and 'action' entries. The first is an example of 'no further action'. Often just a single record exists on cases of this type.

Referred by: Self

Problem: Called, requested help with clothing. Has only one pair of shoes and very little underwear. It would appear that this man is rather simple. He had a period of three years in [*a psychiatric hospital*]. He is now on tablets prescribed by the doctor. He hopes to get a job in a hotel as a kitchen worker as soon as the season starts. He says that he has done this sort of work. He is in receipt of £6.70 from MSS [*Ministry of Social Security*] and pays £5 weekly for lodgings. Discussed case with [*a senior social worker*] and gave line for shoes and underwear to [*a voluntary organisation*]. No follow up.

Sometimes, however, an enquirer may be coded NFA repeatedly as in the next example in which referral sheets report three intake interviews over eight days.

Sheet 1

Referred by: Selves

Problem: Accommodation. Said they needed accommodation straight away. A furnished flat preferably. They were prepared to pay £5 between them. Her mother has asked her to leave home tonight.

Assessment: Explained we had no accommodation to offer but maybe they could get separate accommodation. They refused this and said that I was not trying to help and could they see my senior. [*The senior social worker*] explained that we have no accommodation but they went away saying that we were always finding accommodation for other people and they were always turned away. No further action.

Sheet 2

Referred by: Self

Problem: Accommodation. [*Mr P*] claims that being forced to live in [*an overnight shelter*] has produced in him a state of nervousness and he feels that unless he is helped into alternative accommodation his condition will deteriorate. His family (?) three sons and two daughters, all reside in the [*a town nearby*] area but he feels they are unable to be of any assistance. He is to get in contact with them regarding the possibility of accommodation. He would prefer however to stay in the City area and to live with Mrs B. Contacted Dr [*name of a doctor*] and appointment made for Mr P to be seen at 5.30 today. Mr P to contact YMCA regarding accommodation. No further action.

Sheet 3

Referred by: Selves.

Problem: Accommodation. Evicted from house at [*address*]. Gave them two addresses. However they are leaving City for Glasgow, later this afternoon if they are unsuccessful in obtaining accommodation. It is very possible that this will be the only alternative available. Phoned [*Social Security Office*] who agreed to pay Mr P his money in the early afternoon if he was definitely leaving for Glasgow. No further action.

The next example illustrates cases in which the duty officer recommended some contact with the client beyond the intake interview.

Referred by: Self. Advised by Ministry of Social Security.

Problem: Financial. This man would like a loan of £18.30 to pay the electricity bill. He received a letter from Mr Q about arrears on [*date*] regarding this sum which was due from his previous address [*address given*].

Assessment: He agreed to repay this sum at £1 per week. Has made one payment of £1 but finds he cannot keep this up. He is unemployed and is already paying £5 per week for HP.

135

Action:

His wife is pregnant. They moved into present address at the end of last year. The HP is for furnishings they acquired when they moved in. They were living in one room in [*address*] so had no furnishings for council house. [*Client*] was employed for 7 weeks with body building engineers but was paid off as not suitable for the work. Before that he was employed with the [*name of company*] but was paid off during strike. This week [*client*] received £9.63 unemployment benefit and will get a Giro from Ministry of Social Security tomorrow. Amount not known. He has been told by MSS that his income next week will be £11.55. He has paid his HP instalments regularly apart from week rent is due. He owes [*name of company*] £114.64, [*name of company*] £18.25, [*name of company*] £80. This man feels he will be able to start repaying loan as soon as he is employed but feels he cannot cope with spending £6 on HP weekly. Said a social worker would call and assess situation but could not say when. He said the MSS had explained he might have to wait some time for a visit. Could the social worker write and say the date the call will be made.

In all these examples the client is described as a 'self' referral. The majority of people enquiring personally at a social work department do so on their own behalf, although sometimes they may report that someone else suggested they should call—for example:

Referred by:

Health visitor

Problem:

Living in furnished rooms. Husband away at sea. Goes to parents home at A . . . [*a nearby town*] at weekends. When returned on Monday found tenant above had put nail through pipes. Place flooded and water and electricity cut off. Has coal fire. Neighbour helps. Also friend round the corner. Is due to go to rent tribunal as landlady had asked to leave on March 11th. Said I did not see how we could help and Mrs W will go to A . . . if can't manage. No action.

Duty officers are also responsible for dealing with telephone enquiries either from or about those people who are not already 'cases' in the organisation. In practice the majority of these calls come from members of other professional groups in the form of quite specific requests for the services of the Social Work Department.

Unless the caller asks for a particular social worker by name, telephone enquiries in the City department are directed to the reception office. The receptionists redirect the calls to whichever duty officer is free. The duty officer's task then resembles that of dealing with clients personally. He must construct a documented account of client 'need' as the basis for action at subsequent stages of the allocation routines. Again his primary task is the completion of 'Form A'.

In important respects, however, his task in these cases is considerably simplified. First, the professional—the prison welfare officer, health visitor, doctor or whatever—is likely to present the 'needs' of the client both in a form which is in line with the existing service routines and in a way which is readily reduced to documentary form. Much of the probing, reformulation and editing that the social worker undertakes in the interview with a client himself is redundant here. Second, the 'investigative stance' is redundant here too. The duty officer's task is considerably simplified if he accepts at face value the referral agent's account of client need. And, third, in the case of a referral by telephone the duty officer is seldom in a position to initiate 'action' at the time. The activities of the social worker are therefore largely limited to entering the requirements of the referral agent on the referral sheet and passing this to allocation for the course of action thus requested.

In consequence the entries on such referral sheets are often quite brief. In contrast to self referrals the duty officer is not here generating a body of material upon which a subsequent decision about the client is purportedly based. Rather he is relaying a request from one professional to another about the client. In substantial part 'need' is a construct of the referral agent here. Only rarely is a telephone referral coded NFA. Indeed it was noticeable that even when the duty officer did not accept the grounds of referral, as outlined by another professional, as legitimate, he nevertheless passed the case on to allocation where it tended to be assigned to a caseload. The following is one example of a referral from a doctor:

Referred by:	Dr C acting on behalf of Dr D
Problem:	Miss B has suffered three bereavements recently, one just this week, very distressed. GP

137

anxious about her future plans. Can social worker visit to see if support can be given.

Action: Miss B is not at her own home; may be c/o [*address given*]

In completing this entry, as in making the entry on all referral sheets the duty officer purports to collect and present a body of material upon the basis of which subsequent decisions will be made. The important point to note here, however, is that although it is widely held in the City department (and many aspects of the allocation procedures are based on the assumption that it is true) that decisions on the fact and nature of need and the related decision on whether to allocate the client to a caseload or not, are made at the final stages of the allocation procedure, in practice the structure of the referral sheet and the kind of conversations and interviews the duty officer conducts to complete that sheet render such decisions an intrinsic part of the intake function itself. Given the NFA code or given the kind of statement on a referral sheet that already implies this code, then contact with that case proceeds no further. Given the duty officer's recommendation for a home visit, this action ensues as a matter of course. For, given that the only information available on the case is that presented on the referral sheet, there is no independent basis for questioning the conclusions of the intake interview. Furthermore, in those cases in which the client is referred by some other professional agent, then the Social Work Department most often accepts that agent's construction of the fact and nature of the client's need. That is, the way in which the notion of social need is utilised by social workers in part, at least, reflects the way in which it is utilised by other professional groups. There is operational expression here of the ideology that views the referral agent as a most competent assessor of the nature of social need.

It is ironical that at the third stage of allocation procedures exist for making decisions which, in effect, are made at earlier stages of the client's passage through the agency. For here, as I shall now describe, we find clear operational expression of the view that the professional social worker is the most appropriate assessor of the nature of social need.

Allocation

For allocation purposes the region covered by the City department is divided into three geographical areas, each being manned by one of the three groups of social workers which constitute the fieldwork staff of the agency. This area division embodies the ideology, widely subscribed to within the department, that a social worker provides a most effective service to his client when he is familiar with the population, cultural traditions, other agencies and characteristics of the client's local community.

The fact of three communities and the boundaries of these communities in City was established by a working party within the agency which reported soon after the department was established. All cases taken over from the previous Children's, Welfare and Probation Departments were plotted, by address, on a map of the region. The working party, in a report circulated within the department, explained:

> The geographical areas we have chosen may look clumsy and uneven, but we decided upon them following a detailed account of numbers in receipt of help as of the 30th of September, 1969. We tried to make the areas similar a) numerically and b) in the type of work.

Within these constraints an attempt was made, also, to ensure that the areas represented collections of natural local communities. Social workers who had been brought up in the region were asked for their intuitive feelings on the boundaries of communities which might be used to promote local activity of this sort.

To some extent the area groups are autonomous within the agency. Senior staff make a good deal of this autonomy, although in practice, it is limited since many activities involve the other areas and contact with other agencies, which can only be approached on important matters through senior staff. One area discussed, for example, arrangements for the court duties which social workers perform but the matter could only be resolved by consulting court duty officers in the other areas and by arranging a meeting between the director and the sheriff's clerk. Also the area groups control few resources independent of overall department policy and this limits their effective autonomy.

Throughout the agency maps are available with the area boundaries clearly marked. It is a near invariable practice to assign a client to a social worker who covers the area of the client's address. For the purposes of allocation a client is deemed to belong to the area of the address at which he is staying at the time of the intake interview. Although originally noted simply as a feature for identification, once embodied in organisational documents, this address becomes 'the address' of the client and is subsequently used as a criterion for allocating the case. At the end of each day the duty officers sort the referral sheets into three area groups and each case then passes to one of the three meetings of social workers—the area allocation meetings—held for the most part, daily in the agency.

At this point in the proceedings two areas do differ from the third in the arrangements that they employ. Each morning an allocation meeting is held in these two areas. One group meets at 9.00 a.m. and the other at 9.30 a.m. and in one of the groups there is a system in which, for a week, in turn, social workers are not allocated any cases at all. This gives them an occasional week in which they are able to plan their work ahead, although they usually attend the meeting during these weeks so as not to miss anything. Apart from these minor differences, however, allocation meetings in these two areas are broadly similar.

All social workers eligible for receiving cases are expected to attend these daily meetings but on any one day some are absent because of emergency business, because they are on duty at court or perhaps because they are working away from the office that day. The meetings vary in length, but about 20 to 30 minutes is the norm. The senior social workers in each area take it in turns, week about, to collect the referrals and chair the meetings. On occasions the seniors take the opportunity at these meetings for making announcements to the group—a reminder about the monthly statistical returns, a circular from the director or notice from the administrator about some new procedure—but in the main the business is that of discussing the previous day's referrals to the area and, if necessary, allocating them to the caseloads of workers in the group. This practice is an operational expression of the view that it is the professional social workers who should be assessing the needs of the client and matching those needs with the skills and characteristics of the professional best able to meet those needs. It also reflects the view that as a unit the social workers in each group are responsible for the needs of the 'community' in their area and should be viewing particular requests for help within this context.

The allocation meeting proceeds with the senior social worker reading out the details of each new referral in turn. These may be in the form of the referral sheet but they may also be in the form of letters or documents received by post or as documents completed as a result of court requests for service from the Social Work Department. So far I have described only the reception and intake of personal enquiries and telephone calls. Some 'types' of cases, however, are treated quite separately and I should describe these arrangements before I continue the account of their discussion in the allocation meeting.

Some referrals to the department are made by letter arriving in the post. As such they are dealt with in line with all other post. Incoming mail goes to the personal secretary of the Director of Social Work if it is not otherwise addressed to an individual in the department. (A fairly large proportion is in fact directly addressed.)

The director's secretary sends cases for allocation back to reception, who, on the basis of the client's address, pass them to the relevant allocation meeting, having first checked that the case is not already 'open' and on a caseload. Invariably cases referred by post are allocated either for a social work visit or for a written reply to the original letter. As with telephone referrals, postal referrals seldom appear as 'NFA' cases. In particular, cases which are connected with the Children's Panels never appear as 'NFA'.

'Children's Panel' cases are probably the most significant single group of cases entering the department by post. Initially, usually, the department is involved in receiving a request for a background report from the reporter. This request most often endorses the request from the police which first gave rise to the case. (Anyone may refer a case to the reporter but by far the majority in fact come from the police.) Before being passed to allocation details of the request are entered in a Children's Panel Book at reception. Reception also check to see if the child is 'known' or a member of a family already 'known' to the department. This is important because it is a near automatic practice to assign cases to a social worker if he is already working with some other member of the same family. However, the receptionists' concern for the family unit is frustrated since the central card index system treats the client as an individual unit of need. Receptionists may attempt to deduce the family relationship from information on age, surname and address but given the complex situation of some clients (where the 'family', for example, may be split between addresses and not share the same surname) they do not always succeed. Different ideologies on the unit of need are operative at different stages of the routines. Nevertheless Children's Panel cases are always allocated and a report is always produced.

I have mentioned so far, then, three ways of entry for cases to the allocation stage: telephone referrals and personal callers through reception and intake, and postal referrals touching reception but bypassing the intake stage. Court cases employ a fourth way.

In the City department a limited number of social workers are designated court officers. Initially this was a group with a background in probation but this restriction was subsequently broadened. Each week one social worker acts as court duty officer and attends court for that week. The court duty officer then brings back from the court several types of referral, principally social enquiry reports (SER), fine supervision orders (FSO), deferred sentence supervision, and probation orders. All these cases come to the reception office and are in some repects treated differently from other referrals.

It is the responsibility of the court duty officer to ensure that reception is aware of the court's requests. In most cases, and in all SER cases, he will make a note of this request, while in court, on a 'flimsy' (so termed because thin pieces of paper are used in order that several carbon copies can be made at the time of taking the original note). This is a small blank sheet of paper without printed headings. All give the name of the court, date, name of the sheriff or baillie and name, age, and address of the client. Generally the client is referred to simply by surname. The following are examples of completed 'flimsies'.

> 2 fines not paid £30 and £40
> Wife left him [*date*]. He had woman looking
> after his 2 children - aged 4 and 1 years.
> A . . . [*surname of client*] has not worked since
> September.
> Sheriff wants SER for [*date*]
> He is concerned about this man's children
> According to A sheriff [*the same sheriff*]
> gave him custody of children on [*date*]

> Theft
> Continued until [*date*]
> Employed by City Transport Dept. from whom
> he stole money bag containing £100 in coin
> Sheriff noted that he did not feel C . . . was unduly
> worried by the offence. Agent [*name of agent*].

> Breach of peace
> Ord. to appear [*date*] for SER
> Case No. 651 known to [*name of social worker*]
> Wife also accused in this case — plead N.G.
> Trial on [*date*]

All SERs are then entered in a book before allocation, for the purposes of constructing statistics for central government. In this book is noted the date on which the report is required to be produced. The receptionist also checks the central index to see if the case is 'known' already to the department. These cases are then distributed for allocation by area. Any case which has no fixed abode is sent to the area of the court duty officer concerned. If the case is already known, the receptionist puts as much information on the top of the form as she can find. If a social enquiry report is requested for a client who is already on the caseload of a social worker, that report will generally be produced by the social worker. The allocation problem is thus minimised. However, social workers like the cases to be passed to their seniors for consideration at the allocation meeting so that the seniors will know that the social worker is producing the report and is thus involved in the additional work which this task entails. Thus generally SERs are passed to the allocation meeting even when it is known that they are already on the caseload of one social worker.

A court diary is also kept at reception. The court officer takes the court diary along to court every day. When an SER is requested he then notes in the diary the day on which it should be produced. Subsequent court duty officers are thus able to check at the beginning of their day whether or not they have all the reports that they should have for that time. The court diary and a book containing details of each flimsy are checked against each other. A check is needed since the production of SERs at the appropriate time, as the court demands, is thought to be most important. It is thought to reflect badly on the efficiency of the Social Work Department if a social enquiry report is not produced (although in fact I did not ever encounter such an occurrence).

FSOs and 'Deferred Sentences' are dealt with in a way that is broadly the same as SER type cases but there are some differences. Principally, the same amount of care is not given to recording and checking the records of those cases since the immediate task is not that of producing a specific report for the court on a particular date. But as in the case of SERs reception checks to see whether FSOs and deferred sentences are already known cases and if so scribbles details on the form. They then pass to allocation, whether known or not. A running total for FSOs and deferred sentences is also kept in order to produce statistics for central government.

Finally there are 'probation' cases as a distinct type which may enter the department via the court duty officer. There is not usually any problem in allocating probation cases since in general they will have been visited already for the purposes of constructing a social enquiry report. The person who did the social enquiry report would thus be assigned the case. Generally such a case 'comes back from the court' simply in the form of the court officer saying that the case has been put on probation, although an official order does follow subsequently.

I have paid some detailed attention to the activities of the court duty officer as a route through which cases may be presented for discussion to the allocation meeting because several points are of particular note to our more general concerns. We see here the clearest operational expression of the ideology which designates the referral agent as appropriate assessor of social need. Several 'types' of case in the Social Work Department are direct adoptions of legal designations assigned to clients in the court system. Moreover, these designations are operationally employed by social workers within types of case. It is especially notable that the duplication of recording systems for SERs is atypical of those elsewhere in the department. This stresses the importance attached to completing a task imposed by another agency and one which may be taken as very visible evidence of the department's competence. In the arrangements for court cases we should particularly note that the fact of need is deemed established. Such cases are always allocated. NFA is not a possibility. We should note too that the nature of need is also deemed established, at least provisionally. Not only is it given that the Social Work Department will act; the ways in which it will act, at least initially, are also given quite specifically. Furthermore, in selecting a worker with appropriate skills, the department is heavily dependent upon the needs of the clients as constructed within the court system. That is, in bypassing intake in these cases the department abnegates responsibility for collecting its own information on which the allocation decision may be based.

Let me now return to the description of the conduct of allocation meetings. The meeting proceeds with the senior social worker reading out details of all new referrals. They include referrals in any or even all of the forms that I have now described although referral sheets normally constitute the majority. Except for legal documents and the like, whose pattern is well known to those present, the senior normally reads out the referral sheet, or whatever, complete, with little selection or summary. No particular order in presenting the cases is apparent. They are usually just in the two piles as delivered by the two duty officers and receptionists at the end of the previous day.

Each case is then taken for discussion in turn. This opportunity for discussion is based upon the principle that the group should be making some attempt to establish the needs of the client within a community context and match those needs with the skills and characteristics of the professional best able to meet those needs. But in practice in the City department this kind of discussion actually seldom occurs. Typically in the meetings of these two areas the announcement of a case for allocation is followed by a period of silence, eventually broken by a single statement from one worker that he is prepared to accept the addition to his caseload. The sequence may be repeated several times although occasionally cases are discussed in more detail. Occasionally social workers in the allocation meetings do offer additional pieces of information connected with the case that have apparently not emerged in the intake interview or they may make suggestions for ways of dealing with a case based upon their experience of a case of a similar 'type'. Such comments, however, seldom alter the established nature of need.

The following illustration is a description of one allocation meeting taken directly from my fieldnotes:

> The week in which this meeting was held was the week of Mr Q [*one of the senior social workers*] for leading the allocation meeting. He explained that for allocation on that day there were only three social enquiry reports and one day-nursery application. He read out each of the allocation forms and there was some discussion, consisting mainly of social workers asking for points to be clarified (like a specification of the date on which the SER was requested). On the first case there was some discussion of a previous offence which had been committed by this client. The second SER was for a pair of twins. On the day-nursery application one social worker said that 'the case has been up before'. Another pointed out that 'it is different now' because [*a local voluntary agency*] had been dealing with the case before.
>
> The first case was already known to [*one social worker*] and she wanted to take it but she was soon going on holiday and it looked as if she would be hard pressed to produce the report in time. Mr Q suggested that she should not take it but she was keen to do so and took it in spite of the fact that she would soon be on leave.
>
> No one particularly wanted to take the second case, that of the twins. There was a silence with some small talk to fill in the gap from seniors. Mr Q suggested that someone might like this 'double bill'. Eventually one social worker took it with 'No, but I'll take it'.
>
> Mr Q circulated a boarding out notice for the information of anybody who had not yet seen it and then said that that was all for the allocation meeting.

In this example two points are of note. Although there was some comment in the meeting on these cases the type of need involved was not questioned. 'SER' and 'application for day nursery place' codings were taken as given. Second, although the offer of one worker to take a case was questioned on practical grounds, the 'suitability' of social workers, in terms of their ability to meet a particular kind of social need, was not a matter for open debate. This is typical of allocation meetings in this agency.

As far as the needs of the client are concerned, this lack of discussion is explicable. As I have explained, there is rarely a source of material other than the referral sheet, the 'flimsy' or whatever, on which the area group can base its discussion. This material is presented in a way which validates a prior construction of social need. In many cases a clear and established sequence of routines is already underway and the subsequent course of events (at least in the initial stages) is unproblematic within the agency.

As far as the skills of the worker are concerned, they generally receive even less attention than client need. But this too is explicable for given a particular categorisation of need, several very clear criteria are operative for deciding who is assigned a case. Within fairly narrow limits allocation is determined by the application of these criteria. Negotiation on an individualised basis for the disposal of a case, phrased in terms of the 'skills' and 'abilities', or whatever, of the workers is conducted on only a very limited number of occasions. Thus these allocation meetings, expressly designed to match 'needs' and 'skills' in an individualised way, are, in practice, routinised to a considerable degree.

Amongst the clearest of the allocation 'rules' is that cases already 'known' to a social worker are nearly automatically assigned to him. 'Known' has two meanings here. A social worker may offer to take a case because he had already met the client personally or has some information about him, perhaps through dealings with another client or his knowledge of the area. Indeed, the operation of this practice is based upon the assumption that this is so. Often, on the other hand, a case is said to be 'known' to a worker only in the sense that it has been coded as 'known' at reception. This does not necessarily involve personal contact or knowledge of the case confined to that worker. In this sense 'known' is an administrative category.

Second, it is a nearly invariable practice to assign a case to a social worker if another member of the same family is already an open case on that caseload. This is a direct operational expression of an ideology which views the family as a basic unit of social need. However, it may not always be clear at allocation that in fact clients are related since in other sectors of the agency's administration, and most important in the central index, the client is treated as an individual unit of need. The following fieldnote on an allocation meeting presents a case in point:

> Another client was referred to one worker because he was
> dealing with a family with the same surname. The Senior
> noted; 'we had two Mc . . . families'. The social worker
> replied; 'if he is at the Children's Panels he is not my Mc . . .'.
> Senior social worker; 'There may be some tenuous connection'.

The third criterion operative for allocating a case rests upon its classification as 'easy' or 'difficult'. 'Easy' cases are those which are coded as a 'simple request' at intake and for which relatively simple routines exist. 'Simple' refers to the complexity of arrangements for dealing with the case. More 'difficult' cases are those with an 'underlying need' coded in terms of casework theory at intake and those for which the arrangements for coping with the 'simple request' are more complex; for example arrangements for a funeral. Simple cases are accepted by students under supervision, trainee social workers and those who have been social workers for only a short time.

Fourth, many cases are assigned automatically because social workers have become established as 'specialists' in dealing with a particular type of case. In the main these specialisms are based on categories of case which involve special negotiations with other organisations; for example, schools, hospitals, the courts or adoption agencies. It is thought that inter-organisational relations are simplified if only a small number of social workers represent the Social Work Department. Thus only a limited number of social workers in the department accept adoption cases and many decisions about these cases are made by an adoption group chaired by a principal social worker in the agency. Also, only one social worker in each area performs *curator ad litem* duties. There are three mental health officers in the agency. One social worker has been especially appointed to conduct group work sessions with active and prospective foster parents. One social worker deals with all clients at a local lodgings hostel; another with clients at a mission run by voluntary workers. Two workers in the department are based at a local psychiatric hospital. Their caseload consists of patients referred to them directly from the hospital and all ex-patients of the hospital who are referrals to the Social Work Department. Three workers in the agency are also 'liaison officers' with a school for mentally handicapped children. Clients in the department who have attended this school are passed to their caseloads.

Some members of the department have also become 'specialists' in dealing with a particular type of case, by virtue of having consistently expressed an interest in this type of case and by being known to hold a high proportion of one type of case on their caseload. 'Probation' and 'physically handicapped' are particular examples. Some social workers have successfully overcome opposition to this practice by being prepared to accept a higher caseload because they said they could deal with clients more quickly if given cases of their specialism.

The routine application of these four criteria assigns the great majority of referrals to the caseload of one or other member of the area group. But in addition to these public criteria there are also a number of considerations which those present at the allocation meetings apply to their own caseloads at a particular time. It is generally accepted that each worker should do a 'fair share' of the work coming to the area. On occasions, for example, workers have complained when they felt that they were doing more work in the evenings than some of their colleagues. In practice, however, it is very difficult for each social worker to know how much work he is doing in relation to other members of the department. It is generally agreed that the total number of cases on a caseload gives little indication of the amount of work actually involved in managing the load, so workers fall back on the standard of the number of new cases accepted over a given period. It is thus important for each social worker that he should be seen to accept new cases from time to time. This will be balanced by him against the volume of work currently on hand. Thus social workers reported that they would go into an allocation meeting determined not to accept any case, if at all possible, regardless of 'what came up' (although often they nevertheless 'came out with something'). On other occasions they would feel that 'it is about time I had one'. Moreover, senior staff expect professionals in the department to hold a so-called 'generic caseload'. Social workers, particularly those who are known as specialists, are thus keen to maintain a token number of cases of a range of types and they accept some additions to their caseload with this in mind. These are the criteria operative for cases not otherwise assigned.

Now I explained that there are three area groups in the department and that the description of allocation, above, describes events in only two of these areas. Referrals assigned to the third area are allocated to the social workers in that team in a different way.

Here, each morning at 9.00 a.m. the two senior social workers for that area meet together for about 20 minutes in order themselves to assign the referrals to caseloads. They arrive at their decision in the following way. The two seniors take it in turns, week about, to be 'on allocation'. The worker on duty that week is responsible for collecting the referrals. He then reads out details of the case from the referral sheet or whatever and suggests a general course of action; for example, 'home visit required', 'no further action', and so on. The other senior then comments, sometimes consulting the referral documents as well. Seldom, however, is there very much discussion between the two at this point for the course of action to be taken, as in the case of the other areas, is treated as largely self-evident by this stage. Thus, so far as an assessment of client need is concerned, the different procedures used in this area are in outcome little different from the other two areas. Given my argument that the categorisation of need and the initiation of a routine subsequent upon this categorisation is a function of codings at intake (and earlier), this is not surprising. If a case is to be allocated (all those apart from NFA), the seniors then proceed to discuss who should be assigned a case. Here too, my observations suggest that the criteria employed closely resemble those used in the allocation meetings of the other two areas. Clients 'known' to a worker are assigned to him. Clients from a family assigned to a worker are also assigned to him. There are a number of 'specialists' in particular 'types' of case although all workers, if only in token, are assigned a 'generic caseload'. There is, too, the distinction between an 'easy' and 'difficult' case.

In this area, however, the seniors do appear to give somewhat more explicit attention to the 'capabilities', as they see them, of each social worker than is the case in the open meetings of the other areas. But the main difference in the use of allocation criteria between this area and the other two lies in the overriding importance assigned here to the amount of work occupying a social worker at the time. This criterion operates in the other areas, but only crude estimates of relative workloads are available. In the area where the seniors play a more significant role in making the allocation decision they put this kind of information to more specific use. They maintain a large foolscap-sized book with each page divided into squares, one axis representing dates and the other social workers in the area. Whenever a social worker is allocated a case the type of case is noted in the appropriate square. Cases are 'typed' on the basis of the referral sheet (or other referral documents). There is a significant preference for procedural and legal categorisations as against those reflecting a theoretical account of the problem involved. Examples are 'adoption', 'panel report', 'financial', 'deferred sentence', 'nursery place', 'OPH', 'aid', 'SER', 'electricity bill', 'funeral', 'hand rail', 'marital'. Also noted in this book is information on holiday periods and other occurrences affecting allocation. For example two social workers were on a departmental working party for ten days. This was noted and they did not receive new allocations during that time. Each senior also claims a 'fair knowledge' of the work that each member of their team is involved in at the time. When allocating a case the seniors consult this book and assign the case to a worker who has not had many new cases in the past few days. Other criteria are brought into play only to veto this working rule.

When the cases in this area have been allocated the senior on duty then takes the referral document to a meeting of all members of the area group, starting at 9.30 a.m. each morning. This meeting is referred to throughout the agency as the area's 'allocation meeting' and its conduct closely resembles the allocation meetings of the other two areas—except for the fact that the allocation decision has already been made. The holding of this meeting reflects the view that cases coming to the area are reflective of the life of that community as a unit. It is therefore important that all members of the area group should be fully aware of them and should contribute to the case, if possible, their own suggestions and relevant experiences. But in terms of the specifics of making an allocation decision this meeting has no important role. In practice, however, the conduct of this meeting does not differ significantly from the meetings in the other two areas since there too, in effect, the allocation decision in most cases is made outside the confines of the area group.

In this third area the senior social worker, as in the other areas, chairs the meeting although it is informally conducted throughout. The senior reads out full details of the referrals in turn and, after each, tells the relevant social worker that the case has been assigned to him. A certain tension is apparent at these moments as each worker hopes that he will not suffer an addition to his caseload, and there is an accompanying sense of relief as the majority do not. As one social worker explained: 'You sit there with your fingers crossed behind your back hoping that it will not be you. You don't make eye contact.' A senior, too, said: 'Some of them are under considerable pressure. You can see them sitting there praying that it is not coming to them.'

'No further action' cases are also read out in order to keep members informed about the kind of work coming to the area. On both NFA and allocated cases brief comments may follow the announcement of the referral details. Neither the skills of the worker nor, to any substantial degree, the 'established' needs of the client are discussed. Nor do social workers refuse to accept a case. The following exchange which I quote together with the comments that appear in my original fieldnotes, is the closest approximation to a refusal that I encountered:

Senior social worker:	(to social worker) Can you do this? (Really a a rhetorical question).
Social worker:	Well it won't be this week. (As near a refusal as possible).
Senior social worker:	Well when you can get round to it. (Order reinforced).

In general in this meeting remarks are confined to requests for information on the case, suggestions about future action or comparisons with other cases.

Once a case has been allocated, broadly the same procedures are followed in each of the three areas. The senior writes the name of the relevant social worker on the top of the form, or NFA for cases not assigned if this is not already abundantly clear. At the end of the allocation meeting the referral papers are retained by the senior and are not passed at once to the social worker assigned the case.

Exceptions to this practice are a small number of occasions on which a case is already 'known' to a social worker and the senior judges that the documents involved in 'registering' the case (described below) will already have been completed. (This judgment is sometimes wrong.) Some seniors enter the name of the social worker, the name and type of case and the date of allocation in an 'allocation book' which they retain for their own use. Except in the third area, however, these books do not play any part in subsequent case allocations.

The seniors then pass the referral sheets to the secretaries in the central reception office of the agency. It is at this point in the procedure that the files and agency records on which reception routines are based are constructed. Except for clients already indexed (in which case a second entry may be made or an addition made to the existing card) a receptionist types out a card for the central index file corresponding to each referral document. She takes the information for this card from the referral document itself. I have explained that the function of this card is that of facilitating the necessarily rapid routines of the intake and other procedures. It is a small card and contains the simplest categorisation of need to be found in documentary form within the agency. Since there is seldom sufficient space on the card for replicating all the available 'assessment' information, the receptionist extracts what seems to her to be the simplest statement of need and that statement of need which renders the client manageable for intake purposes. Two typewriters with different sized typefaces are used in this task. Receptionists explained that the use of one typewriter allowed for a longer statement of client need than the use of the other. When the cards are typed they are placed in their alphabetical position in the index file.

The referral sheets for allocated cases are then attached to other papers (Form B) which are routinely completed after a social worker's first visit on a case in this agency and placed by the receptionist in the social worker's pigeon hole. A social worker assigned a case in the morning meeting can usually pick up these papers any time after mid-afternoon the same day. All cases listed as allocated in the index file also have a case number typed on to the card alongside the name of the social worker. Once assigned a number a client is 'registered' in the department and fully established as a 'case' in the agency. All such cases are entered in a 'numbers book' containing the case number, name of client and name of social worker holding the case. The NFA referral sheets are stored, in alphabetical order by surname, in the filing cabinet which is housed in the reception room.

Again, however, there is a distinct procedure for 'types' of cases

rooted in the legal system. Any 'flimsy' case involving the production
of a report for the court is not immediately entered into the central
index. An entry is made in the 'flimsy' book mentioned earlier and
a copy of the 'flimsy' itself is retained at reception as a check on the
progress of this type of case. A card for the central index is entered
only when the report that the social worker assigned the case
produces, is eventually typed up. Only then is the case assigned a
number and 'registered'. And it is only with the filing practices of
registration that the procedures for allocation cases in this agency
are finally complete.

I have described in this chapter the organisational routines in a
social work agency for coping with the allocation task. I have
described these routines as being divided into three distinct stages
and I have dealt separately with reception, intake and allocation
itself. As an observer I watched the passage of different cases
through *each stage in turn*. In the next section of this chapter I
shall supplement this account by describing the sequence of routines
with respect to particular clients as I followed the passage through
several stages of a *number of cases in turn*.

Again I am taking up Denzin's (1970) suggestions on methodological triangulation. This account of the construction of social
need in an agency context is based not only upon data collected in
different ways but also upon the use of these data to describe the
same events from different points of view.

Cases of 'need'

This section of the chapter presents material on the construction of a
number of specific cases of 'need' in the City department. The
collection of these data were described earlier (the only point to add
being that the conversations at the reception window reported here
are based on notes made by one of the receptionists and are not
available in all instances). These specific cases were simply selected
as the five who were interviewed by one social worker during the
afternoon session of his day as duty officer. In presenting these cases
in considerable detail I have three purposes in mind. First, they are
intended to provide fuller illustration of a number of points that
have so far been made in only general terms. Second, and perhaps
most important, they are intended in particular to illustrate the
processual character of social need. This far we have stood, as it
were, at each stage of the process and 'watched the clients go by'. In
joining even a small number of clients and going through the entire
process *with* them, we shall see that aspects of the way in which the
agency constructs client need emerge, which might otherwise have
remained obscured. Third, I hope that these descriptions of five

cases may be of substantive interest in their own right. There are in the research literature very few observational accounts of the details of what is actually involved in the practice of even small sectors of professional social work. They may be useful for secondary analysis in related research or as material for teaching purposes.

Case 1—Mrs W

Mrs W called at the reception window of the City Social Work Department towards the start of one afternoon and asked to see a social worker. She had with her a little boy, about seven years old. The receptionist took Mrs W's name and address and consulted the index file. There was no card of this name in the index so Mrs W was shown to the room of one of the duty officers. This social worker then interviewed Mrs W.

SW:	Now you have some problem?
Mrs W:	It's electricity bills.
SW:	[*Standing up and moving over towards her to look at the bills which she had in her hand*] Now what is that?
Mrs W:	This one is for £27. I didn't use that much electricity. I don't use the light very much and we don't use the heaters and I make the bed up by 10 o'clock. I don't use that much. I went to the electricity board and they said it was the Town. But I went to the Town and they said it was the electricity board. I really don't think I've used that much.
SW:	So you think that the meter is at fault?
Mrs W:	They said that I could have a new meter but that I would have to pay £4.10 if they put it in. Why should I pay that? If the meter's at fault they should put it right. They said I should come up here.
SW:	This is the Social Work Department.
Mrs W:	They said that I was on a high rate E and D. There are cheaper rates of F and H. I don't use much electricity. There is my neighbour who has a heater and she's on cheaper rates. I don't use the storage heater.

SW:	Would you like me to phone the electricity and tell them that you think that your meter is wrong. I'll give them a call and say that you think your bill is too high.
Mrs W:	I am afraid to put on the electricity. The bills are so high that a bill might come one day that I couldn't pay. My husband works but I can't work.
SW:	What does your husband do?
Mrs W:	He's a digger. You see I'm afraid to sleep at nights for the worry. There's no need for me to get a breakdown just because of this electricity bill. I'm in a new and modern house and I shouldn't be worried about that.

[*At this point the social worker telephoned the Electricity Board.*]

SW:	[*On the telephone*] I want to query an account. I have here [*he gave the name and address of the client*]. She was referred to the 'Town'. I wonder if you could tell me what this is about. Now exactly what would that be. I wonder if it is the city architects. This is a corporation bill. She paid the bill today. But it was suggested that she might be able to pay at a lower rate. She's thinking that the bill is rather high.
SW:	[*To the client*] Have you been there a long time?
Mrs W:	Nine months.
SW:	It would be very high in the winter time?
Mrs W:	It was £22 for only 8 weeks. I'm afraid to use it. I don't do cooking in the day.
SW:	Is it storage heaters that you have?
Mrs W:	Just one. I haven't been using it. I use the paraffin heater. It is in the house to see. In a modern house it's something to have to use a paraffin heater in the house. It's a fine thing that I can't sleep at nights for fear of the bills.
SW:	[*Resuming his telephone conversation with the Electricity Board he arranged for an inspector from the Board to call at the client's home and discuss the bill and the meter.*]

Mrs W:	[*Interrupting the telephone conversation*] I'll be in during the mornings.
SW:	[*On the telephone*] She is in every forenoon.
SW:	[*To client*] Now your bill is down a bit from the last time.
Mrs W:	But what will it be like in the winter time? A bill could come in so big that I wouldn't be able to pay.
SW:	[*He now took from the client the full names of herself, her husband and her address. This social worker has a technique of getting names by taking a guess at what the christian name is and then asking if that is right*] Is it A . . . W then?
Mrs W:	A . . .
SW:	Not a bad guess. Well this man will come and see you then and you can tell all your trouble to him.
Mrs W:	But he said he would come before.
SW:	I think that he will come this time now that I've spoken to him.
Mrs W:	But it was three months.
SW:	If he doesn't come you'll come back here will you?
Mrs W:	Yes.
SW:	But from what you have told me it does sound as if the bills are quite high roundabout. [*This is a reference to the fact that Mrs W had compared her bills with her neighbours and the social worker suggested that some of these were high too.*]
Mrs W:	But the highest I ever had for the gas was £15 and I had a gas fire then.
SW:	Where were you before?
Mrs W:	[*Gave an address*]
SW:	Well that's about all then; you'll come back and see me. And we'll see about this 'Town' business. You'll see Mr K [*who was to visit Mrs W from the Electricity Board*].

Mrs W:	You've no idea how much trouble I had with the storage heater in the winter. I went to this person and that person and none of them would accept responsibility for it. They all passed me on to someone else. I then went down to the blind and they fixed it. [*The client wore dark glasses so I assume that she was partially sighted although this cropped up at no other point in the conversation and the cue was not taken up by the social worker.*]
SW:	And that is just your one boy [*pointing to the child with her*].
Mrs W:	No he's not mine. He's my grandchild.
SW:	So there's just the two of you in the household? [*i.e. Mrs W and her husband*].
Mrs W:	Yes.
SW:	Does he work? Is he in regular work?
Mrs W:	He has to work.
SW:	So there is just the two of you?
Mrs W:	Yes.
SW:	Will he have to come out if there is this strike?
Mrs W:	Well the employer is keeping him on. He's a grand boss.
SW:	Yes, I see that he's not really a builder. He works on the machinery. But I suppose if the others come out he might have no work to do. But at the moment he'll be in work then. Well, Mr K will be round to see you. [*The client left.*]

After the interview the duty officer filled out a referral sheet on Mrs W consulting notes that he had made during their conversation. The following is the referral sheet on the case.

Name:	Mr A . . . W
Address:	[*address*]
Referred by:	Wife at office.
Problem:	Paid electricity account today £32.20. Com-

plained of high cost especially as she had not been using the storage heater and had otherwise tried to conserve electricity. Had also complained to Hydro Board of being charged on higher rate of tariff compared to her neighbours. Mrs. W is disappointed over lack of action by Electricity Board who have referred her 'to the Town'. ? department. I rang Board who promised to send their Mr. K to investigate Mrs. W's complaint. She said they had previously arranged for someone to call but no one appeared. I invited Mrs. W to return here if Mr. K did not appear and further contact could be made with Board. Self and husband in household. He is a 'digger driver' with [name of builder] and is in steady employment. Social worker [name] [date].

The referral sheet was also noted as 'not known'.

On the basis of Mr and Mrs W's address this sheet then passed to one of the area teams. It was the team in which the senior social workers initially assign the case. My notes on the morning discussion of this particular case read as follows:

SSW A read over the referral sheet. He said that he thought this case would be one quite clearly for no further action. He said that, apparently, they just wanted the tariff changed and that he would say 'no further action' because they were quite capable of getting in contact with the Electricity Board and getting this done for themselves. SSW B agreed with this and added that there was no shortage of money, the husband was in regular work, and there were no children involved since only the married couple themselves were occupying the house.

The referral sheet was marked NFA and was taken to the subsequent allocation meeting with the other referral papers for that day.

When the case came up for discussion senior social worker A read out the referral sheet in its entirety and said that he had decided no further action was required. He said the problem was not a 'financial difficulty' but simply that the electricity bill was too high. The following discussion then occurred.

SW 1:   She should have gone to the Town Council. It wasn't really a case for the Social Work Department, at all. If she wants the rate changed because she is in a corporation house she has to get the approval of the Town Council before the Electricity Board will do it.

SW 2:	How much did you say the bill was?
SSWA:	£32. I think that that is not too bad.
SW 2:	What!—just with her and her husband?
SW 1:	She could be on the wrong rate. Or perhaps she has switched off the wrong switch or perhaps it involves some HP debts.
SW 3:	She could be on a white meter . . . or we don't know . . .
SW 4:	[*The duty officer who had taken the referral.*] But she'll be back to this department if Mr K from the Electricity does not call.

After this meeting the papers were taken to reception. The referral sheet was placed in the NFA file and the following card typed for the central index.

Name:	Mr A . . . W
Address:	[*address given*]
Referred by:	
Date of referral:	[*date given*]
Assessment:	Electricity Board Office who are to send out a man to investigate.

Case 2—Mr D

The next client interviewed by the duty officer was Mr D. He called at the reception office with his wife and asked:

Mr D:	Is this the welfare place?
Receptionist:	Yes. Would you like to see someone?
Mr D:	A welfare officer or someone like that.
Receptionist:	Have you seen anyone here before?
Mr D:	No.

The receptionist also requested his name and address and asked him to wait in the waiting room. The cards were checked and Mr D was coded 'Not known'. He was then taken with his wife to see the duty officer. The following is my record of the intake interview.

Mr D: We are in digs. We have to leave by [date]. We are on the housing list and we wonder if you could help us to get a house more quickly. We are expecting a child in September.

[Mr D also explained that he and his wife were lodging with a relative in a sub-let room of a council property. This is not allowed and when they went to the Housing Department to ask to be put on to the housing list they had to say where they were staying at the present time and thus it was discovered. In any case an informer in the block of flats in which they were staying had already sent an anonymous letter to the Housing Department informing them of the clients occupying a sub-let room.]

SW: How long have you been on the list? When you say not very long is that six weeks or six months?

Mr D: Three weeks.

SW: That's not very long. You know you should have to be a year on the list before you can get a house.

Mr D: They said perhaps six months—for a G type house.

[This is a type of low standard house.]

SW: But if you get a G type house you will not get out of that you know. Are you prepared for that?

Mr D: Well that's up to ourselves.

SW: Yes that's so. Now, Mr . . . [The social worker then takes the name of both Mr and Mrs D]. Now just where is it that you are living now?

Mr D: [Gives the address]

SW: What is it you have, one or two rooms?

Mr D: Just one room.

SW: And how much are you paying for that?

Mr D:	£5 per week.
SW:	That's rather high isn't it, £5 per week?
Mr D:	That includes our meals as well.
SW:	Oh that includes your board as well—as well as the rent. Now are you working? Unemployed?
Mr D:	I'm at [*name of a company*].
SW:	As a packer?
Mr D:	No . . . just as a general labourer.
SW:	How long have you been at [*present address*]?
Mr D:	Nine weeks.
SW:	And before that?
Mr D:	[*Gives address*] with my mother.
SW:	So you have to get out by the end of the month?
Mr D:	Yes
SW:	G type houses are fairly big. So it would be a high rent. They are quite big for you.
Mr D:	Well we'll take anything just now.
SW:	You're quite definite are you?
Mr D:	Yes.
SW:	Do you have any clubs, etc?
Mr D:	Financially we are quite all right. It's just the housing.
SW:	So what you want is for a social worker to come out and recommend you for a house. Is that what you want? What would you do if there was no G house?
Mr D:	I don't know.
SW:	What about your mother?
Mr D:	She is in the same position.
SW:	What about your people, Mrs D?
Mrs D:	They live out in the country.

SW:	So that wouldn't be any good for your work, would it? Have you been in contact with any councillors or any officials or is it that you have just asked personally at the Housing Department?
Mr D:	No I've just asked myself.
SW:	Right, we'll see what we can do [*the clients leave.*]

The duty officer then completed the following referral sheet.

Name:	Mr D [*age given*]
Address:	[*address given*] (brother-in-law)
Referred by:	Self and wife [*name of wife*] [*age of wife*] who is expecting a child in September.
Problem:	Accommodation. Paying £5 weekly for board and lodgings but have been asked to leave by [*date*] by Housing Department or the house-holder would face eviction. Seen here 8 to 9 weeks previously c/o his mother at [*address*] Can't return there—no sub-lets per Housing Department regulations. Wife's parents in country, applicant must remain in city for his job as labourer with [*company*]. Here he earns approximately £16 per week. Name on housing list for three weeks and been told they might possibly be offered 'G type' housing after 6 months on list. He would accept such accommodation despite the penalty involved. Wanted to know if this department could help him find a house. Social worker would contact him but it was unlikely Housing Department sould bend their regulations [*Name of Social Worker*] [*Date*]

The sheet was also marked 'not known'.

Now this case also went to the area team in which the seniors meet before the allocation meeting. Again it was quickly decided that the case could not be followed up nor allocated. One of the seniors would simply write saying that there was nothing the Social Work Department could do to help. At the allocation meeting the social workers present were informed of this fact without further discussion.

One of the seniors then wrote the following letter to Mr D.

Dear Mr D

Following your visit to this office yesterday we have considered whether this Department could help you with housing and very much regret that we are unable to do so.

As [*the duty officer*], the person you saw, told you we do not have housing available ourselves and the allocation of housing is a matter for the Housing Department. I feel that I can only suggest that you continue to press the Housing Department and if necessary consult your local councillor in this matter if you feel your case is not being given the attention you feel it requires.

I would like to say once again how much I regret the department are unable to help you and do hope that you will be successful in the near future in finding accommodation for yourself and wife.

Yours sincerely,
[*signed*]
Senior Social Worker

A copy of this letter was attached to the allocation sheet. When both were passed to the reception office they were deposited in the NFA file and the following card was entered in the central index for future reference:

Name:	Mr D [*age*]
Address:	c/o [*address*]
Referred by:	Self
Date of referral:	[*date*]
Assessment:	Accommodation problem.

Case 3—Mrs B

When Mrs B called at the reception office she was accompanied by a man and two children, but it was Mrs B herself who spoke to the receptionist:

Mrs B:	Can I see someone?
Receptionist:	Have you seen anyone before?
Mrs B:	Oh yes, about six months ago but I can't remember his name.
Receptionist:	Was it just the once you saw him?
Mrs B:	Yes.

The receptionist then took Mrs B's name and address, asked the group to wait in the waiting room and told them that they would be able to see someone. She checked the central index under the name of Mrs B (she assumed the rest of the group to be Mrs B's family) and located two cards. The one dated earlier read:

Name:	Mrs B
Address:	[*same address*]
Marital status:	divorced
Referred by:	self via [*a local voluntary agency*]
Date of referral:	[*date given, about five months earlier*]
Assessment:	financial difficulties

And the second card read:

Name:	Mrs B
Address:	[*address given*]
Marital status:	
Referred by:	[*name of lawyer*]
Date of referral:	[*date given, about 2½ months earlier*]
Assessment:	M.O.S.S.?

Since the case was not 'registered' on either card, it was coded NFA and the receptionist extracted the previous referral sheets. These were as follows.

Name:	Mrs B
Address:	[*address given*]
Children:	male 5, female 3
Referred by:	self via [*a local voluntary agency*]
Problem:	Financial, Mrs B is divorced from her husband. Receives £9 weekly from Social Security. Her little boy is due to start school next term and she's been told by the [*voluntary agency*] to request an educational grant to help clothe him.
Assessment:	Appeared to be a case justifying an extra grant for clothing from Ministry of Social Security.

Action:	Confirmed with school welfare department that I cannot help a family in receipt of Ministry of Social Security. Advised Mrs B to apply by post to Ministry of Social Security for an extra grant. No follow up. [*name of social worker*] [*date*]
Name:	Mrs B
Address:	[*address given*]
Children:	male 6, female 4
Referred by:	[*name*] lawyer (who can be contacted for further information)
Problem:	Mrs B was working until December. Since then has been claiming from Ministry of Social Security and receiving £12 per week. Recently she took in a lodger—a man of around her own age who pays £4 per week board. She informed the Ministry of Social Security of this who said she would get 3 weeks' allowance and then it would be stopped as Ministry of Social Security assumes the lodger is intending to support her.
Action:	Phoned Ministry of Social Security who said that position would be reconsidered next week and a decision would be arrived at but the assumption was no more money would be given. Asked about appeal and was told that pending appeal allowance would still be paid. Informed Mrs B of this and of appeals procedure and that she could be represented at the appeal if she wished. Gave her the address of claimants' union. Mrs B going back to her lawyer when she left and advised her that should she have any further difficulty she could contact the Social Work Department again. [*name of social worker*] [*date*]

When the receptionist took the group to the duty officer's room she brought these referral sheets with her and gave them to him. Only Mrs B entered the room. The man and two children waited outside and were not referred to throughout. The intake interview proceeded as follows.

SW: Well Mrs . . . [looks at referral sheet] B, what
                 is your problem today?

Mrs B: Well the Social Security has stopped my
                 money. The chap who stays with me, my chap
                 . . . but he has to keep my two kiddies as well.
                 And he has to support his wife as well. Now
                 my chap will support me and he knows that if
                 he takes me he's got to support me but he is a
                 bit annoyed that he is expected to support the
                 kids as well. Now my solicitor is going to
                 appeal but while the appeal is on the Social
                 Security have taken in my book and stopped the
                 allowance. I thought that while I was appeal-
                 ing I could get my money. Otherwise they will
                 say that if he has kept me and the kids for a
                 month he can do it always. I can't get the
                 money from my husband. They say that they
                 can't get money from a man who is not
                 working.

SW: So what would you like us to do?

Mrs B: Well I think I should get the money while my
                 appeal is going through. [At this point the
                 duty officer took from the client details of her
                 marital status—ages of the children and
                 name and address of the man with whom she
                 was living. From that point onwards the duty
                 officer referred to the co-habitee as Mr B]

SW: Does Mr B work?

Mrs B: Yes, but he has a lot to do. My solicitor said
                 that he would get in the appeal for the 1st
                 August but he can't do it just at the moment
                 because he is going on holiday and he doesn't
                 know all that much about the rules and reg-
                 ulations at Social Security and Welfare. He
                 said that I should come here and find out
                 about it to see what will happen to it this
                 month. I thought if I came here someone
                 would know about these things. I came to see
                 someone who knows about this. And this is
                 the only place.

SW: I'll phone about this. [He telephones the So-
                 cial Security office and asks if the allowance

165

> can be restored. He refers to the client by
> name and there is a pause while the person he
> talks to consults a senior. The social worker
> reports that the senior confirms the ruling
> that while an appeal is in progress allowances
> can be stopped.]

Mrs B: What annoys me is that B [*referring to Mr B
          by christian name*] should be expected to pay
          both. [*ie. his own wife and children and Mrs
          B and her children*]

SW: [*After the phone call*] He has checked with the
          supervisor and the payments cannot continue
          until the appeal.

Mrs B: But why should B pay for it all? He gets the
          whole thing loaded on to him. He is annoyed
          that K [*Mrs B's ex-husband*] should get away
          with it all scot free.

[*K is a musician in a group, currently living with another woman,
and claiming that he only works two nights a week and thus has
insufficient money to pay the amount to Mrs B which she was
awarded at the divorce. K is drawing Social Security and this annoys
Mrs B even more*]

SW: But if your husband does not work then they
          can't make him pay.

Mrs B: [*there is a pause here with neither client nor
          the social worker speaking*] So . . . we'll just
          have to see what happens . . . well I'll . . .
          [*gets up to go*].

          [*The social worker forestalls her*]

SW: Did Social Security warn you that this would
          happen?

Mrs B: Well I wrote and told them that E has come
          to stay . . . I did not do anything behind their
          backs. I didn't want to do anything that
          would get me into trouble. They said they
          could stop it anytime they wanted.

SW: But it will be a bit of time before the appeal
          comes through now won't it? If your solicitor
          is on holiday. Would you like a social worker
          to come and see if anything could be done?

Mrs B:	But what can be done? I don't see that anything can be done.
SW:	But perhaps someone could look into your circumstances. Perhaps a letter to the Social Security would do more than a telephone call. I have known cases where writing a letter has helped.
Mrs B:	This is annoying that K does not work. I have a court order for £9 but I've not seen anything of it.
SW:	Well maybe you can expect a call from a social worker to see if anything can be done.
Mrs B:	Thank you very much. [*client leaves*]

At the end of this interview the duty officer filled up the third referral sheet on this case.

Name:	Mrs B
Address:	[*address*] (She is a householder)
Children:	male [*name given*] 6½ female [*name given*] 4 and a child expected in September.
Referred by:	self
Problem:	Paramour is B . . . E, an electrician who supports his separate wife and children. Mrs B is divorced and her former husband has re-married and has a family. He has not supported applicant or his children [*names given*] and his earnings, playing in a group, are uncertain and her solicitor is unable to enforce a decree of maintenance. She has been receiving £11.25 Social Security until [*date*] when it was withdrawn and B is expected to maintain the entire household. Her solicitor [*name given*] has advised her to appeal against the Social Security decision but I today confirmed that the allowance would not be restored until the appeal was heard. For visit by social worker. Signed [*name of social worker*] [*date given*]

Mrs B's address fell in an area covered by one of the first two groups that I described earlier. It was therefore taken directly to the relevant allocation meeting by the senior social worker 'on duty' that week. The senior read out the details of all the allocation papers and then returned to consider each in turn. Mrs B was the fourth case for consideration. My fieldnotes record the following discussion.

SSW:	This is another one of those cases.
SW 1:	Can we really allocate this one—the one about Social Security? There is really little we can do.
SSW:	Well she has been referred to us for help.
SW 1:	But she can't eat that.
SSW:	Social Security has cut her benefit. I think it could go a lot deeper than that. But they just won't pay. She was getting £11.25 a week.
SW 2:	It's just one of those cases. It's the kind of thing where she has to prove that she is not co-habiting.

[*Several social workers then spoke of cases of their own in the past where the allowance had been cut off and they had been unable to get Social Security to restore it prior to an appeal. A number of these cases involved an unsupported mother co-habiting.*]

SW 1:	But she is maybe needing more help. She might be wanting to kick the man out. She must be wondering what to do. She is probably wondering what to do and perhaps needing more help.
SW 2:	Sometimes they make these decisions, just on the basis of slippers lying by the fire or something like that.
SW 3:	Well, I'll take it.

The senior then noted the name of this last social worker on the bottom of the referral sheet, and at reception a further index card was made up before the referral papers were passed to the worker assigned the case. This third entry in the central index was based upon the sheet just completed and read:

                     Case No 7185
                     [*name of Social Worker*]

Name: Mrs B

Address: [*address given*]

Marital status: divorced

Age: [*not given*]

Referred by: self

Date of referral: [*date given*]

Assessment: Ex-husband not maintaining children

Case 4—Mrs F

Mrs F arrived at the department in the middle of the afternoon and
called at the reception office requesting to see a social worker. There
was no entry under her name in the central index so she was taken to
the duty officer.

The intake interview began in the following way.

SW:	Well . . . ?
Mrs F:	I've been waiting for five weeks now for some-one to call. My husband has multiple sclerosis. She was coming to see him.
SW:	Who was this?
Mrs F:	Mr F

[*The social worker establishes that Mr F is Mrs F's husband and he
notes her full address.*]

SW:	Who was it you said was going to call?
Mrs F:	A Mrs Y.
SW:	I don't know anyone by that name. Was it from this office?
Mrs F	[*Hesitantly*] Yes. He has multiple sclerosis. It's a crippling disease. They never recover.
SW:	Yes I know. I'll just go downstairs and check the records. I think it may be a health visitor.

The duty officer then left the room and consulted the central
index. Here he located the following card entry on Mr F.

	Case No 6247
Mrs X	[*Name of social worker*]
Name:	Mr A . . . F
Address:	[*address given*]
Marital status:	
Age:	[*not given*]
Referred by:	Miss S health visitor
Date of referral:	[*date given*]
Assessment:	PH [*Physically Handicapped*], bath rail and seat requested.

On the duty officer's return the interview continued.

Mrs F:	It was a young girl that I saw.
SW:	I see from downstairs that someone was to come for a bath rail. Did you not get that? Is he in a wheel chair?
Mrs F:	No. He can walk with sticks.
SW:	I am surprised that you didn't get that. They normally send the workman from the city architects round quite quickly to that.
Mrs F:	I have myself and the two children and we are needing clothes. He hasn't got any clothes either. Some of the children are needing shoes. He has his pension. I have my pension book here. [*She takes her pension book out of her handbag*]
SW:	[*Taking the pension book.*] So what do you have? I see that you have a pension of £15.50. And you have family allowance. How much is that?
Mrs F:	£1.80.
SW:	£1.90 do you mean?
Mrs F:	Oh yes. I get muddled up with the new decimals. It used to be £1. 18s. and that's why I keep thinking that it's £1.80.
SW:	So that makes . . . [*He adds up the figures.*]

Mrs F:	Then I have had £3 off for the rent. And I have a gas fire . . . we can't have a coal fire because I can't carry the coal and of course he can't so we have to have a gas fire on.
SW:	Well that is taken into account you know in the book. When they are calculating that they take in rent and electricity and things like that and you just have to learn to manage on that amount. Well anyway someone will be down. They are usually very quick with these things. [*Client leaves.*]

On the basis of this interview the duty officer completed the referral sheet. Mr F remained 'the client' in this case.

Name:	Mr F
Address:	[*address given*]
Referred by:	Wife at office.
Problem:	Husband is disabled with multiple sclerosis. Two months ago a request for aids was passed to this office but apparently no one has called at [*address given*]. There is an additional request now for clothes.
Assessment:	Invalidity benefit £17.65, family allowance £1.90, total £19.55 per week.
Action:	Told Mrs F a social worker would be in touch. [*date given*] [*name of social worker*]

He also noted across the top of the form 'case known to Mrs X'.

This case fell in the same area as Case 3, Mrs B, and was discussed at the same allocation meeting. Again, the senior read out the sheet in its entirety and said that it was noted as a case for Mrs X. Mrs X explained that Mrs F had in fact been seen at the office by a student working under her supervision. Without further debate she accepted the case and took the referral sheet. It was assumed to be a 'continuing case' and did not go back to reception for further documentation.

Case 5—Miss G

Miss G called at the reception window of the department towards the end of the afternoon and asked to see a social worker. The receptionist took Miss G's name and address and consulted the index file. There was no card of this name in the index so Miss G was shown to the room of one of the duty officers. It had been a busy afternoon in the department and the duty officer was interviewing at the time. Miss G waited a few moments until the previous interview was completed and was then asked by the duty officer to come in and take a seat. The duty officer then interviewed Miss G.

SW: Now Mrs . . . ?

Miss G: I'm known by my maiden name. Miss G.

SW: Divorced . . . ?

Miss G: Separated. I'm hoping to get a divorce for cruelty.

SW: Now what is it . . . ? Someone will call and get full details later but can you tell me something about it now . . . ?

Miss G: Well we used to live in R but then we came back from R and got the flat with £150 from me. He was joint owner with the flat in both our names and I was supposed to be a joint owner but I can't get my things now. [*It seems that Miss G is in fact still married. She used to live with her husband in R but for some reason returned to City. They then bought a flat, with at least some of her money —the £150.*] He wanted access to P [*the daughter of the marriage*]. The sheriff gave him access once a week. Well he was weird. He was taken with melancholy and he acted most strange with boys in the house. He paid excessive attention to wind and some of the comments were obscene. He was rushing around the house and I have known him not speak for three days. He always said how melancholy he was and how he liked dark and dreary colours. He was most weird. He was acting strange. He gets access once a week and he takes her on the milk round that he does.

SW: And this is what is worrying you? P being on the milk float with him?

Miss G:	Yes and the strange things he tells her. And when she comes home she cries. And sometimes she thinks that we are bad and then gets all upset because she must know that we aren't bad. She is all confused. [*The social worker asks for the name and address of Miss G's husband.*]
SW:	What day does he take her out?
Miss G:	It's various days. He has listed the days that he's supposed to be off but in fact he works overtime. Sometimes he takes her when he's working. And he took me to court in January. I was told not to interfere with the access arrangements. And the judge didn't even read what I said. When I went to court before I wrote down about the strange things that he was doing and the judge didn't even read it. In the legal system they're not interested in persons. They're only interested in rules. I've been sentenced all along and I've not done anything wrong. The courts are supposed to pass judgment but in fact they pass sentence. All the time I've been trying to get a quick solution. I said that I would settle for my personal belongings and £150 because I want to get a quick solution. All the time I've been trying to find some quick way out but that doesn't seem possible.
SW:	Was your solicitor there?
Miss G:	Yes but the law is not interested in people. The neighbours have had to get the sanitary down twice for the mess that he has left the place in [*she is referring to the flat currently occupied by her husband*].
SW:	Who told you that?
Miss G:	The neighbours tell me.
SW:	Now . . . where was it that you were today?
Miss G:	At the Citizens Advice.
SW:	And they sent you here?
Miss G:	Yes.

SW:	. . . for casework.
Miss G:	He won't let me in. I think he may have had a conversion done and there is something funny about it. Perhaps it was a homer [*job done by workers in their spare time*] and the Building Society don't know about it. Because he won't let me in and he has had all the locks changed. I've been down sometimes and my father has been down sometimes because there are some of my father's things in the flat as well. But he won't let us in.
SW:	Perhaps he just wants to be spiteful. Who is your solicitor? [*The client gives the name of her own solicitor and also that of her husband.*]
SW:	So your worry is for the daughter?
Miss G:	Well yes . . . and some of her things are in the flat. Her cot and her bath are there. She has to sleep with me at the moment. And this is not so good as she is getting older. She is beginning to lie awake waiting for me to come to bed now. I have been in contact with the RSPCC before. He said that we had to form a relationship but I can't. When he comes and takes P, I just push her out through the door and when he brings her back he just pushes her back again.
SW:	You don't talk to each other?
Miss G:	Oh no, he just speaks jibberish. And she calls him 'the man'. And she calls my father daddy. She hasn't got this from us because we don't call him 'the man'. I'm frightened of him. I don't go down there alone any more. I'm really frightened of him.
SW:	Why did you come up here? [*i.e. Why did you move to City from R?*]
Miss G:	I kept thinking about the dogs. I thought it was the dogs. I think I was going neurotic myself and when you're neurotic you don't really understand why you do want things. He was acting so strange that I thought it was

	maybe all the dogs that were chasing him. And there was this carry on with the boys.
SW:	What boys were these?
Miss G:	Oh they were just friends, boys about 15 to 18.
SW:	What are you living on now . . . a job?
Miss G:	I'm a night auxiliary nurse but I'm starting teaching after the holiday—in September.
SW:	Where is it that you're a nurse at? [*Suggests the name of a hospital.*]
Miss G:	Yes.
SW:	So someone can come in the day?
Miss G:	Yes. I shall probably be in bed.
SW:	Resting?
Miss G:	I would think that he would pay the £150 and let me have my things to get me out of the way. Any decent person would let me have the £150 to get things over. Any decent person would move out of the flat and let me have it. I used to think that it was the husband who had to get out and leave the flat to the wife and kids but apparently that's not so. I got a few of the belongings back the other week but they were in a dreadful state. There's not really much. Just personal odds and ends and a few presents. And the £150.
SW:	Quite a complicated problem you have.
Miss G:	Yes. I'm just trying to find a quick way out. That's all I've been trying to do all along to try and find a quick way out but there doesn't seem to be one. It's been going on for nearly a year now. Since last July.
SW:	But there is not a quick way out.
Miss G:	Anyone decent would just give me the £150.
SW:	But he's spiteful.
Miss G:	That is why he takes P. He was really odd. He had two cars. And when I put P to the baby minder when I was working in R I had to go

and get her in the snow and all that, while he had a Humber Super Snipe and a mini van just standing there. He always had debts for cars. And there were bits and pieces all over the living room. He used to bring pieces in and polish them. And there was the top of a car being remoulded on the dining room table. But he hasn't got one of the cars now. He was in debt to a company for it and he sold the car which he shouldn't have done and I think they caught him. Because he hasn't got it now.

SW:	You feel that you came off worst . . .?
Miss G:	I've had no help. All along I've had no help.
SW:	So . . . if I got someone to see . . . it is P that we have to be concerned about.
Miss G:	Yes. She does not like seeing him.
SW:	Has he got relations? She can't just be walking about the streets when he has her for the day. She can't just be with him on the milk float all the time.
Miss G:	Yes there is his mother. She goes there sometimes. But I don't want her to go there.
SW:	What about on a wet day?
Miss G:	She goes there and to the flat. She sleeps in the afternoon. She doesn't sleep with us but when she goes with him she sleeps.
SW:	You don't know what she's been doing there?
Miss G:	She doesn't say what she's been doing. She's not washed before she comes home, and sometimes her dress is creased but she's quite clean. And that's unusual because she's not clean in the afternoon when she's at home. She must have been sitting about or something. I would like to know about the state of the flat, if it's clean. Someone said they saw him taking her out with someone else, a woman.

SW:	So there is a housekeeper . . . shall we say, staying there.
Miss G:	Well . . . I don't know who she is. I suppose you could say that.
SW:	Well at least there is a woman there. So she would be in during the day, if I knocked at the door it would be this lady who would open it.
Miss G:	Well, she may be working.
SW:	Oh she works in the day. Well, I'll pass this on to the area that deals with your road and someone will call. P is the main concern.
Miss G:	But the sheriff did not like the welfare to be involved. When I was contacting the RSPCC he asked what the RSPCC had to do with it. He didn't think that was anything to do with the welfare.
SW:	Well, we'll see what can be done . . . [*client leaves*].

After the interview the duty officer filled out a referral sheet on Miss G consulting notes that he had made during their conversation.

Name:	Miss G [*age given*]
Address:	c/o parents [*address*]
Children:	female: P (3½) [*the child is known by Miss G's married name*]
Referred by:	Self. Sent here from Citizens Advice Bureau for casework. Separated from husband for about one year. He is [*name*] [*age given*]. A [*name of firm*] dairy roundsman who lives at [*address*]. A house jointly owned by himself and applicant. She can't get into the house for her belongings and there may be a girl-friend living with her husband. The sheriff granted the husband access to his daughter and he calls for her on one day each week at 10.00 a.m. and returns her to her mother at 6.00 p.m. The child has referred to her grandfather as being bad and it is alleged her father is putting these ideas into her head.

177

Assessment: Applicant's solicitor is [*name and firm*] while [*name of solicitor*] acts for husband. Mr A for the RSPCC has also reported to the court about the child. Miss G makes various allegations about her husband's mental state, his conduct, his obsession for cars, etc. She feels she had a raw deal from her solicitor and court. She is an auxiliary nurse (night shift) at [*name of hospital*] but on [*date*] will start teaching at [*name of school*]. Husband contributes £4 weekly for P's [*the daughter's*] maintenance. [*date given*] [*signature of social worker*]

It then occurred to the duty officer that perhaps the agency would have some record on the client, but filed under Miss G's married name. He consulted the central index and found a card on P, Miss G's daughter. It read:

    Case No 6519
    Mr Z [*name of social worker*]

Name: [*Miss G's married surname*] P

Address: [*address given*]

Date of birth: [*date given*]

Referred by: mother

Date of referral: [*date given*]

Assessment: Nursery place required.

The duty officer then wrote across the top of the referral sheet 'Case No 6519, application for nursery placement in the name of Mr Z'. He noted the address on the referral sheet (Miss G's parent's address) and placed this piece of paper in the basket of the area which covered this address.

The next morning the case of Miss G was allocated at the morning meeting of the area group. Again it was the same meeting as that at which Cases 3 and 4 were discussed. The senior read out the first four referral sheets before coming to Miss G, she being the fifth. He noted that the case was 'down to Mr Z', referring to the duty officer's notes written across the top of the form. Addressing Mr Z, the senior social worker said, 'It is down to you for a nursery place but maybe you haven't had much to do with it.' He added, 'She was sent here by the Citizens Advice for casework—that is how it was put.' He then read out the referral sheet on Miss G in full adding '[*the name of the road*] no less'. (The address of Miss G's parents indicated a 'respectable' area of town). Thereafter this allocation entailed virtually no comment at all. The senior simply handed the referral sheet to Mr Z who took it and retained it at the end of the meeting. The referral sheet did not go to reception and an index card on Miss G was not made up that day.

The next day, however, the social worker, Mr Z, checked the index file. He could not recall details of the 'nursery placement' case that he had been assigned and wanted to 'refresh his memory' by referring to the index card on P (Miss G's daughter). He also checked to see if there was a card on Miss G and discovered that there was not. He pointed this out to the receptionist, who, later that day, typed the following index card.

Case No 6519
SW Mr Z [*name of Mr Z's area group*]

Name:	G Miss (Married name M)
Address:	[*address given*]
Marital status:	Separated
Date of birth:	[*Date given*]
Referred by:	Self
Date of referral:	[*Date given*]
Assessment:	Separated from husband. Feels she has had a raw deal from her solicitor and court.

Miss G was also assigned a number which 'registered' her in the agency. In this way she became a 'case' in the department, allocated to a social worker's caseload.

This concludes my description of the allocation of five specific cases in this department.

Discussion

It is, as I have observed, a part of the conventional wisdom of current social work in Britain that clients of social work agencies are 'in need', that social workers possess skills appropriate to meet those needs, that the needs are infinitely variable and demand individual assessment and that caseload allocation consists of the attempt to assess these needs and match them to the skills of professionals best able to meet them. Caseload allocation is the activity of establishing the fact and nature of social need. In this final part of this chapter I am going to discuss how it is that welfare professionals do come to establish this fact in particular cases and how in these cases they establish the particular nature of need. I have taken the view that it is an intrinsic part of a sociological account of social need to give an account of the way in which the fact and nature of need comes to be taken as a fact by social workers and enshrined within the documents and practices of their agencies.

In previous sections of the chapter I described the allocation arrangements in one agency. I then described what happened to several clients who either became 'cases' or were routed away from the agency in line with these arrangements. I shall now highlight particular features of allocation in the City department and then spell out some points relevant to the more general themes of this book.

It is clear that 'social need' is not a single concept with some universal definition but rather several different notions that are used in a number of very different ways. These different concepts of need can be described as ideologies with variation on at least three dimensions: the unit, cause and assessor of social need. Moreover, I have indicated that in examining the activities of a professional group we should not necessarily expect to find consistent operational usage of a single ideological stance since 'need' will be employed as a practical resource in a range of situations to accomplish a number of specific operational tasks. The ethnography in this chapter is offered as an example of these processes at work. The description reveals operational practices in the allocation procedures of one social work agency that are in line with a rather wide range of ideological positions. Let us consider each dimension of social need in turn.

1 The unit of need

The view that the individual client is the primary unit of social need finds operational expression in important sectors of the established allocation procedures of the City department. Most significant of all the majority of the filing systems used in the agency are based upon the individual unit. Cases are 'registered' and numbers assigned to individual clients. A social worker's caseload consists of so many individual cases. And the central index file has a separate card entered for each individual person in contact with the agency. Thus if several enquirers call at the office together only one may become 'the case'. The unit of need in Case 3 described above, for instance, was deemed to consist of 'Mrs B' and not, say, as we could envisage, of 'Mrs B and Mr E'. (And there are, of course, several other possibilities.) Thus an enquirer from a family with other members in regular contact with the department remains 'not known' to the agency at the reception stage if he is not 'a case' as an individual in his own right. Operational philosophies based upon the individual as the unit of need are particularly influential at the earlier phases of the allocation procedures, although throughout 'types' of need are conceived of and applied on an individualistic basis. The client is managed as a discrete entity. This ideology considerably simplifies many agency tasks, particularly in the documentation of social need.

However, although this ideology is a significant one it is not applied with total consistency throughout the agency. At some stages in the allocation routines an ideology is apparent that dictates the community as the major unit of social need. This stance finds particular expression in the establishment of the three areas, each serviced by a group of professionals whose work centres upon that area. This stance also finds expression in the holding of the allocation meeting at which the area group is thought to be the most appropriate group to consider the case. Thus each of the cases discussed above was referred by the duty officer to one of the area groups, deemed to cover the 'community' within which that particular problem could be understood. And each case was allocated to a social worker within that group. This ideology provides a ready criterion for dividing up the work of the department into manageable area teams.

The family is also viewed as an important unit of social need. For in several ways the family, too, as a unit, is embodied within the allocation procedures of the department. A social worker already dealing with one member of a family will nearly automatically be assigned any other member of that family should they too become a 'case' of the agency. (And assuming that the family connections do, in fact, become apparent.) Factors endemic to the family situation are assigned such importance in the practice of social work that, at least in aspects of the allocation routines, the family itself is treated as a unit of social need. This ideology provides a ready criterion for the non-problematic assignment of a number of cases at the allocation stage. Thus by moving in operation from one ideological position to another along the dimension of the unit of need, the notion may be used as a resource to manage the task of allocation within the agency.

2 The causes of need

Predominantly, on the ideological dimension referring to the causes of need, the allocation routines in the City department consist of an operational expression of the view that psychodynamic factors are the major causes of social need. The dictates of this stance find wide expression in the agency. First, the detailed intake interview reflects the view that clients' needs are not self-evident. A distinction is drawn between the 'presenting problem' and the 'underlying needs', and the intake interview is held to draw out the distinction between these two. Second, the psychodynamic ideology highlights the importance of the therapeutic relationship in casework practice. The systems in the department by which the duty officer collects information but refrains from action appropriately part of the casework relationship, commenced only after allocation of the case, probably to another, more 'suitable' worker, reflects this concept. This too is why a careful records search at reception, undertaken to discover whether the client is already 'known' (and has then already established a relationship), is held to be important. And this too is why it is almost automatic that a client 'known' to a worker is again assigned to that caseload. A change of social worker is deemed detrimental to the treatment relationship.

This ideology provides a rationale which is convenient for the allocation of a number of cases coming into the agency. More significant than this, however, the therapeutic ideology allows for the construction of social need by professional personnel in forms which are amenable to management within the terms of the established agency practices. 'Presenting problems' can be reinterpreted and replaced with a statement of the 'real' underlying need. Similarly certain cases may be dispensed with by being defined as 'no more' than a 'simple request'. No 'real' need is deemed to exist and the case may be assigned either to some other agency or to junior personnel. In the City department this practice is evidenced in the assignment of 'easy' cases either to students or inexperienced workers.

At some points in the allocation procedures material factors are also deemed significant as major causes of social need. Certain 'types' of need embodied within the agency's practices reflect resources which the department has available for meeting need in material form. Cases dealt with under Section 12 of the 1968 Act, for instance, are termed 'financial'. Most notably, however, need is viewed as dependent upon material factors in those areas in which the administration of a service resource is a particularly complex affair. The clearest examples are 'nursery place application', 'home helps', and 'old people's homes'. This ideology allows for the separate treatment of these types of cases and the administration of these services as separate entities. 'Home helps', in particular, is a distinctly separate sector of the agency, conceptualised throughout in terms of the material causes of need. Here 'assessment' of need consists simply in the calculation of the number of hours of help required each week. There is no attempt to detect an 'underlying need' in this sphere of° agency affairs. Again we can see that movement along a particular ideological dimension facilitates the accomplishment of certain management tasks.

3 The assessor of need

The predominant ideology about the assessor of social need, embodied operationally in the allocation procedures of this department, is that professional social workers are seen as the most appropriate assessors of need. This philosophy is expressed in the holding of both the intake interview and the allocation meetings. It is felt that the client himself is not capable of assessing his own real needs since this is a skilled task best performed by the welfare professional. The client is only able, it is thought, to announce his initial requests. The social worker must start 'where the client is' (the principle of acceptance) but then proceed to disclose the true underlying need. Thus clients are interviewed at some length by the duty officer with the objective of providing a statement of their request for help, as they see it, but followed by a body of data which will permit of professional assessment subsequently by a team of social workers pooling their knowledge, experience, insights and other social work skills. Cases are therefore passed to one such group where the opportunity of making such a professional assessment does arise. Indeed for cases assigned to one of the areas the task of assessing need is viewed as such a complex matter that it is deemed best undertaken by two senior social workers in consultation.

However, there are parts of the allocation routines in which an operational philosophy derived from quite a different ideology of assessment is implemented. Here the assessment of need is still viewed as a task for experts but is delegated to other professionals acting as referral agents. At intake, in particular, quite separate practices are apparent for dealing with cases designated 'in need' by another professional health or welfare worker. Distinct routines, however, are most clearly apparent in the way in which the social work agency manages 'court' cases. Here definitions of 'types' of need, rooted in the legal system, are adopted, largely without question, by the Social Work Department. Indeed such cases completely bypass intake, the stage at which social workers normally generate a body of material upon which to base their own assessment of need. Although these practices do deprive the Social Work Department of control of important aspects of the management of some 'types' of case—since here the fact and nature of need is taken as given—there are advantages. Principally, inter-agency co-operation is facilitated and this is especially important where the other agency is rather powerful, in relation to social work, as are the courts. It is of note that less credence is attached to the assessment of the referral agent when the referral is from a relative, neighbour, friend or some non-professional person.

Finally, in some limited aspect of allocation the client is himself deemed an appropriate assessor of need. The principal example of this practice is the way in which requests for the home help service are dealt with at reception. I have already noted that this service is administered quite separately in the City department. By coding this type of case as rapidly as possible and passing it to the home help sector, the receptionist maintains this separation. In general, however, there are major disadvantages from the professionals' point of view in accepting the client's own assessment as depicting the state of real need. Again we are seeing how different notions of need are used to accomplish different organisational and administrative tasks.

Now by referring to these variations in ideology and by noting the way in which the various notions of need are embodied operationally in the allocation procedures of the agency a good deal of what happens in allocation as a matter of organisational routine is explicable. We can understand, for instance, why a search for previous mention of cases in particular agency records takes place at reception. We can see why clients are interviewed by the duty officer, why he asks them what their problem is but why he asks them a good deal more besides. We can see why he should write notes on a referral sheet and why he passes this sheet to a particular group of colleagues in the agency. We can understand too that a meeting should be held to select a particular one of these colleagues as being best suited to accept an addition to his caseload.

However, a careful review of the cases presented in detail in this chapter also reveals aspects of events of allocation which are not explicable in terms of the professionals' service ideology, even given the observation that different phases of these events are the operational expressions of different ideologies of social need. At various phases of allocation events occur from time to time which clearly are at variance with the operational philosophies which the procedures purportedly embody.

Thus, for example, we may ask of the case of Mrs W (Case 1), who presented an electricity bill at the department and who was interviewed by a social worker, why it is that no record of her name was entered in the central index given that this index is specifically designed to record all those individuals who have had any contact with the agency. Similarly, we may ask why Mr W should be recorded as a client (NFA) in the agency files although he in fact did not have any contact at all with the Social Work Department. Again, given that clients known to a worker are routinely assigned to that same worker's caseload at allocation, we may ask why Mrs B

(Case 3) was coded 'not known' and assigned to a new worker even though on two previous occasions she had been interviewed by a social worker from the City department and even though this information was readily available to all those present at the allocation meeting at which her case was discussed. Conversely, we may ask why Mrs F (Case 4) was deemed known to a social worker and automatically assigned even though she had in fact not met the worker concerned. These are the kind of questions we may pose about the management of particular cases, answers to which are not forthcoming simply by appealing to the professionals' ideologies and operational philosophies.

I am therefore going to take one of the cases that I have described, the last one, Miss G (Case 5), and explore it in a little more detail in this respect. Bearing in mind the different ideologies of need operationally expressed in particular and different parts of the allocation routines, a number of questions arise. For in important respects the allocation of Miss G (and this case is but just one example) was not handled in line with the operational philosophies which are manifestly embodied in the agency's allocation procedures. It is important to stress that I am not adopting here any independent criteria as an observer, so I am not, in that sense, 'criticising' either the allocation procedures in general or the management of Miss G's case in particular. It is simply that if, in trying to understand the administration of the agency, we confine ourselves to (1) acknowledging that 'need' is not a simple concept but a complex ideology and (2) seeing that different aspects of the agency's administration implement different ideologies of need, some data still remain unexplained. Some questions remain.

First, we may ask why Miss G was coded as 'not known' at reception given that in fact she had recently been to the agency requesting a nursery place for her child, and given too that sets of records are kept at reception specifically designed to record contacts of this kind. Why did the search of agency records not reveal her previous contact with the department, why was the record of her previous contact filed under the name of her daughter, and why was she, in her previous request, classed as a referral agent and not a client?

Again the formulation of Miss G's request for help is puzzling in view of the claim that the intake interview and referral sheet serve in the first instance to provide a clear statement of the client's problem as the client presents that request. Miss G's statements entailed, minimally, requests for help (a) in obtaining a divorce as rapidly as possible and (b) in recovering her property and £150. Why was Miss G's request for a hastened divorce and legal settlement not considered and why did the referral sheet not mention her divorce or the

£150? The duty officer repeatedly asked her to present her problem as a request for help because of worry about her daughter, P. This perhaps reflects a 'human growth and development' approach to social problems, widespread in social work. Even so we would have expected such an interpretation to appear as a part of the duty officer's 'assessment' of the 'underlying need'. Certainly, we would expect a clearer statement of the presenting problem to the allocation meeting than actually occurred.

Third, there is the view that a client's needs should be met within the context of the community within which those needs arise and by those workers who are most likely to have local information helpful in this respect. In view of the information that emerged from the intake interview, it is possible that Miss G could have been assigned to the area that covered her flat. In dealing with the case it is arguable that familiarity with that flat, the neighbours mentioned by Miss G, her husband and his girlfriend would be of greater value than knowledge of Miss G's parents' home. Yet in spite of a procedure specifically designed to establish a community location for client need, Miss G was automatically assigned to the area of her then current 'c/o' address. I am not arguing that she was assigned to the wrong area. The point is that in a situation of clear alternatives the matter was not seen as one for debate.

Fourth, in spite of the arrangements for a discussion of Miss G's case and the opportunity for a group assessment of the skills of the worker best suited to meet her need, neither the needs of the client nor the skills of the worker received any attention at all. No reference was made to the information on the body of the referral sheet in allocating the case. Indeed the note 'known to Mr Z' was sufficient for the senior to suggest that the case would be assigned to Mr Z, even before he read out the details to the area group.

Finally, given that routines exist for a careful check of whether or not any social worker has had previous contact with a case and given that Miss G was specifically assigned to Mr Z on this basis it is surprising that in fact Mr Z knew nothing about her, had never met her nor any member of her family. The one member of staff who had met Miss G and did know a good deal about her and her problems was never considered for the assignment.

Thus in spite of careful records search, a detailed interview, and a meeting to discuss the case (amongst others), Miss G was assigned to a worker who did not know her, did not necessarily work in the area most closely connected with her case, and for whom no evidence was produced to suggest that he was any more suited to take the case than any other fieldworker in the agency. If we confine ourselves to appealing only to those ideological principles about the nature of need and service provision purportedly embodied in agency practices, it is difficult to see, so far as the outcome of this allocation is concerned, why the case could not as well have been assigned randomly.

Clearly a further step in the argument is required. The point is that not only is the administration of the agency a function of the professionals' ideologies of need, but also in important respects 'need' is a function of its administrative context. The allocation routines operate, not only to implement certain views about the nature of client need, but also in fulfilment of the requirements of smooth and efficient organisational management. In this last section of the chapter I shall highlight these latter aspects of the allocation arrangements. I shall suggest that the needs of Miss G were constructed and managed, at least in substantial part, in line with these administrative constraints.

I pointed earlier to the fact that the allocation task is a complex one. However, we have seen also that for the smooth running of the agency allocation should be completed rapidly and without disturbance to other agency business, both because it occurs so frequently and because service provision does not begin until it is completed successfully. In so far as we can generalise from the case study of the City Social Work Department these constraints are reconciled by an allocation procedure which is highly routinised, rigidly segmented and heavily dependent upon documentary material.

1 The allocation procedures are highly routinised

The management of social need is simplified through the operation of a set of routinised arrangements which in practice obviate the necessity for the individualised consideration of each case. This routinisation consists of the categorisation of a case and then almost automatic implementation of a set of procedures dependent upon the category employed. This arrangement entails a limitation to the total number of categories in the set (and the possible subsequent lines of action, too), the assignment in general of only one category to any one case, and the treatment of cases as individual units for categorisation purposes. This routinised nature of the proceedings has several important effects.

First, at all stages of allocation the activity of agency personnel consists, at least in major part, of an attempt to confer upon the client one of a relatively small set of existing categories of social need (or 'need-related' categories). The task of most members of the organisation involved in allocation is achieved once this task is accomplished. Thus the supposedly highly individualised nature of client need is severely restricted. Second, categorisation is achieved by initiating search procedures aimed at eliciting 'relevant facts'. Once sufficient data are at hand to justify a particular code, the search ends; often regardless as to whether or not further search would permit an alternative code. A 'satisficing' rather than a 'maximising' strategy is employed; that is, the 'first available' rather than the 'ultimate best' fit between client and need code is made. Third, decisions are often, in effect, taken at a phase in allocation prior to that phase at which the decision is supposedly made. This is particularly true of the allocation meetings. Most of the important decisions for this phase are in practice taken at the intake interview. Similarly coding at reception affects assessment by duty officers.

2 The allocation procedures are rigidly segmented

The management of social need is further simplified through a segmentation of the procedures into the three clear phases of reception, intake, and allocation itself. Different personnel are involved at each phase, at a different time and in a different place. Since a rigid division of labour assigns separate tasks to separate segments of the routine, members of the organisation are frequently unaware, in any detail, of what activity at the other stages involves. This segmented nature of the proceedings also has some important effects.

First, neither the clients themselves nor any member of the staff of the agency has an over-view of the allocation arrangements. Principles embodied in practices at one phase may be alien to principles operationalised elsewhere. Even in those instances in which staff do have experience of more than one phase of the events—as do field-workers who act as duty officers and who, as members of a team, also attend some of the allocation meetings—only rarely does this experience relate to the separate phases *of the same case*. Second, data generated at each phase for use at the next may well prove redundant. This is particularly true of information on the referral sheet. Third, information collected and used for a particular purpose at one phase may be employed in a quite different way at another stage. For example, the meaning of 'known' changes in important ways between the reception and allocation stage. The client's address is taken first as a feature for identification, second as a location for future contact and then as an indication of community origin. Fourth, as client need is processed through the three phases agency staff are concerned only with the completion of those tasks which form a part of the phase with which they are concerned. And, fifth, since decisions at later phases are heavily (usually totally) dependent upon earlier categorisations, these codings are taken as establishing the fact and nature of need.

3 The allocation routines are heavily dependent upon documentary material

It is an important part of the routine management of social need in the agency that need is rapidly reduced to, and largely handled in, documentary form. In this way need can be stored for future reference, passed from person to person and there is always physical evidence of the location of a case. This significant role of organisational records in the allocation routines also has five important effects.

First, the reduction of need to a documentary form further strengthens the establishment of the fact and nature of need at early phases of the routines. Second, in search procedures documented 'facts' are assigned credence over other materials. Third, search procedures are not undertaken for materials which cannot be reduced to documentary form. Fourth, the activities of personnel at some stages of allocation (especially intake) are almost entirely oriented towards the completion of specific documents. The structure of these documents structures their activities. And fifth, throughout allocation, documents must be generated as material for future searches.

We can now return to the example of the case of Miss G. By referring to these general characteristics of the allocation procedures in City Social Work Department—their routinised and segmented nature and the role of documentary material—it is now possible to suggest answers to the questions that were raised earlier.

First, Miss G was classed as an entirely new case at reception because a search of the central index revealed no card in her name. This was a direct result of the way in which her 'needs' had been categorised and documented during her previous contact with the agency. Coded then as a 'nursery place application' an established routine was automatically applied. (The name of P, the daughter, was entered in the waiting list, nominally assigned to a social worker and so on.) Since to fit in with the index system 'the client' must, at that stage, be an individual and must be assigned to only one need code, the 'need' for a nursery place was documented as the need of P with Miss G noted only as the 'referral agent', deemed herself not to be in need. Although there is no evidence to suggest that Miss G's situation at her first visit was substantially different from her situation at the visit described in detail here she was not then 'in need', a coding which resulted from the way in which nursery places are administered in this agency. On Miss G's second visit the standard search procedure of records, generated previously, established that 'not known' code, at which point the search ceased.

Second, although I can by no means claim to present a complete

189

analysis of the transcript of the interview between Miss G and the duty officer, reference to the administrative constraints under which this interview is conducted begins to suggest lines along which we may understand the questioning of the social worker, and his completion of the referral sheet. Much of the material in Miss G's opening statement is not readily presentable in terms of the available need categories nor are the lines of action which Miss G is suggesting established lines of action in the agency. (For instance, the social worker regards her complaints against 'the law' as matters that are rightly the concern of her solicitor.) The duty officer's questions may thus be viewed as a search for material which will permit a coding of need and disposal of the case to allocation. He seems to view a focus on Miss G's daughter P as the most hopeful approach to completing this task. However, this is not an entirely successful search from the duty officer's point of view and he finally falls back on the residual category of 'casework' in completing the referral sheet.

Third, the community within which Miss G's need was viewed as appropriately sited was decided upon administratively. It was not made in line with the principles which the area division purports to reflect. As with categories of need, each client is routinely assigned only one address for administrative simplicity. Since it must always be possible to contact the client readily and since it is very much simpler to note the postal address of the client's current residence than to make some attempt to assess the client's 'real' local community, Miss G was coded at her 'c/o' address. Her assignment to one of the area teams followed automatically upon this coding, even though there are good grounds for believing, in line with the notion of the local community, that this may not have been in her best interests.

Fourth, we can understand why neither the needs of Miss G nor the skills of Mr Z were assessed at the allocation meeting of the area group. Once designated 'known to Mr Z' the referral sheet information on Miss G was redundant, as was any discussion of her case, as far as allocation was concerned. The fact, and this is the fifth point, that Mr Z had actually not met (and could not remember) Miss G or P was not assigned credence over and above the 'fact' that, as a result of agency routines and documentation procedures Miss G was 'known' to a social worker and deemed to be in need, constructed in such a way that the need was best met by the skills of this particular professional. That is, I am arguing that not only is 'need' here a professional and specifically situated construct but also that it is, in substantial part, an administrative construct used for distinct management and organisational purposes. The case of Miss G is an illustration of this more general argument.

Summary

In previous sections of this book I have suggested that 'social need', when discussed within the context of welfare services, may be viewed as a professional accomplishment, as a social process in itself and as situated within a particular organisational environment. In this chapter, drawing upon data collected through fieldwork observation, and in other ways, I have presented material illustrative of these aspects of social need. In describing the reception, intake and allocation arrangements in a local authority Social Work Department I have detailed here one example of the way in which the social needs of welfare clients are professionally constructed.

The allocation task represents an organisational dilemma to a social work agency. On the one hand allocation is deemed the task of matching the particular needs of clients with the special skills of particular workers in a highly individualised way. On the other hand it is a management requirement that allocation should be conducted rapidly and repeatedly in standard ways in order to confine the occurrence of unpredictable events to strictly limited and clearly established organisational locales.

The data that I have presented in this chapter suggest that this dilemma is resolved, as follows. While 'meeting the needs of clients' remains the predominant requirement of professional activity throughout an agency, the ways in which 'the needs of clients' are constructed by professionals varies with the practical and organisationally situated purposes for which the notion is being used at any particular time. The reception, intake and allocation routines in the City department are a case in point. Employing the framework for describing variations in ideologies of need that emerged from the exploratory stages of this research I noted that very different notions of the unit, cause and assessor of need are embodied in different stages of the procedures as members of the agency are faced with particular management tasks. That is, the complex of client need becomes manageable because procedures are operative for establishing need in manageable form. Moreover, the fact that these allocation procedures are highly routinised, rigidly segmented and heavily dependent upon documentary material, both accentuates and obscures from the view of agency members the administrative components of the way in which the needs of particular clients are construed.

I am suggesting that so far as the functioning of the personal social services is concerned, social need is in substantial part an administrative construct. It is not a single, simple concept but rather a complex of interrelated assumptions, and ideas, which are used by welfare workers as resources for the accomplishment of the organisational task of client management. That is why I have suggested throughout the discussion that any notion of social need held independent of the concepts or practices of those workers and independent of the organisational contexts within which it is operationally employed is of only limited value in explanatory research. In a brief final chapter I shall recall not only the theoretical and methodological implications of this point but also its significance in terms of the policy question with which the book began.

Conclusion

Chapter seven

Overview

In this concluding chapter I shall summarise briefly and bring together the central themes of this book. I shall also highlight the main implications of the empirical materials I have presented in Part three and of the arguments that I have tried to develop throughout. In the Introduction I said that I thought a systematic study of the management of 'social need' was potentially fruitful on three counts: (1) theoretically in terms of our understanding of the concept of 'social need' and of the way in which social work agencies function to meet 'need', (2) methodologically in terms of exploring appropriate strategies for the study of social work and related agencies, and (3) in terms of social policy and practice so far as 'need' played an important part in assumptions which were basic to the reorganisation of British social work. I shall again use these three headings to arrange the comments in this chapter.

However, it should by now be clear that the division between questions of theory, methodology, policy and practice has in outcome proved artificial to a substantial degree. Indeed, throughout I have tried to show that questions of policy and practice cannot be debated independently of a discussion of certain theoretical issues central to research in the field of social work. Likewise the research techniques I adopted reflected a particular theoretical approach. I have been especially critical of some empirical studies which, in pursuit of practical and policy relevance have glossed over theoretical and methodological questions to confusing effect. Nevertheless on occasions the above tripartition does have pragmatic utility and I shall use it here.

Theory

My central theoretical concern has been that of attempting to locate a sound formulation of the concept of social need. This concern arose from a dissatisfaction with the way in which the concept had been used both in the policy debate preceding the reorganisation of British social work and within the predominant tradition of research in Britain into the functioning of social work and welfare services. On the basis of a review of the policy and research literature and in looking at my own research data subsequently, the approach which sought to define need as a property of the individual in terms of some objective and universally applicable criteria appeared clearly inadequate. In particular, I came to reject the view that social need could be studied as independent of the concepts and precepts of professionals and laymen and independent of the contexts within which the notion is utilised.

It is true that there have been attempts to modify the traditional approach by pointing, for example, to the fact that there are clearly variations in subjective definitions of social need. In practice, however, such modifications have had little lasting effect upon the way in which the idea of 'need' has been used. All too often the approach has been to note the variations or complexities but then gloss over them. Seldom have they been developed empirically in any systematic way. It seemed that the resulting confusion was such that it could be clarified neither by minor modifications to the traditional approach nor by yet further empirical research along traditional lines. What was required was an analytic framework to *take account* of the complexities, focusing upon the fact that the study of 'need' entails not only the study of subjective concepts (or belief systems or whatever) but also those actual practices through which need is socially constructed in operative form.

Thus, following Berger and Luckmann (1967) and others, I have taken the general view that for the purposes of explanatory research 'social need' is fruitfully seen as the objectification of a set of subjective phenomena. An adequate theory of need must therefore minimally offer (a) a framework for describing different subjective notions of need and (b) a framework for describing the way in which these notions become 'objective facticities'; that is, the way in which they are employed socially to construct the realities of need in particular contexts.

Now the context in which I have been most interested here is that of the recently reorganised local authority social work organisations both in Scotland and in England and Wales. So, rather than seeking out some supposedly independent criteria, I attempted to describe the subjective notions of need that social workers do actually hold and moreover the ways in which these subjective notions do become objectified in the actual working out of social work agencies. Throughout, I have viewed the phenomenon of social need, as it is empirically encountered within the organisation of the social services, as closely dependent upon the precepts and concepts of professional workers who employ the term and closely dependent too upon the agency contexts within which it is employed.

At this point, however, I should reiterate some limitations in this general approach. First, although I have argued that we can treat 'social need' as a professional and organisational construct, this should not be taken to imply that it is exclusively so. Undoubtedly the notion of social need is employed by clients and other lay publics in situations quite outside the context of the formally organised provision of social services. A study of broader scope would examine these other uses and the relationships between them. In outline, however, I would suggest a research approach for this task similar to that which I have adopted here for the study of 'need' as a professional and organisational phenomenon. Second, we should recall that the approach I have taken does not purport to explain the causes or rates of occurrence of those social conditions, psychological states or whatever that may be construed by professionals or laymen as constituting social need. I have simply suggested that the construction and use of 'social need' as a research topic in its own right is of primary concern.

So, I attempted to develop a framework that would allow for the description of sets of interrelated precepts and concepts which professional social workers actually do employ to construe 'social need' as the appropriate object of their professional practice. The ideas of a multi-dimensional professional ideology and a related set of operational philosophies (Strauss, 1964; Marx, 1969) were introduced to the analysis. Exploratory empirical material indicated that variations in the models of need adopted by social workers can be described as variations on at least three major dimensions of a professional ideology of social need. These dimensions refer to the unit, assessor and causes of need. (And it may be that further data would suggest additional dimensions which were not evident in these particular materials.) I noted, moreover, that so far as the operational expression of these ideological positions in the form of institutionalised procedures is concerned no single consistent stance is apparent. Rather different operational philosophies are implemented in different spheres of the agency's routines. The next stage of the analysis therefore consisted of a study of the different situations in which different ideologies gained operational effect.

At this point I focused the research upon one particular aspect of agency affairs, the reception, intake and allocation practices. I also adopted the case study approach. Within these limitations I suggested that 'need' functions within a social work organisation in substantial part as an administrative construct. That is, it is employed by professional personnel as a resource to accomplish specific management and organisational tasks.

Conclusion

In so far as we can generalise from the department I studied in greatest detail, in the sphere of allocation the practitioners' management of social need takes place in the following way. First, as a solution to the organisation's central division of labour problem, different ideologies of need gain inconsistent operational expression in agency procedures in a way which facilitates either the disposal of cases or their unproblematic allocation to the caseloads of members of staff. The outcome is a set of procedures which are highly routinised, quite rigidly segmented and heavily dependent upon documentary material. These features in turn place constraints upon the way in which the needs of particular clients are then construed. Again, however, by drawing upon different ideologies with respect to different 'types' of clients and by constructing the needs of the same client in slightly different ways at different stages of the routines, 'need' is used as a resource by professional social workers and others to facilitate the smooth running of agency affairs. It is in this sense that 'need' is to be viewed as a professional and an administrative accomplishment.

A final note on the generality both of these comments and of the more detailed points in the ethnography that I have presented is called for here. It is clear that I have examined in any detail only a limited number of organisations, that many of my comments derive from a single case study and that I have focused primarily upon just one sphere of agency affairs. In so far as we can generalise, however, this much is apparent. On the one hand we may explain the administrative procedures of a social work organisation as the operational expressions of certain professional ideologies of need. On the other hand certain ideologies of need gain operational effect because of the administrative functions that they fulfil. In short the relationship between professional ideologies and patterns of administration in the organisation of social work practice is a complex one because in important respects it is a reflexive one. The theoretical significance of the materials I have described is that they point to the complexities of this relationship which I have tried to explore.

Methodology

The central problem involved in empirically studying social need within welfare organisations in a way that is consistent with the theoretical approach that I have tried to pursue is that the collection of several different kinds of data is required. I have explained that I adopted an approach which stems from the fact that: 'Since society exists as both objective and subjective reality, any adequate theoretical understanding of it must comprehend these aspects' (Berger and Luckmann, 1967, p. 149). The same is true of an adequate empirical understanding and I have tried to pursue the methodological implications of this point in the study of social work agencies.

Stated in this general form the point that Berger and Luckmann are making is not, of course, very new. However, it has not, as yet, been taken very seriously so far as the research designs of the majority of studies in the field of social work are concerned. At various points in this report I have expressed two reservations about the methodology of many studies conducted within the dominant tradition of research into the functioning of the British welfare services. First, I described a serious neglect of observational material. Second, I have suggested that many studies are over-dependent upon a single data source. There is a third and related reservation which I have touched upon but not stated quite so clearly. It is that (in the absence of direct observations) interview material, questionnaire responses, official statistics and the opinions of professional assessors have all been taken as valid measures of objective phenomena. Drawing, as a theoretical basis for study, upon the traditional notion of social need, researchers have not been sensitised to the fact that much of their material is potentially reflecting welfare workers' professional ideologies. By making a distinction in this study between professional ideologies on the one hand and operational philosophies which are the actual practices of service delivery, on the other, and by attempting to explore the relationships between the two, I have been forced to consider the status of different kinds of data a little more carefully.

I have described the way in which I made use of three types of data. During the early stages of the project in which I was primarily concerned with establishing a framework for mapping variations in ideologies of need, I did rely quite heavily upon interview materials. But as I became increasingly interested in the way in which these ideologies are actually utilised I increasingly employed an observational methodology. I also studied agency records within the context of a review of the filing system of the agencies and I supplemented this study with observations of the record-keeping practices of social work professionals and clerical and secretarial staff. I took both the entries in these records and the way in which they are generated and utilised as indicative of the process of the objectification of social need. Thus, in line with the dictates of a strategy of 'methodological triangulation', I attempted to use different kinds of material to explore different facets of the phenomenon of social need. In particular I made use of observational data to examine the way in which the notion of need is operationally employed by welfare professionals within the context of social work agencies.

In conclusion, however, I should also note that the research methods adopted here have not been used without some reservations. In practice the distinction between data of varying status has not been as sharp as the above discussion implies. In particular I necessarily relied on accounts from personnel in the agency for a description of some practices that could not be observed. Undoubtedly too there are other kinds of data that could fruitfully be used to supplement this research. Although in my order of priority the question 'How many?' is preceded by the question, simply 'How?', additional quantitative measures would undoubtedly add precision to the account. It might also be possible to devise some experimental project which would illuminate facets of an agency's intake and allocation routines. Interviews with clients and referral agents about their notions of social need would allow us to explore more fully how it is that their constructs impinge upon those of the social workers. We could also explore 'need' in other than organisational domains, although, as I have noted, this would extend the study considerably.

Finally, by way of methodological comment, I should stress that an emphasis upon the importance of observational data is not intended to gloss over the difficulties involved in collecting this kind of material in the field of social work. I have noted that the spatial and temporal dispersal of such social work practice militates against the use of observational techniques, and if the individual client career is taken as the basic unit of analysis the researcher may indeed be required to observe in many different places over an extended period of time. However, there are other possible units of analysis such as the accomplishment of a particular agency task. I have studied caseload allocation. Another study might focus, say, upon the procedures involved in 'closing' a case. The activities of a particular group of agency personnel, senior social workers, for example, may also be used as the basic unit for observation. By taking some unit other than the client career as the basis for sampling events and situations to be reviewed the practical difficulties involved in observational research can be substantially reduced.

Another restriction on the use of observational methods in research in social work has been the assumed 'confidential' nature of much of the material that the researcher might wish to collect. I have noted, however, that although a great deal of material of various kinds is 'confidential', in the sense that an observer is required not to disclose the personal identity of the individuals involved, this does not usually act as a bar to his collecting observational data for research purposes. So far as the research reported in this book is concerned only a proportion of the material that I wished to collect was 'confidential' in the sense that it was available only in very private situations normally restricted from the view of all but the client and a single professional. (Even in the intake interview the presence of an observer in the role of 'student', 'colleague', or 'research worker' was viewed as acceptable.) There are, as I have noted, good organisational reasons for this state of affairs. Given the procedures I have described, details of enquiries (and subsequently 'cases') must be readily and routinely available to, and regularly passed among, not only up to thirty or forty professionals but also a range of clerical and secretarial staff within the agency. Under these conditions, consultations and written records acquire a certain openness which facilitates the research fieldworker's tasks. The interests of researcher and agency staff are in perhaps surprisingly close accord at this point for the placing of material under restricted access creates 'trouble' so far as both are concerned.

Yet a further restriction on the use of observational techniques has been the assumed impact of the 'observer effect'. It is argued that the presence of a researcher is likely to change in important ways the events and situations he seeks to describe. In particular it is possible that professionals and others may change their behaviour, temporarily, to conform to these patterns which they perceive the researcher to expect. However, so far as the aspects of social work practice which I have observed are concerned, I have reported that agency routines are so firmly established that it is difficult to envisage temporary and *ad hoc* change which would not be very apparent because of its disruptive effect. As Becker (1970) notes;

> What [*a person*] is involved in at the moment of observation is as a rule much more important to him than the observer is . . . [*The*] presence in the observational situation of the very social constraints the sociologist ordinarily studies makes it difficult for the people he observes to tailor their behaviour to what they think he might want or expect. However much they want to, the real consequences of deviating from what they might otherwise have done are great enough . . . that they cannot (pp. 46-7).

Certainly during reception, intake and allocation in a social work agency the disadvantages of not doing what is typically done would far outweigh the most tentative advantages of attempting to conform to some other supposed ideal.

In short, what I am suggesting is that, although there are difficulties in collecting observational data on social work practices, these difficulties appear surmountable to a considerable degree. They are certainly not so severe as to justify the neglect of this type of research hitherto. The fact remains that students have not under-taken observational work in the field of social work primarily because their predominant theoretical stance, rooted, as it is, in the traditional notion of social need, has not assigned a significant role to data of this kind.

Policy

I explained in the early chapters of this book that the topic at the centre of the research report—namely, the relationship between social need and the organisational and administrative structures of the welfare services—was rooted in the policy debate that preceded the reorganisation of British social work. Through an examination of the arguments of the Seebohm and Kilbrandon reports, and the Scottish White Paper, *Social Work and the Community,* I tried to make explicit that model of service provision upon which major changes in the administration of social work services in Scotland and in England and Wales were based.

I argued that within this model one central assumption played a crucial role. It was believed that the existing categories of social work and social need perpetuated 'rigid' and 'artificial' distinctions and persisted only because the organisational structures within which the welfare workers functioned prohibited the use of an alternative set of ideas. It was assumed that reorganisation would lead to the adoption and operational application of what were deemed to be more accurate notions of real need. It was this assumption which I proposed to review.

Now let us at this point return to the basis upon which I suggested this examination should proceed. I sought to establish that the government reports in which the policy debate was set out consisted in substantial part of sets of factual assertions, for I argued that, in general, the activity of producing such reports is a scientific enterprise because it is conducted within what we may call a context of assertion. The importance of this point is that it established that the assumption I had highlighted as central to the policy debate was amenable to conceptual analysis according to the canons of social scientific research and likewise to bombardment with empirical data. It was sensible to ask in this context 'Is it clear?' and 'Is it true?'

On inspection, the concept of social need contained within the body of policy I reviewed soon evidenced important deficiencies. The formulation closely resembled what I later termed the traditional notion of need. That is, it was assumed that some universal and objective criteria are possible. But what is odd, from a social scientific point of view, is that, although criticism of the existing services was based upon their embodiment of artificial notions of need, no specification was given of criteria for determining what a closer approximation to reality might be. Only this much was clear.

Notions of need adopted by professionals, it was argued, should be held independently of the organisational contexts within which they are utilised. Categories of need dependent upon administrative and legal constraints were deemed indicative of a serious service deficiency.

However, when I collected material on this theme, I suggested that a view of need denying its contextual character pays little attention to the social realities of the way in which the concept actually does function within the provision of the social services. Throughout, the data generally indicated a close and reflexive relationship between notions of need and patterns of administration within the reorganised social work agencies.

Recall, in particular, the case study of City Social Work Department. I described here the clear predominance in use of categories of need with a legal or administrative basis. First, there are those categories which reflect a liaison relationship with some other institution: a school for educationally subnormal children, a lodging hostel, or a psychiatric hospital. Second, there are categories derived from the courts such as 'SER', 'FSO' or 'Probation', or from the Children's Panel, a quasi-legal institution. Third, there are those categories which reflect resources administered separately within the agency; for example 'financial' or 'old people's home'. And fourth, there is a set of codings which are based upon specific agency procedures. 'Open', 'closed', or 'no further action' cases, for example, are very clearly administrative categories. I noted that a group of codings, for example, 'preventive', at first sight appear to reflect an alternative framework for categorisation purposes, but that in practice they serve only as residual codes where no specific legal or administrative procedures serve further to designate the case.

I suggested also that 'need' consists not merely of such legal and administrative categories but also of their embodiment within relatively complex professional ideologies of need. And when we examine the way in which these sets of ideas are operationally employed we see that, in substantial part, they are employed as professional resources to administrative effect.

Thus the 'policy' conclusions of this report do not differ from those which I have already discussed as potentially furthering our theoretical and empirical understanding of the way in which welfare agencies function to meet social need. My argument is, first, that the phenomenon of social need is itself more complicated than is suggested by the traditional notion as embodied in the model upon which the reorganisation proposals are based. Second, the relationship between professional ideologies and patterns of administration in social work is similarly more complex than that which is assumed in the view that the creation of Social Work and Social Services Departments alone would result in a radical reformulation of the way in which the notion of need is operationally utilised within the organised provision of social work services. Although the materials I have presented are by no means conclusive, they are strong enough to cast serious doubt upon the conceptual soundness and empirical validity of an assumption that is fundamental to the organisational structure of British social work.

Bibliography *

Albrow, Martin (1968), 'The Study of Organisations — Objectivity or Bias?' in Gould, J. (ed.), *Penguin Social Science Survey*, Harmondsworth, Penguin.

Armstrong, D. M. (1973), *Belief, Truth and Knowledge*, Cambridge, Cambridge University Press.

Becker, Howard S. (1970), *Sociological Work: Method and Substance* London, Allen Lane.

Benney, Mark and Hughes, Everett C. (1956), 'Of Sociology and the Interview: Editorial Preface', *American Journal of Sociology*, vol. 62, no.2.

Berger, Peter and Kellner, Hansfried (1970), 'Marriage and the Construction of Reality: An Exercise in the Microsociology of Knowledge', ch. 2 in Dreitzel, Hans Peter (ed.), *Recent Sociology, No. 2: Patterns of Communicative Behaviour*, New York, Macmillan; London, Collier-Macmillan.

Berger, Peter L. and Luckmann, Thomas (1967), *The Social Construction of Reality*, London, Allen Lane.

Bittner, Egon (1965), 'The Concept of Organisation', *Social Research*, vol. 32, no. 3, reprinted as ch. 17 in Salaman, Graeme and Thompson, Kenneth (eds), *People and Organisations*, London, Longman for the Open University Press.

Bloor, David (Undated), 'Wittgenstein and Mannheim on the Sociology of Mathematics', Unpublished paper (mimeo), University of Edinburgh, Science Studies Unit.

Blum, Alan F. (1970), 'The Sociology of Mental Illness', ch. 2 in Douglas, Jack D. (ed.), *Deviance and Respectability: The Social Construction of Moral Meanings*, New York, London, Basic Books.

Bradshaw, Jonathan (1972), 'The Concept of Social Need', *New Society*, vol. 19, pp. 640-43.

Braybrooke, David and Lindblom, Charles E. (1970), *A Strategy of Decision: Policy Evaluation as a Social Process*, New York, Free Press; London, Collier-Macmillan.

*British government publications are listed in date order under HMSO.

Cicourel, Aaron V. (1964), *Method and Measurement in Sociology*, New York, Free Press; London, Collier-Macmillan.

Cicourel, Aaron V. (1968), *The Social Organisation of Juvenile Justice*, New York, John Wiley.

Davies, Bleddyn (1968), *Social Needs and Resources in Local Services*, London, Michael Joseph.

Denzin, Norman K. (1970), *The Research Act in Sociology: A Theoretical Introduction to Sociological Methods*, London, Butterworths.

Douglas, Jack D. (1967), *The Social Meanings of Suicide*, Princeton University Press.

Douglas, Jack D. (ed.) (1970), *Deviance and Respectability: The Social Construction of Moral Meanings*, New York, London, Basic Books.

Douglas, Jack D. (ed.) (1971), *Understanding Everyday Life: Towards the Reconstruction of Sociological Knowledge*, London, Routledge & Kegan Paul.

Dreitzel, Hans Peter (ed.) (1970), *Recent Sociology, No. 2: Patterns of Communicative Behaviour*, New York, Macmillan; London, Collier-Macmillan.

Emerson, Joan P. (1970), 'Behaviour in Private Places: Sustaining Definitions of Reality in Gynecological Examinations', ch. 3 in Dreitzel, Hans Peter (ed.), *Recent Sociology, No. 2: Patterns of Communicative Behaviour*, New York, Macmillan; London, Collier-Macmillan.

Etzioni, Amitai (1960), 'Two Approaches to Organisational Analysis: A Critique and a Suggestion', *Administrative Science Quarterly*, vol. 5, pp. 257-78.

Etzioni, Amitai (1965), 'Organisational Control Structure', ch. 15 in March, J. G. (ed.), *Handbook of Organisations*, Chicago, Rand McNally.

Filmer, Paul; Philipson, Michael; Silverman, David and Walsh, David (1972), *New Directions in Sociological Theory*, London, Collier-Macmillan.

Freidson, Eliot (1970), *Professional Dominance: The Social Structure of Medical Care*, New York, Atherton Press.

Galbraith, J. K. (1958), *The Affluent Society*, London, Hamish Hamilton.

Garfinkel, Harold (1964), 'Studies of the Routine Grounds of Everyday Activities', *Social Problems*, vol. 11, pp. 225-50.

Garfinkel, Harold (1967), *Studies in Ethnomethodology*, Englewood Cliffs, New Jersey, Prentice Hall.

Geertz, Clifford (1964), 'Ideology as a Cultural System' in Apter, David E. (ed.), *Ideology and Discontent*, New York, Free Press, pp. 46-76.

Gilbert, Doris C. and Levinson, Daniel J. (1956), 'Ideology, Personality and Institutional Policy in the Mental Hospital', *Journal of Abnormal and Social Psychology*, vol. 53, pp. 263-71.

Glaser, Barney G. and Strauss, Anselm L. (1967), *The Discovery of Grounded Theory*, London, Weidenfeld & Nicolson.

Gold, Raymond L. (1958), 'Roles in Sociological Field Observations', *Social Forces*, vol. 36, no. 3.

Goldberg, E. Matilda with Mortimer, Ann and Williams, Brian T. (1970), *Helping the Aged: A Field Experiment in Social Work*, London, Allen & Unwin.

Goode, William, J. and Hatt, Paul, K. (1952), *Methods in Social Research*, New York, McGraw-Hill.

HMSO (1960), *Report of the Committee on Children and Young Persons* (The Ingleby Report), Cmnd 1191, London.

HMSO (1963), *Children and Young Persons Act,* London.

HMSO (1963), *Prevention of Neglect of Children* (The McBoyle Report), Cmnd 1966, Edinburgh.

HMSO (1964), *Children and Young Persons, Scotland* (The Kilbrandon Report), Cmnd 2303, Edinburgh.

HMSO (1965), *The Child, The Family and the Young Offender,* Cmnd 2742, London.

HMSO (1966), *Social Work and the Community,* Cmnd 3065, Edinburgh.

HMSO (1968), *Children in Trouble,* Cmnd 3601, London.

HMSO (1968), *Report of the Committee on Local Authority and Allied Personal Social Services* (The Seebohm Report), Cmnd 3703, London.

HMSO (1968), *Social Work (Scotland) Act,* London.

HMSO (1969), *Children and Young Persons Act,* London.

HMSO (1970), *Local Authority Social Services Act,* London.

Hall, A. S. (1974), *The Point of Entry*, London, Allen & Unwin.

Hall, Phoebe (1976), *Reforming the Welfare*, London, Heinemann.

Hey, Anthea and Rowbottom, Ralph (1971), 'Task and Supervision in Area Social Work', *British Journal of Social Work*, vol. 1, no. 4.

Holman, Robert (1970), 'Combating Social Deprivation', ch. 4 in Holman, Robert (*et al.*), *Socially Deprived Families in Britain*, London, The Bedford Square Press of the NCSS.

Jeffreys, Margot (1965), *An Anatomy of Social Welfare Services: A Survey of Social Welfare Staff and their Clients in the County of Buckinghamshire*, London, Michael Joseph.

Johnson, John M. (1975), *Doing Field Research,* New York, Free Press; London, Collier-Macmillan.

Junker, Buford, H. (1960), *Field Work: An Introduction to the Social Sciences*, Chicago and London, University of Chicago Press.

Kitsuse, John I. and Cicourel, Aaron, V. (1963), 'A Note on the Use of Official Statistics', *Social Problems,* vol. 11, pp. 131-9.

Lang, K. and Lang, G. E. (1960), 'Decisions for Christ: Billy Graham in New York City' in Stein, M., Vidich, A. J. and White, D. M. (eds), *Identity and Anxiety*, Chicago, Ill., Free Press.

Lazarsfeld, Paul F. and Menzel, Herbert (1961), 'On the Relation between Individual and Collective Properties' in Etzioni, Amitai (ed.), *Complex Organisations: A Sociological Reader*, New York and London, Holt Rinehart & Winston.

Lindblom, Charles E. (1964), 'The Science of "Muddling Through"', in Gore, William J. and Dyson, J. W. (eds), *The Making of Decisions: A Reader in Administrative Behaviour,* New York, Free Press, pp. 155-69.

Macintyre, Alasdair (1964), 'A Mistake About Causality in Social Science' in Laslett, Peter and Runciman, W. G. (eds), *Philosophy, Politics and Society* (2nd Series), Oxford, Blackwell.

Manning, Peter K. (1967), 'Problems in Interpreting Interview Data'. *Sociology and Social Research,* vol. 15, pp. 302-16.

Martin, F. M. and Murray, Kathleen (eds) (1976), *Childrens Hearings,* Edinburgh, Scottish Academic Press.

Bibliography

Marx, John H. (1969), 'A Multi-dimensional Conception of Ideologies in Professional Arenas: The Case of the Mental Health Field', *Pacific Sociological Review*, vol. 12, no. 2.

Matza, David (1969), *Becoming Deviant*, Englewood Cliffs, NJ, Prentice-Hall.

Meyer, John E. and Timms, Noel (1970), *The Client Speaks: Working Class Impressions of Casework*, London, Routledge & Kegan Paul.

Miller, S. M. (1952), 'The Participant Observer and "Over-Rapport"', *American Sociological Review*, vol. 17, pp. 97-9.

Mills, C. Wright (1940), 'Situated Actions and Vocabularies of Motive', *American Sociological Review*, vol. 5, pp. 904-13.

Moser, C. A. (1958), *Survey Methods in Social Investigation*, London, Heinemann.

Murray, George (1976), 'Juvenile Justice Reform', ch. 1 in Martin, F. M. and Murray, Kathleen (eds), *Children's Hearings*, Edinburgh, Scottish Academic Press.

Packman, Jean (1968), *Child Care: Needs and Numbers*, London, Allen & Unwin.

Perkin, Harold (1969), *The Origins of Modern British Society, 1780-1880*, London, Routledge & Kegan Paul.

Perrow, Charles (1961), 'The Analysis of Goals in Complex Organisations', *American Sociological Review*, vol. 26, pp. 854-66.

Perrow, Charles (1963), 'Goals and Power Structures—A Hospital Case Study' in Friedson, E. (ed.), *The Hospital in Modern Society*, New York, Free Press.

Reid, William J. and Shyne, Ann W. (1969), *Brief and Extended Casework*, New York, London, Columbia University Press.

Rein, Martin (1969), 'Research Design and Social Policy' in Ryan, William (ed.), *Distress in the City: Essays on the Design and Administration of Urban Mental Health Services*, Cleveland and London: The Press of Case Western Reserve University.

Rowntree (1969), *Social Work in Scotland: Report of a Working Party on the Social Work (Scotland) Act 1968*, Edinburgh, Department of Social Administration, University of Edinburgh.

Rubington, Earl and Weinberg, Martin S. (1968), *Deviance: The Interactionist Perspective*, London, Collier-Macmillan.

Rubington, Earl and Weinberg, Martin S. (1977), *The Study of Social Problems: Five Perspectives* (2nd edn), New York, Oxford University Press.

Scheff, Thomas J. (1966), *Being Mentally Ill: A Sociological Theory*, London, Weidenfeld & Nicolson.

Schutz, Alfred (1967), *Collected Papers: Vol. 1: The Problem of Social Reality*, ed and intro. by Maurice Natanson, The Hague, Martinus Nijhoff.

Scott, Robert A. (1969), *The Making of Blind Men: A Study of Adult Socialization*, New York, Russell Sage Foundation.

Scott, Robert A. (1970), 'The Construction of Concepts of Stigma by Professional Experts', ch. 9 in Douglas, Jack D., (ed.) *Deviance and Respectability: The Social Construction of Moral Meanings*, New York, London, Basic Books.

Seed, Philip (1973), *The Expansion of Social Work in Britain*, London, Routledge & Kegan Paul.

Silverman, David and Jones, Jill (1976), *Organisational Work. The Language of Grading the Grading of Language*, London, Collier-Macmillan.

Sjoberg, Gideon and Nett, Roger (1968), *A Methodology for Social Research*, New York, Harper & Row.

Smith, Gilbert (1971), 'Some Research Implications of the Seebohm Report', *British Journal of Sociology*, vol. XXII, no. 3.

Smith, Gilbert (1973), 'Ideologies, Beliefs, and Patterns of Administration in the Organization of Social Work Practice: A Study with Special Reference to the Concept of Social Need'. Unpublished PhD Dissertation, University of Aberdeen.

Smith, Gilbert (1978), 'The Meaning of "Success" in Social Policy', *Public Administration*, vol. 56 (Autumn).

Smith, Gilbert and Harris, Robert (1972), 'Ideologies of Need and the Organisation of Social Work Departments', *British Journal of Social Work*, vol. 2, no. 1.

Smith, Gilbert and Stockman, Norman (1972), 'Some Suggestions for a Sociological Approach to the Study of Government Reports', *Sociological Review*, vol. 20, no. 1.

Spencer, John (1973), 'People in Social Work. Miss Megan Browne, O.B.E. Retirement', *BASW News*, 17 May, in *Social Work Today*, vol. 4, no. 4.

Strauss, Anselm (*et al.*) (1964), *Psychiatric Ideologies and Institutions*, New York, Free Press.

Sudnow, David (1965), 'Normal Crimes: Sociological Features of the Penal Code in a Public Defender Office', *Social Problems*, vol. 12, no. 3.

Sudnow, David (1967), *Passing On: The Social Organisation of Dying*, Englewood Cliffs, New Jersey, Prentice Hall.

Sumner, Greta and Smith, Randall (1969), *Planning Local Authority Services for the Elderly*, London, Allen & Unwin.

Thomas, N. M. (1973), 'The Seebohm Committee on Personal Social Services', ch. 6 in Chapman, Richard A. (ed.), *The Role of Commissions in Policy Making*, London, Allen & Unwin.

Timms, Noel and Rita (1977), *Perspectives in Social Work*, London, Routledge & Kegan Paul.

Torgerson, Warren S. (1958), *Theory and Methods of Scaling*, New York, John Wiley; London, Chapman & Hall.

Townsend, Peter (1968), 'Family Welfare and Seebohm', *New Society*, vol. 12, pp. 159-60.

Townsend, Peter and Wedderburn, Dorothy (1965), *The Aged in the Welfare State*, London, Bell.

Turner, Roy (ed.) (1974), *Ethnomethodology*, Harmondsworth, Penguin.

Voysey, Margaret (1975), *A Constant Burden*, London, Routledge & Kegan Paul.

Wareham, Joyce (1970), *Social Policy in Context*, London, Batsford.

Webb, Eugene J., Campbell, Donald T., Schwartz, Richard D. and Sechrest, Lee (1966), *Unobtrusive Measures: Nonreactive Research in the Social Sciences*, Chicago, Rand McNally.

Wessen, Albert F. (1958), 'Hospital Ideology and Communication Between Ward Personnel' in Jaco, Gartley E. (ed.), *Patients, Physicians and Illness*, Chicago, Free Press.

Bibliography

Weiss, D. J. and Dawis, R. V. (1960), 'An Objective Validation of Factual Interview Data', *Journal of Applied Psychology*, vol. 44, pp. 381-4.

Wheeler, Stanton (1967), 'Criminal Statistics: A Reformulation of the Problem', *Journal of Criminal Law, Criminology and Political Science*, vol. 58, no. 3.

Wheeler, Stanton (ed.) (1969), *On Record: Files and Dossiers in American Life*, New York, Russell Sage Foundation.

Wilson, Bryan R. (ed.) (1970), *Rationality*, Oxford, Blackwell.

Zald, Mayer N. (ed.) (1965) *Social Welfare Institutions: A Sociological Reader*, New York, John Wiley.

Zimmerman, Don H. (1966), 'Paper Work and People Work: A Study of a Public Assistance Agency', Unpublished PhD Dissertation, University of California, Los Angeles (Microfilm, University Microfilm Ltd).

Zimmerman, Don H. (1969a), 'Tasks and Troubles: The Practical Bases of Work Activities in a Public Assistance Organisation', ch. 8 in Hansen, Donald A. (ed.) *Explorations in Sociology and Counselling*, Boston, Houghton Mifflin.

Zimmerman, Don H. (1969b), 'Record-keeping and the Intake Process in a Public Welfare Agency', ch. 11 in Wheeler, Standon (ed.), *On Record: Files and Dossiers in American Life*, New York, Russell Sage Foundation.

Zimmerman, Don H. (1971), 'The Practicalities of Rule Use', ch. 9 in Douglas, Jack D. (ed.), *Understanding Everyday Life: Towards the Reconstruction of Sociological Knowledge*, London, Routledge & Kegan Paul.

Zimmerman, Don H. and Pollner, Melvin (1971), 'The Everyday World as a Phenomenon', ch. 4 in Douglas, Jack D. (ed.), *Understanding Everyday Life: Towards the Reconstruction of Sociological Knowledge*, London, Routledge & Kegan Paul.

Zimmerman, Don H. and Weider, D. Lawrence (1971), 'Ethnomethodology and the Problem of Order: Comment on Denzin', ch. 12 in Douglas, Jack D. (ed.), *Understanding Everyday Life: Towards the Reconstruction of Sociological Knowledge*, Routledge & Kegan Paul.

Index

Index

clarity, as criterion in assessing
   government reports, 20, 36, 202
client career, 200
clients, 2, 8, 50, 55, 61, 65, 66, 84,
   91; as cases of 'need', 153-79; at
   intake, 129, 132-3; at reception,
   123-4; views of allocation, 188
client's problems, *see* social problems
clinical trial, *see* experimental study
closed cases, 125, 126-7, 200, 203;
   see also case
committee of enquiry, 20-5, 202
commonsense constructs, 72
community, 17, 19-20, 30-34, 181,
   190; care, 42, 49-52, 56
compulsory powers, 33-4
confidentiality, 115, 200
context of assertion, 21, 22-4, 37, 202
contextual determination of meaning,
   principle of, 70
conventional wisdom, 179
correlations, 45, 47, 48
court work, 97, 139, 152, 183; cases
   for, 141-4

'daft laddie', research stance, 93
data; analysis, 42; collection, 43
   (summarised, 199); *see also*
   methodology; research methods
data, for allocation, 188
Davidson, K., x
Davies, B., 42, 46-48, 56
Dawis, R., 114
'death', 70, 75, 79-82
decision-making, 57, 101, 110,
   149-50, 188
delinquency, juvenile, 3, 17, 18, 25-7,
   28-32
Denzin, N., 9, 94, 95, 96, 116-17,
   152; *see also* methodological
   triangulation
'difficult' cases, 146, 149; *see also*
   'easy' cases
disability, 70
disjointed incrementalism, 57-8, 70
division of labour, 198
doctor, 112; *see also* referral
documentary, basis of allocation, 122,
   189; *see also* files
documents, *see* files
Douglas, J., 7, 68, 70-1
Dreitzel, H., 68
duty officer, 129-138 *passim,* 152;
   and cases of 'need', 153-79 *passim*

'easy' cases, 146, 149, 182
effectiveness, of services, 62, 65-6
elderly, 49, 50-1, 53-4, 106, 108; *see
   also* old people, homes application
'eligibility', for service, 75, 77-8, 82
Emerson, J., 70
ends, in policy analysis, *see,* means
   and ends
England, 3, 4, 13, 29. 36, 43, 196,
   202
ethnography, 76, 119, 198; *see also*
   observational data
ethnomethodology, 68
Etzioni, A., 8, 58
evaluation, 59, 62-3, 67
experimental study, 43, 59-63, 200

family, 17, 18-20, 31, 33, 34, 49, 83,
   180, 181; *see also* ideologies of
   need, unit (family)
files, 90, 102-3, 104-5, 184;
   construction and use of in cases of
   'need', 153-79 *passim*; documents,
   10, 78-9, 93, 114, 139, 151, 181,
   190; effects of, 189; official
   statistics, 25, 42, 48, 49, 51, 199;
   records, 8, 9, 78, 81, 98, 113, 115,
   116-17, 126, 130, 186; statistics, 8,
   9, 10, 113; *see also* documentary,
   basis of allocation
Filmer, P., 68
financial provision, 52-5, 61, 97, 131,
   182, 203
Friedson, E., 7

Galbraith, J., 53
Garfinkel, H., 68, 75
Geertz, C., 100
'generic'; caseload, 148-9;
   departments, 13, 16
Gilbert, D., 99
Glaser, B., 94
'going native', 96; *see also* participant
   observation
Gold, R., 96
Goldberg, E., 43, 59-63, 66
Goode, W., 92, 93
government commission, *see*
   committee of enquiry
government report, *see* committee of
   enquiry
grounded theory, 94

Hall, A., 90
Hall, P., 3, 6, 21

Index

National Assistance Board, 53-5
Nett, R., 94, 96, 114
'no further action', 126-7, 133, 137-8, 141, 150-1; examples, 133-6
Nuffield Provincial Hospitals Trust, ix
nursery place application, case of, 171-9, 185, 189

'objective facticities', 196
objectivity, 63, 64, 69-70, 196, 198
observational data, 74, 76, 79, 80, 82, 120-1; and 'participation', 98; comparison with interviews and files, 9, 116-17; difficulties in collection, 8, 93, 115, 201; lack of, in social work research, 64, 114, 199; on five cases, 153-79; see also participant observation; methodological triangulation
observer, 96; see also participant observation
observer effect, 8, 201
official statistics, see files
old people, see elderly; homes applications, 130, 182, 203
Open University, x
operational philosophies, 100, 103-12 passim, 125, 181, 183-5; summarised, 197-8
ordinal data, 47
organisational structure, of social work, 14-15, 16, 32, 34, 36, 89, 91; see also adminstration
'orthodox' stance, in studying organisations, see traditional approach

Packman, J., 42, 43-6, 47
Paper Work and People Work, 75-9
participant, 96, 98; see also observational data
participant observation, 7, 10, 92, 95, 113; see also, 'going native'; observational data
Passing On: The Social Organization of Dying, 79-82
Perkin, H., 24
Perrow, C., 99
personal incapacity score, 49, 50
personal social services, 3, 30, 34, 118
planning, 42-3, 65
Planning Local Authority Services for the Elderly, 55-9

policy, *see* social policy
policy makers, 35
Pollner, M., 69, 70, 71, 72
poor law, 109
poverty, 53, 105
practicalities of research, 92, 95
practice, 16; in relation to methodology, policy and theory, 195
practitioner, 64, 66, 75; *see also* professionals
presenting problem, 107-8, 182
'preventive' cases, 131-2; as residual category, 203
principle of acceptance, 183
probation, 29, 34, 35, 104, 139, 147, 203; cases, 143
problems, *see* social problems; presenting, 132-3
professional ideology, 8, 9, 59, 99-112, 118, 180, 185, 187; as multi-dimensional, 112; in interviews, 114; summarised, 197; *see also* ideologies of need
professional skills, *see* specialist skills
professionals, 53, 58, 65, 69, 83, 84-5, 100, 118, 191; and laymen, 196-7; interaction with clients, 8 (examples, 153-79); perspective of, 45, 63, 184; problems of, 43; research on, 113, use of official categories by, 46
Psychiatric Ideologies and Institutions, 100
psychiatric social work, 34, 129

qualitative data, 200
questionnaires, 42, 44, 51, 199

rational planning, 58
rationality, 22-3, 37
reception, 77, 120-1, 123-9; of cases of 'need', 153-79 *passim;* summarised, 191
receptionists, 115, 116, 127, 137, 141-2, 151, 199; and cases of 'need', 153-79 *passim*
records, *see* files
reference group, 50; *see also* relative deprivation
referral, 90, 130, 138, 189; from doctor, example, 137; from health visitor, example, 136; from lay person, 184; letter, 140-1; of cases of 'need', 153-79 *passim;* 'self',